초급 Junior

VOCA 3000

■ 이홍배   육군 사관학교 졸업
　　　　　미국 브라운 대학교 석사 · 박사(언어학)
　　　　　서강대학교 교양 영어 주임교수
　　　　　미국 브라운 대학교 객원교수
　　　　　서강대학교 영어영문학과장
　　　　　국제문화교육원 원장
　　　　　한국 영어영문학회 회원
　　　　　한국 언어학회 회원
　　　　　한국 생성문법학회 회원
　　　　　서강대학교 영어영문학과 교수 역임

TOEFL · TOEIC · TEPS 보카바이블

초급 Junior VOCA 3000

저 자 이홍배
발행인 고본화
발 행 반석출판사
2025년 10월 10일 초판 6쇄 인쇄
2025년 10월 15일 초판 6쇄 발행
홈페이지 www.bansok.co.kr
이메일 bansok@bansok.co.kr
블로그 blog.naver.com/bansokbooks

07547 서울시 강서구 양천로 583. B동 1007호
(서울시 강서구 염창동 240-21번지 우림블루나인 비즈니스센터 B동 1007호)
대표전화 02) 2093-3399 **팩 스** 02) 2093-3393
출 판 부 02) 2093-3395 **영업부** 02) 2093-3396
등록번호 제315-2008-000033호

Copyright ⓒ 이홍배

ISBN 978-89-7172-852-9 (13740)

■ 교재 관련 문의: bansok@bansok.co.kr을 이용해 주시기 바랍니다.
■ 이 책에 게재된 내용의 일부 또는 전체를 무단으로 복제 및 복제하는 것을 금합니다.
■ 파본 및 잘못된 제품은 구입처에서 교환해 드립니다.

머리말

영어 실력의 척도라고 할 수 있을 만큼 영어의 어휘력은 영어학습에 있어서 필수적인 요소이다. 그래서 영어를 배우는 사람이라면 누구나 한번쯤은 **어떻게 하면 어휘력을 향상시킬 수 있을 것인가?** 하는 문제에 부딪치게 된다.

많은 사람들이 이처럼 어휘력 향상 문제에 대하여 깊은 관심을 갖고 있으면서도 이에 대처할 수 있는 마땅한 어휘학습서를 연구·개발 시키는 면에서 여지껏 황무지 상태를 면치 못하고 있음은 어휘학습서의 개발이 영어를 모국어로 하지 않는 어느 한 사람의 힘 만으로 단기간 내에 이루어질 수 없기 때문이다.

이러한 현실로 인하여 몇 권의 한국인용 어휘학습서에 의존하여 각기 나름대로의 해결 방법을 모색하고 있는 실정인데, 그 중에서 Levine이 지은 *20000 VOCABULARY*는 비교적 조직적이면서 과학적인 방법으로 어휘력 증가에 접근하고 있다. 원래 이 책은 약 3,000개의 단어를 근간으로 하여 미국 고등학생들의 어휘력을 향상시키기 위하여 미국인이 쓴 책으로서, 우리나라의 실정으로는 이미 상당한 수준의 어휘력이 있는 사람이 보다 체계적으로 어휘를 정리하는데 적합한 책이 아닌가 하는 것이 필자의 견해이다.

그러나 이 책에 대하여 우리나라 영어 학도들의 입장에서 약간 아쉬운 점이 있다면, 그것은 *20000 VOCABULARY*에서 학습시키는 상당한 수의 단어들이 우리가 흔히 접하는 단어가 아니기 때문에 이 책을 철저히 학습한 사람도 영문서적을 읽는다거나 각종 영어 시험에서 실제로 유익하게 활용할 수 없다는 사실이다. 뿐만 아니라 *20000 VOCABULARY*에서 학습시키는 단어가 실제로 약 3,000개에 지나지 않기 때문에 이를 완전히 습득했다 해도 영어 어휘력을 증가시키는 데는 부족한 점이 있다.

여기서 필자는 *20000 VOCABULARY*의 부족한 점을 보충하면서 우리나라 영어 학도들의 현실에 적합한 새로운 어휘 학습의 방법을 제시하고자 일련의 어휘학습서를 내게된 것이다. 이 어휘학습서는 *20000 VOCABULARY*에 나오는 근간단어를 포함하지 않으면서 우리가 중급 또는 고급 영문서적을 읽는데 반드시 알아야 하는 단어 약 8,000개를 정선하여 독자 자신의 어휘력 수준에 맞추어 스스로 학습할 수 있도록

초급 Junior VOCABULARY (근간단어 3,000개)
중급 College VOCABULARY (근간단어 5,000개)로 구분하였다.

어휘력이란 단순히 한 단어의 뜻만을 아는 것이 아니기 때문에, 단어의 뜻을 암기하는 것만으로는 효과적인 어휘 학습 방법이 되지 못한다. 그러기에 이 책에서는 정확한 발음과 간결한 정의에 의하여 우선 그 뜻을 안 다음 명쾌한 예문들에 의한 다양한 문제를 통하여 반복 학습 시킴으로써 그 의미와 용법을 완전히 습득하게 되는, 이른바 **인지론적 방법(Cognitive Approach)**을 어휘학습에 시도하였으며 매 과(LESSON)를 시작하기 전에 자신의 어휘력 수준을 진단해 볼 수 있는 Self-test를 실시함으로써 지속적인 흥미유지와 문제의 다양성을 기했다.

초급 Junior VOCABULARY의 구성

1. 중학교 영어 교과서 및 초급 수준의 영문서적 독서나 이 수준에 해당하는 각종 영어 시험에 나오는 단어들 중 가장 빈도(頻度)수가 많은 3,000개의 단어를 정선(精選)하여 근간(根幹)으로 하였다.

2. 총24개 과(LESSON)로 구성하였으며 매 과마다 단어의 뜻 및 그 동의어(SYNONYM), 반의어(ANTONYM), 파생어(DERIVATIVE)들을 수록하였다.

3. 매 과(LESSON)마다 근간단어에 대한 이해와 숙달을 돕기 위하여 응용문제를 구성하였으며, 9가지 이상의 상이한 문제형식을 취하였다.

4. 매 과(LESSON)마다의 예문 및 연습문제 중 초급수준 이상의 중요한 단어 및 숙어에는 주해를 달아 놓았다.

5. 근간단어에 대한 발음은 국제 음성기호로 표시하였고, 우리말 역어(譯語)는 사용빈도가 으뜸이며 가장 대표적인 의미를 일관성있게 달았으며, 그 용례에 있어서 현저한 차이가 있을 경우에는 1, 2로 구분하였고, 이에 대한 명쾌한 예문을 통하여 이해력을 촉진시키고 응용력을 함양할 수 있도록 하였다.

CONTENTS

▶ 머리말 / 3

▶ **Lesson 1** 8
  • 종합 연습 문제 16

▶ **Lesson 2** 18
  • 종합 연습 문제 27

▶ **Lesson 3** 30
  • 종합 연습 문제 39

▶ **Lesson 4** 42
  • 종합 연습 문제 51

▶ **Lesson 5** 54
  • 종합 연습 문제 63

▶ **Lesson 6** 66
  • 종합 연습 문제 75

▶ **Lesson 7** 78
  • 종합 연습 문제 87

▶ **Lesson 8** 90
  • 종합 연습 문제 99

▶ **Lesson 9** 102
  • 종합 연습 문제 111

▶ **Lesson 10** 114
  • 종합 연습 문제 122

▶ **Lesson 11** 125
  • 종합 연습 문제 134

▶ **Lesson 12** 137
  • 종합 연습 문제 146

CONTENTS

▶ **Lesson 13** 149
　· 종합 연습 문제 158

▶ **Lesson 14** 161
　· 종합 연습 문제 169

▶ **Lesson 15** 172
　· 종합 연습 문제 181

▶ **Lesson 16** 184
　· 종합 연습 문제 193

▶ **Lesson 17** 196
　· 종합 연습 문제 205

▶ **Lesson 18** 208
　· 종합 연습 문제 217

▶ **Lesson 19** 220
　· 종합 연습 문제 229

▶ **Lesson 20** 232
　· 종합 연습 문제 241

▶ **Lesson 21** 244
　· 종합 연습 문제 253

▶ **Lesson 22** 256
　· 종합 연습 문제 265

▶ **Lesson 23** 268
　· 종합 연습 문제 277

▶ **Lesson 24** 280
　· 종합 연습 문제 289

▶ **찾아보기 / 292**

초급 Junior

VOCA 3000

반석출판사 Bansok

LESSON 1

Self-test 1

적당한 단어를 골라 빈칸을 채우라.

1. When water _____, it is full of *bubbles*.
   (A) boils (B) freezes

2. Many people *resort* to the beaches in _____ weather.
   (A) cold (B) hot

3. Let's all *cooperate* to get the work done _____.
   (A) quickly (B) slowly

4. He was _____ because his name was *omitted* from the list.
   (A) invited (B) not invited

5. They put the *blame* for the _____ on the driver of the car.
   (A) success (B) accident

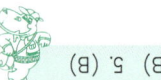

1. (A) 2. (B) 3. (A) 4. (B) 5. (B)

New Vocabulary -1

abroad
[əbrɔ́ːd]
adj. 해외로, 해외에서
syn. overseas
He lived *abroad* for many years; he knows several foreign languages.

affect
[əfékt]
v. 영향을 미치다, 감동시키다
The small amount of rain last year *affected* the growth of crops[1].

attend
[əténd]
v. 출석하다, 다니다
n. attendance
All children over seven must *attend* school.

---

1. crop[krɔp] *n.* 농작물

blame [bleim]
n. v. 비난(하다), 책망(하다)
I have done my best; neither praise[2] nor *blame* can affect me now.

bubble [bʌ́bl]
n. 거품, 기포(氣泡)
Children like to make *bubbles* with soap and water.

cemetery [sémitri]
n. 묘지, 공동 묘지
syn. graveyard
There are many tombs[3] in the *cemetery*.

commendation [kɔmendéiʃən]
n. 칭찬, 추천
syn. praise, compliment
ant. blame, insult
He was given a *commendation* for bravery[4] after he saved the little children from the fire.

conflict [kɔ́nflikt]
n. 투쟁, 전투
syn. fight, war, battle, struggle
ant. reconciliation
Some people think that there is a great deal of *conflict* between religion[5] and science.

cooperate [kouɔ́pəreit]
v. 협력하다, 협동하다
n. cooperation
adj. cooperative
The children *cooperated* with their teachers in keeping their classrooms clean.

curious [kjúəriəs]
adj. 알고 싶어하는, 호기심이 강한
syn. inquisitive
ant. incurious, indifferent
I am *curious* to know what my teacher said to my mother.

Practice 1

위 단어를 사용하여 아래 문장을 완성하라. 필요시 단어를 적절한 형태로 변형하라.

1. The news of his mother's death _____ him deeply.
2. _____ is a place for burying the dead.
3. He is planning to go _____ next year for his study.
4. He doesn't _____ church very often.
5. If a child a _____, he is always asking questions.

---

2. praise[preiz] *n.* 칭찬   3. tomb[tu:m] *n.* 무덤   4. bravery[bréivəri] *n.* 용감한, 용기   5. religion[rilídʒən] *n.* 종교

New Vocabulary -2

delicious
[dilíʃəs]

adj. 맛있는, 맛좋은
syn. sweet-tasting
We had some *delicious* cakes after dinner.

direct
[dirékt/dai-]

v. 지도하다, 감독하다
syn. conduct, command
There was nobody to *direct* the workmen.

adj. 똑바른, 곧은
ant. indirect
Which is the most *direct* way to London?

draw
[drɔː]

v. 끌다, 잡아끌다, 잡아당기다
syn. drag, haul
Draw your chair nearer to the table.

empire
[émpaiər]

n. 제국, 제왕의 영토
syn. realm
The United States was once a part of the British *Empire*.

event
[ivént]

n. 사건, 대사건, 우발 사건
syn. accident, happening, incident
The discovery of America was a great *event*.

failure
[féiljə]

n. 실패, 실수
v. fail
ant. success
Success came after many *failures*.

file
[fail]

n. 서류철, 철해 놓는 곳
Please put these letters in the main *file*.

v. 철하다, 철하여 정리하다
The secretary *filed* the cards in order[6].

frank
[fræŋk]

adj. 솔직한, 정직한
syn. candid, honest
ant. deceitful, dishonest
He was *frank* to admit[7] that he had not studied the lesson.

---

6. in order : 순서대로, 질서있게   7. admit[ədmít] *v.* 인정하다

generate	*v.* 발생시키다, 일으키다
[dʒénəreit]	**syn.** produce, make
	We know that heating water can *generate* steam.

halt	*v.* 정지하다, 멈춰 서다(세우다)
[hɔ:lt]	**syn.** stop
	ant. start
	The soldiers *halted* and rested from their march.

Practice 2

위 단어를 사용하여 아래 문장을 완성하라. 필요시 단어를 적절한 형태로 변형하라.

1. Her graduation from college was a(n) _____ I did not want to miss.
2. What _____ food you've cooked!
3. The picnic was a _____ because it rained.
4. If you want my _____ opinion, I don't think the plan will succeed.
5. The company _____ operations[8] during the strike.

New Vocabulary -3

| horn | *n.* 뿔, 경적 |
| [hɔ:rn] | A goat has two *horns* on its head. |

individual	*adj.* 개인의, 개개의
[indivídjuəl]	A teacher cannot give *individual* attention if his class is large.
	n. 개인, 사람
	syn. person
	The rights of the *individual* are more important than the rights of society as a whole.

interval	*n.* 시간의 간격, 사이, 휴지(休止)
[íntərvəl]	**syn.** pause, break
	There was a long *interval* before he replied[9].

| knot | *n.* 매듭 |
| [nɔt] | The *knots* on your package must be tied tightly. |

---

8. operation [ɔpəréiʃən] *n.* 가동(稼動), 작업   9. reply [riplái] *v.* 대답하다

liberal
[líbərəl]

adj. 1. 개방적인, 자유로운
He is *liberal* in his views on government.

2. 일반 교양의
ant. professional
They want their children to have a *liberal* education.

magnificent
[mægnífisnt]

adj. 장엄한, 장대한, 근사한
syn. grand, splendid
n. magnificence
The king was wearing a *magnificent* gold crown.

mental
[méntl]

adj. 마음의, 심적인
ant. physical
Keeping *mental* health is very important in modern society.

momentary
[móuməntəri]

adj. 순식간의, 잠깐 동안의
syn. transient
ant. everlasting
Her feeling of danger was only *momentary*; it soon passed.

neutral
[njú:trəl]

adj. 중립의, 중성의
He remained *neutral* in the argument[10] between his two friends.

omit
[oumít]

v. 빠뜨리다, 생략하다
ant. add
He made many mistakes in spelling by *omitting* letters.

Practice 3

위 단어를 사용하여 아래 문장을 완성하라. 필요시 단어를 적절한 형태로 변형하라.

1. We didn't think that you would come here, because your name was _____ from the list.

2. The judge in a court[11] must be _____ in a trial[12].

3. Each _____ leaf on the tree is different.

4. There is a(n) _____ of a week between Christmas and New Year's Day.

5. There are probably as many kinds of _____ illnesses as there are kinds of physical illnesses.

---

10. argument[á:rgjumənt] *n.* 논쟁   11. court[kɔ:rt] *n.* 법정, 법원   12. trial[traiəl] *n.* 재판, 공판

New Vocabulary -4

peacock
[píːkɔk]
n. 공작새
A *peacock* can fly only short distance.

pioneer
[paiəníər]
n. 개척자, 선구자, 주창자
syn. forerunner
John Glenn was a *pioneer* in space travel[13].

pray
[prei]
v. 기도하다, 빌다
I will *pray* to God for your safe return.

pronounce
[prənáuns]
v. 1. 발음하다
n. pronunciation
The teacher *pronounced* each word slowly.

    2. 선언하다, 표명하다
n. pronouncement
The doctor *pronounced* that the man was dead.

race
[reis]
n. 1. 인종, 혈통, 민족
There are mainly three kinds of *races* in the world; the white *race*, the black *race*, and the yellow *race*.

    2. 경주, 경기, 시합
Please tell me which horse won the *race*.

relative
[rélətiv]
n. 친척, 일가, 인척
He has many *relatives* in the United States.

adj. 상대적인, 비교상의
ant. absolute
East is a *relative* term; for example, Seoul is east of Incheon but west of Choonchun.

resort
[rizɔ́ːrt]
v. 1. 자주 가다, 흔히 다니다
When we were high-school students, we *resorted* to the restaurant.

    2. 원조를 구하다, 호소하다
He always *resorted* to asking his friends for money.

rub
[rʌb]
v. 문지르다, 비비다
He *rubbed* his hands together to warm up.

---

13. space travel : 우주 여행

shadow [ʃǽdou]	***n.*** 그림자, 그늘 **syn.** shade He walked along in the *shadows* hoping no one would recognize[14] him.
situation [sìtʃuéiʃən]	***n.*** 형편, 형세, 경우 **syn.** condition, case I'm in a difficult *situation* and I don't know what to do.

Practice 4

위 단어를 사용하여 아래 문장을 완성하라. 필요시 단어를 적절한 형태로 변형하라.

1. People of many _____ settled in the United States.
2. My uncle is my nearest _____.
3. With the light behind him, his _____ could be seen on the wall.
4. The doctor is regarded[15] as a(n) _____ in operating human hearts.
5. There in nothing that we can do now but _____ to God for help.

New Vocabulary –5

sore [sɔər]	***adj.*** 쓰린, 아픈 **syn.** aching, painful His *sore* leg made walking difficult.
spread [spred]	***v.*** 펴다, 펼치다, 유포하다 ***p., pp.*** spread, spread His sister *spread* a cloth on the table.
stomach [stʌ́mək]	***n.*** 위(胃), 배, 복부 It is unwise to swim on a full *stomach*[16].
suitcase [súːtkeis]	***n.*** 소형 여행가방 **cf.** trunk He took two *suitcase* with him on the trip.
talent [tǽlənt]	***n.*** 재주, 재능, 수완 The girl has a *talent* for music.

14. recognize[rékəgnàiz] ***v.*** 알아보다   15. regard[rigɑ́ːrd] ***v.*** 간주하다   16. on a full (an empty) stomach : 배가 부를〔고플〕때에

throne [θroun]	***n.*** 왕위, 왕좌, 왕권 He was only 15 years old when he came to the *throne*.
transfer [trǽnsfə(:)r]	***n.*** 이전, 전근, 양도 He has asked for a *transfer* to another job. ***v.*** 옮기다, 전임시키다 The football player is hoping to *transfer* to another team soon.
usage [júːsidʒ]	***n.*** 사용, 용법 **syn.** treatment ***v.*** use Machines soon wear out[17] under rough *usage*.
vowel [váuəl]	***n.*** 모음 **ant.** consonant The *vowels* in the English language are represented by a, e, i, o, u, and, sometimes, y.
withdraw [wiðdrɔ́ː]	***v.*** 움츠리다, 철수하다 ***p., pp.*** withdrew, withdrawn He quickly *withdrew* his hand from the hot stove.

Practice 5

위 단어를 사용하여 아래 문장을 완성하라. 필요시 단어를 적절한 형태로 변형하라.

1. _____ are more difficult to pronounce than consonants.
2. It is not wise to work on an empty _____.
3. The general decide to _____ the troops[18] from the present position.
4. The boy showed a real _____ for painting.
5. This farm has been _____ from father to son for generations[19].

해답					
Practice 1	1. affected	2. Cemetery	3. abroad	4. attend	5. curious
Practice 2	1. event	2. delicious	3. failure	4. frank	5. halted
Practice 3	1. omitted	2. neutral	3. individual	4. interval	5. mental
Practice 4	1. races	2. relative	3. shadow	4. pioneer	5. pray
Practice 5	1. Vowels	2. stomach	3. withdraw	4. talent	5. transferred

17. wear out : 닳아 떨어지다   18. troop[truːp] ***n.*** (보통 ***pl.***) 군대, 부대   19. for generations : 여러 세대 동안

Lesson 1 종합 연습 문제

1 네 개의 단어 중 다른 셋과 관련이 없는 것을 골라 공란에 그 번호를 써넣어라.

_____ 1. (A) compliment (B) commendation (C) approach (D) praise
_____ 2. (A) attend (B) draw (C) haul (D) drag
_____ 3. (A) candid (B) curious (C) frank (D) honest
_____ 4. (A) interval (B) omit (C) break (D) pause
_____ 5. (A) splendid (B) neutral (C) magnificent (D) grand
_____ 6. (A) race (B) situation (C) condition (D) case
_____ 7. (A) aching (B) painful (C) delicious (D) sore
_____ 8. (A) conflict (B) event (C) struggle (D) fight
_____ 9. (A) obey (B) command (C) conduct (D) direct
_____ 10. (A) happening (B) event (C) incident (D) pioneer

2 왼쪽에 주어진 우리말과 같은 뜻을 가진 단어를 골라 그 번호를 공란에 써넣어라.

_____ 1. ~에게 영향을 주다 (A) conflict (B) cooperate (C) affect (D) attend
_____ 2. 비난 (A) blame (B) responsibility (C) stomach (D) talent
_____ 3. 맛있는 (A) incurious (B) delicious (C) dull (D) candid
_____ 4. 개척자 (A) bubble (B) consonant (C) peacock (D) pioneer
_____ 5. 친척, 인척 (A) neutral (B) relative (C) uncle (D) resort

3 왼쪽에 주어진 단어와 반대되는 뜻을 가진 단어를 골라 그 번호를 공란에 써넣어라.

_____ 1. compliment (A) conflict (B) blame (C) success (D) failure
_____ 2. indifferent (A) delicious (B) dull (C) curious (D) magnificent
_____ 3. deceitful (A) dull (B) grand (C) neutral (D) frank
_____ 4. momentary (A) everlasting (B) transient (C) liberal (D) important
_____ 5. withdraw (A) haul (B) draw (C) advance (D) cooperate

4. 괄호 속에 주어진 우리말과 같은 뜻을 가진 단어를 사용하여 문장을 완성하라.

1. Although he was a F_____E at school, he became a successful man later. (실패작)
2. He was so C_____S to know what was in the letter that he opened it, even though it was addressed to his sister. (호기심이 강한)
3. Will you be quite F___K with me about this matter? (솔직한)
4. In their school they have an I_____L of ten minutes for recess[20]. (시간의 간격)
5. The police watched the cafe to which the robber was known to R____T. (자주 가다)

5. 이탤릭체로 된 단어와 같은 뜻을 가진 단어를 골라 그 번호를 공란에 써넣어라.

_____ 1. Steam can *generate* electricity by turning an electric generator[21].
(A) change   (B) produce   (C) stop   (D) spread

_____ 2. He earned high *commendation* from the people for his bravery.
(A) reward   (B) pride   (C) praise   (D) consideration

_____ 3. The policeman *halted* the speeding car[22] to see if the driver was drunk.
(A) stopped   (B) found   (C) chased   (D) caught

_____ 4. I have a *sore* throat from cold.
(A) strong   (B) weak   (C) clear   (D) painful

_____ 5. I will show you the *magnificent* palace of the king.
(A) grand   (B) ancient   (C) colorful   (D) dull

Answers

1. 1. C 2. A 3. B 4. B 5. B 6. A 7. C 8. B 9. A 10. D
2. 1. C 2. A 3. B 4. D 5. B
3. 1. B 2. C 3. D 4. A 5. C
4. 1. FAILURE 2. CURIOUS 3. FRANK 4. INTERVAL 5. RESORT
5. 1. B 2. C 3. A 4. D 5. A

---

20. recess[risés/ríːses] *n.* 휴식   21. generator[dʒénəreitər] *n.* 발전기   22. speeding car : 과속 차량

LESSON 2

Self-test 2

적당한 단어를 골라 빈칸을 채우라.

1. The rider *cursed* his _____ horse.
   (A) great (B) bad

2. An *absolute* ruler can do just as _____.
   (A) people tell him (B) he pleases

3. There is usually a *ceremony* when a new building is _____.
   (A) opened (B) destroyed

4. The _____ was sent to him by *freight*.
   (A) letter (B) box

5. The *peak* of the roof is the _____ part of the house.
   (A) highest (B) lowest

1. (B) 2. (B) 3. (A) 4. (B) 5. (A)

New Vocabulary -1

absolute
[ǽbsəluːt]
adj. 절대적인, 비할 바 없는
ant. relative
He is a man of *absolute* honesty.

agency
[éidʒənsi]
n. 대리점
The Ford Company has *agencies* all over the country.

attitude
[ǽtitjuːd]
n. 태도, 자세
syn. manner
He took a sympathetic[1] *attitude* toward my situation.

---

1. sympathetic [simpəθétik] *adj.* 동정어린, 동정심 있는

blank [blæŋk]	***adj.*** 공백의, 백지의, 빈 **syn.** empty Please write your name in the *blank* space at the top of the page.
bulk [bʌlk]	***n.*** 양, 용적, 부피 **syn.** volume A vast[2] *bulk* of coal is still stored in the basement[3].
ceremony [sérimәni]	***n.*** 의식, 의례 Their marriage *ceremony* was performed in the church.
commerce [kɔ́mә(ː)rs]	***n.*** 상업, 무역 거래 **syn.** trade ***adj.*** commercial Our country has grown rich because of its *commerce* with other nations.
confuse [kәnfjúːz]	***v.*** 혼돈하다, 혼란시키다 **syn.** embarrass, puzzle, confound ***n.*** confusion Even their own mother sometimes *confused* the twins.
copper [kɔ́pәr]	***n.*** 구리, 동(銅) *Copper* is easily shaped into thin sheets or fine wire[4].
curse [kәːrs]	***v.*** 저주하다, 욕설을 퍼붓다 He *cursed* the poor waitress who had spilled[5] soup on him.

Practice 1

위 단어를 사용하여 아래 문장을 완성하라. 필요시 단어를 적절한 형태로 변형하라.

1. He stood there in a threatening _____.

2. _____ is an excellent conductor[6] of heat and electricity.

3. He _____ when a car almost hit him.

4. Long ago some rulers had _____ power.

5. If you try to learn too many things at the same time, you may get _____.

---

2. vast[væst] ***adj.*** 거대한, 막대한   3. basement[béismәnt] ***n.*** 지하실   4. fine wire : 가는 철사   5. spill[spil] ***v.*** 흘리다, 엎지르다
6. conductor[kәndʌ́tәr] ***n.*** 전도체

New Vocabulary -2

delight
[diláit]
n. 기쁨, 환희
syn. pleasure
ant. sorrow, grief, despair
Moving pictures[7] give great *delight* to millions of people.

disappear
[disəpiər]
v. 사라지다, 없어지다, 소멸되다
syn. vanish, fade
ant. appear
The little boy *disappeared* around the corner.

drift
[drift]
n. v. 표류(하다)
The boat was taken out to sea by the *drift* of the tide.

employ
[implɔ́i]
v. (사람을) 쓰다, 고용하다
syn. hire, engage
That big factory *employs* many workers.

evidence
[évidəns]
n. 증거(물), 증언
syn. proof, testimony
adj. evident
adv. evidently
When the police arrived, he had already destroyed all the *evidence*.

faculty
[fǽkəlti]
n. 1. 재능, 능력
syn. capability, capacity
John has the *faculty* to learn languages easily.

2. 교직원, 교수진
That will be discussed in the next *faculty* meeting.

financial
[fainǽnʃəl]
adj. 재정적인, 재정상의, 회계의
syn. fiscal, monetary
n. finance
Before he decides to study abroad, he has to solve *financial* problems.

freight
[freit]
n. 운송 화물
syn. cargo
This aircraft[8] company deals with *freight* only; it has no travel service.

---

7. moving picture : 영화   8. aircraft[ɛ́ərkrɑːft/-kræft] *n.* 항공기(의 총칭)

generous
[dʒénərəs]

adj. 인심 좋은, 관대한
syn. liberal, lavish
ant. mean
n. generosity
It was very *generous* of them to share their meal with their poor neighbors.

handy
[hǽndi]

adj. 편리한, 손재주 있는
syn. convenient
There were *handy* shelves[9] near the kitchen sink.

Practice 2

위 단어를 사용하여 아래 문장을 완성하라. 필요시 단어를 적절한 형태로 변형하라.

1. He was very _____ in his treatment of the captives[10].
2. He has a great _____ for arithmetic[11].
3. The city of London is a great _____ center in Europe.
4. The steel manufacturing company[12] _____ most of young men in town.
5. This _____ must be carefully handled when loading.

New Vocabulary -3

horrible
[hɔ́rəbl]

adj. 무시무시한, 무서운
syn. ghastly, hideous, frightful, horrid
n. horror
I have never seen such a *horrible* car accident.

industrious
[indʌ́striəs]

adj. 근면한, 부지런한,
syn. diligent, busy
ant. lazy
An *industrious* student usually has good grades.

intimate
[íntimit]

adj. 친밀한, 친분이 두터운
syn. familiar
n. intimacy
adv. intimately
Although my brother knew many people, he had few *intimate* friends.

---

9. shelf [ʃelf] *n.* (*pl.* shelves) 선반   10. captive [kǽptiv] *n.* 포로   11. arithmetic [əríθmətik] *n.* 산수   12. steel manufacturing company : 철강 제조 회사

knowledge [nálidʒ/nɔ́l-]	*n.* 지식, 아는 것 A baby has no *knowledge* of good and evil.
liberty [líbərti]	*n.* 자유, 해방, 석방 **syn.** freedom **ant.** slavery They fought to defend their *liberty* against the invaders.
majesty [mǽdʒisti]	*n.* 장엄, 위엄 **syn.** greatness, grandeur, dignity They were inspired[13] by the *majesty* of the snow-covered mountains.
mention [ménʃən]	*v.* 언급하다, ~에 관해 말하다 Do not *mention* the terrible accident before the little children.
monument [mɔ́njumənt]	*n.* 기념물, 유적, 기념비 **syn.** statue The ruins of the castle is an ancient *monument*, which the government pays money to preserve[14].
nickname [níkneim]	*n.* 별명, 애칭 He got the *nickname* "Fatty" because he was very fat.
onion [ʌ́njən]	*n.* 양파 *Onion* has a very strong smell and taste.

Practice 3

위 단어를 사용하여 아래 문장을 완성하라. 필요시 단어를 적절한 형태로 변형하라.

1. He is a(n) _____ student and deserves[15] good grades.

2. The _____ of the Niagara Falls attracts a number of visitors.

3. I heard many _____ stories from my grandfather when I was young.

4. She opened the cage and gave the bird its _____.

5. He has a good _____ of the French history.

---

13. inspire[inspáiər] *v.* ~에게 영감을 주다, 격려하다   14. preserve[prizə́ːrv] *v.* 보존하다   15. deserve[dizə́ːrv] *v.* ~을 받을 만하다

New Vocabulary -4

peak
[pi:k]
n. 절정, 꼭대기, 정점
syn. summit, top
ant. foot, bottom
The mountain *peak* is covered with snow all the year.

pit
[pit]
n. 구덩이, 구멍, 갱(坑)
syn. hole
Water collected in the *pit* left when the old tree was uprooted[16].

preach
[pri:tʃ]
n. v. 설교(하다), 전도(하다)
Many people went to church to hear him *preach*.

proof
[pru:f]
n. 증거, 증명
syn. evidence
v. prove
We must wait for better *proof* before we believe.

rag
[ræg]
n. 넝마 (조각), 걸레 (조각)
adj. ragged
She wiped[17] her boots with a *rag*.

release
[rilí:s]
v. 풀어놓다, 석방하다
ant. hold
After he was *released* from prison, he came home directly.

responsibility
[rispənsəbíləti]
n. 책임, 의무
adj. responsible
Now that[18] you are 13, you should have more sense of *responsibility*.

rude
[ru:d]
adj. 버릇없는, 무례한, 교양 없는
syn. impolite
ant. polite
It is *rude* to stare[19] at people or to point with a finger.

scorn
[skɔ:rn]
n. 경멸, 멸시
We feel *scorn* for a traitor.

---

16. uproot[ʌprúːt] *v.* 뿌리째 뽑다   17. wipe[waip] *v.* 닦다, 씻다   18. now (that): ~이니까, ~인 이상   19. stare[stɛər] *v.* 노려보다 (at)

	v. 경멸하다, 멸시하다
	syn. despise, contempt
	ant. respect
	The woman *scorned* my offer of help.

shallow	*adj.* 얕은, 천박한
[ʃǽlou]	ant. deep
	The lake is too *shallow* for swimming.

Practice 4

위 단어를 사용하여 아래 문장을 완성하라. 필요시 단어를 적절한 형태로 변형하라.

1. Do you have any _____ that you weren't there at 9 o'clock last night?
2. The nurse will be _____ from duty at seven o'clock.
3. Most pupils feel _____ for those who cheat in the exam.
4. He _____ that God would soon destroy the evil world.
5. Don't be so _____ to your teacher.

New Vocabulary -5

soul	*n.* 영혼
[soul]	syn. spirit
	ant. body, flesh
	They were praying for the *souls* of the dead.

sprinkle	*v.* 흩뿌리다, 살포하다
[spríŋkl]	syn. scatter
	ant. gather, collect
	He *sprinkled* sand along the icy path[20].

stoop	*v.* 몸을 굽히다, 굴복하다
[stu:p]	syn. bend
	He *stooped* to pick up the paper.

sum	*n.* 1. 금액, 액수
[sʌm]	syn. amount
	He paid the *sum* of $10 for a new bag.

---

20. icy path : 빙판길

	2. 총계, 합계
	The *sum* of 2 and 3 is 5.
talkative [tɔ́ːkətiv]	*adj.* 수다스러운, 말이 많은
	ant. quiet
	No men likes *talkative* women.
throughout [θruːáut]	*adv.* 완전히, 모조리, 빠짐없이
	ant. entirely
	The woodwork[21] in the house was rotten *throughout*.
	prep. ~의 구석구석까지, ~의 도처에
	His name is famous *throughout* the world.
transport [trænspɔ́ːrt]	*v.* 수송하다, 운송하다
	n. transportation
	Wheat is *transported* from the farms to the mills.
utter [ʌ́tər]	*v.* 발언하다, 말하다
	syn. speak
	n. utterance
	He was gone before she could *utter* a word.
	adj. 전적인, 완전한
	syn. complete
	She is an *utter* stranger to me.
voyage [vɔ́idʒ]	*n. v.* 항해(하다)
	syn. navigation
	The *voyage* from England to India used to take six months.
wither [wíðər]	*v.* 시들다, 말라빠지다
	syn. fade
	The grass *withered* in the sun.

Practice 5

위 단어를 사용하여 아래 문장을 완성하라. 필요시 단어를 적절한 형태로 변형하라.

1. Many people believe in the immortality[22] of the _____.

---

21. woodwork[wúdwəːrk] *n.* (집 따위의) 목조 부분   22. immortality[iməːrtǽləti] *n.* 불멸, 불후성(不朽性)

2. The flowers _____ in the cold.

3. She _____ her head to get into the car.

4. We _____ ashes on the icy sidewalk[23] this morning.

5. The goods were _____ by rail and ship.

Practice 1	1. attitude	2. Copper	3. cursed	4. absolute	5. confused
Practice 2	1. generous	2. faculty	3. financial	4. employs	5. freight
Practice 3	1. industrious	2. majesty	3. horrible	4. liberty	5. knowledge
Practice 4	1. proof	2. released	3. scorn	4. preached	5. rude
Practice 5	1. soul	2. wither(ed)	3. stooped	4. sprinkled	5. transported

23. sidewalk [sáidwɔːk] *n.* (포장된) 인도, 보도

Lesson 2 종합 연습문제

1 이탤릭체로된 단어와 같은 뜻을 가진 단어를 골라 그 번호를 공란에 써넣어라.

_____ 1. a great *faculty* for music   (A) member   (B) capability
                                                                                             (C) audience   (D) knowledge

_____ 2. clear *evidence*   (A) proof   (B) knowledge
                                                 (C) situation   (D) agency

_____ 3. a bulk of *freight*   (A) weight   (B) surprise
                                                 (C) failure   (D) cargo

_____ 4. a *handy* little box   (A) relative   (B) heavy
                                                 (C) convenient   (D) cheap

_____ 5. a *horrible* accident   (A) dangerous   (B) ghastly
                                                 (C) sore   (D) big

_____ 6. the *majesty* of the mountains   (A) grandeur   (B) faculty
                                                 (C) monument   (D) honor

_____ 7. the *peak* of a mountain   (A) foot   (B) summit
                                                 (C) height   (D) horn

_____ 8. *rude* remarks   (A) loud   (B) impolite
                                                 (C) direct   (D) candid

_____ 9. to *sprinkle* water on the road   (A) scatter   (B) draw
                                                 (C) drink   (D) gather

_____ 10. large *sum* of money   (A) spending   (B) peak
                                                 (C) amount   (D) resort

2 왼쪽에 주어진 우리말과 같은 뜻을 가진 단어를 골라 그 번호를 공란에 써넣어라.

_____ 1. 흩뿌리다   (A) pour   (B) halt
                                  (C) scorn   (D) sprinkle

_____ 2. 시들다   (A) rub   (B) utter
                                (C) wither   (D) resort

_____ 3. 상업   (A) commerce   (B) industry
                                (C) finance   (D) freight

_____ 4. 저주하다   (A) release   (B) curse
                                (C) blame   (D) pray

_____ 5. 설교하다   (A) utter   (B) mention
                                (C) preach   (D) affect

Lesson 2 종합 연습 문제

3 왼쪽에 주어진 단어와 반대되는 뜻을 가진 단어를 골라 그 번호를 공란에 써넣어라.

_____ 1. vanish (A) disappear (B) spread
                       (C) appear   (D) attend

_____ 2. generous (A) liberal   (B) mean
                        (C) special   (D) common

_____ 3. industrious (A) handy   (B) diligent
                          (C) lazy   (D) agricultural

_____ 4. release (A) hold   (B) work
                       (C) withdraw   (D) draw

_____ 5. rude   (A) frank   (B) low
                       (C) peak   (D) polite

_____ 6. scorn   (A) contempt   (B) wet
                       (C) cooperation (D) respect

_____ 7. shallow (A) delightful (B) shade
                       (C) deep   (D) delicious

_____ 8. soul   (A) straight   (B) body
                       (C) haul   (D) grand

_____ 9. absolute (A) relative (B) present
                        (C) intimate (D) diligent

_____ 10. delight (A) pleasure (B) sorrow
                        (C) horror   (D) scorn

4 괄호 속에 주어진 우리말과 같은 뜻을 가진 단어를 사용하여 문장을 완성하라.

1. It is R__E to say you don't like hot food, when she spent so long preparing it. (무례한)
2. He seemed to S____N women, and never married. (경멸하다)
3. He becomes very T_____E when he gets drunk. (수다스러운)
4. His A_____E toward school changed from dislike to great enthusiasm[24] .(태도)
5. He is a member of the college F_____Y. (교수진)

5 가장 적합한 단어를 골라 빈칸을 채우라.

_____ 1. We need a great _____ of coal for this coming winter.
           (A) empire   (B) pit   (C) bubble   (D) bulk

---

24. enthusiasm [inθjúːziæzəm] ***n.*** 열성, 열의

_____ 2. To his great _____ he passed the examination easily.
   (A) delight   (B) despair   (C) faculty   (D) convenience

_____ 3. There was not enough _____ to prove him guilty of the crime.
   (A) faculty   (B) evidence   (C) conflict   (D) neutral

_____ 4. Though he didn't have much money to give, he was very _____ with his money.
   (A) curious   (B) magnificent   (C) generous   (D) neutral

_____ 5. They built a _____ in memory of Abraham Lincoln.
   (A) monument   (B) cemetery   (C) freight   (D) majesty

6 왼쪽에 주어진 단어의 적당한 파생어를 사용하여 문장을 완성하라.

1. *horrible*   The little girl has a _____ of snakes and spiders[25].

2. *intimate*   The _____ with which the two friends talked showed how fond[26] they were of each other.

3. *confuse*   If you write more clearly, you will prevent the _____ of your readers.

4. *utter*   His crazy _____ disappointed everyone around him.

5. *proof*   In order to _____ the servant's honesty, she left a bag containing money on the table.

Answers

1. 1. B 2. A 3. D 4. C 5. B 6. A 7. B 8. B 9. A 10. C

2. 1. D 2. C 3. A 4. B 5. C

3. 1. C 2. B 3. C 4. A 5. D 6. D 7. C 8. B 9. A 10. B

4. 1. RUDE   2. SCORN   3. TALKATIVE   4. ATTITUDE   5. FACULTY

5. 1. D 2. A 3. B 4. C 5. A

6. 1. horror   2. intimacy   3. confusion   4. utterance   5. prove

---

25. spider[spaidər] *n.* 거미   26. be fond of ~ : ~을 좋아하다

LESSON 3

Self-test 3

적당한 단어를 골라 빈칸을 채우라.

1. My feet were *damp* from walking home in the _____.
   (A) sun (B) rain

2. When he learned that he had _____ the test, he felt *relieved*.
   (A) passed (B) failed

3. He could not resist[1] the *attraction* of a(n) _____ girl.
   (A) pretty (B) ugly

4. The woman showed *mercy* to the hungry beggar and gave him _____.
   (A) no food (B) some food

5. _____ are *tame* animals.
   (A) Cows and hens (B) Tigers and lions

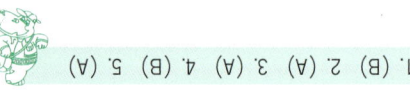
1. (B) 2. (A) 3. (A) 4. (B) 5. (A)

New Vocabulary -1

academic
[ækədémik]
adj. 학원의, 학구적인
syn. scholastic
The *academic* year begins when school opens in March.

ahead
[əhéd]
adv. 전방에[으로], 앞에[으로]
Tom was a quick walker, so he soon got *ahead* of the others.

attraction
[ətrǽkʃən]
n. 매력, 유혹, 끄는 힘
syn. charm
v. attract
He cannot resist the *attraction* of the sea in hot weather.

---
1. resist[rizíst] *v.* 이겨내다, 견디다

blaze
[bleiz]

n. 불길, 광휘
syn. flame
I put some wood on the fire and it soon burst into a *blaze*.

challenge
[tʃǽlindʒ]

v. ~에 도전하다
I *challenged* him to game of tennis.

commit
[kəmít]

v. 1. (죄, 과실을)범하다, 저지르다
A man who steals *commits* a crime.
2. 위임하다, 위탁하다
n. commitment
He *committed* himself to the doctor's care.

congress
[kɔ́ŋgres]

n. 국회, 의회
syn. parliament, assembly
In some countries, the *congress* is composed of a Senate[2] and a House of Representatives[3].

correction
[kərékʃən]

n. 정정, 수정, 교정
v. correct
Teachers usually make *corrections* in red ink.

damp
[dæmp]

adj. 습기 있는, 축축한
syn. wet, moist
ant. dry
If you sleep between *damp* sheets, you will probably catch cold[4].

demand
[dimǽnd]

v. 요구하다, 필요로 하다
syn. require, request, claim
ant. waive, grant
This sort of work *demands* great patience[5].

Practice *1*

위 단어를 사용하여 아래 문장을 완성하라. 필요시 단어를 적절한 형태로 변형하라.

1. Our school _____ the neighboring school's team to a game of football last week.
2. In the U. S. A., the _____ is the law-making body, consisting of the Senate and the House of Representatives.

---

2. Senate [sénit] *n.* (미국의) 상원   3. House of Representatives : 하원   4. catch cold : 감기 들다   5. patience [péiʃəns] *n.* 인내, 끈기

3. If you fall into a river your clothes will be wet; if you walk in the rain for a short time they will be _____.

4. History and French are _____ subjects; typewriting and bookkeeping[6] are commercial subjects.

5. Columbus was _____ of his times in his belief that the world was round.

New Vocabulary -2

disappoint
[disəpɔ́int]

v. 실망시키다, 실망하다
syn. despair
n. disappointment
I was *disappointed* when I heard you couldn't come to the party.

drown
[dráun]

v. 물에 빠져 죽다, 물에 빠뜨리다
The fisherman almost *drowned* when his boat was overturned[7].

encourage
[inkʌ́ridʒ]

v. 용기를 복돋우다, 격려하다
syn. hearten, incite, inspire
ant. discourage, disappoint
The teacher's praise *encouraged* the students to study hard.

evident
[évidənt]

adj. 명백한, 분명한
syn. plain, clear, obvious, apparent
ant. ambiguous
n. evidence
It is now *evident* that, if I don't study hard, I'll fail the course.

fable
[féibl]

n. 우화(寓話), 지어낸 이야기
He read stories to the children from an old book of *fables*.

firm
[fəːrm]

adj. 굳은, 단단한
syn. solid, hard, stiff
ant. loose
We build houses on *firm* ground.

---

6. bookkeeping[búkkiːpiŋ] *n.* 부기(簿記)   7. overturn[ouvərtə́ːrn] *v.* 뒤집다, 뒤집히다

frequent
[frí:kwənt]

adj. 자주 일어나는, 빈번한
syn. common, numerous
ant. rare
n. frequency
Sudden rainstorms are *frequent* on this coast.

genius
[dʒí:njəs]

n. 천재, 수재
Important discoveries and inventions are usually made by men of *genius*.

habor
[há:rbər]

n. 항구
syn. port
The ship is in the *harbor* of New York.

howl
[haul]

v. 울부짖다, 노호(怒號)하다
syn. yell, shout
The dogs were *howling* at the stranger.

Practice 2

위 단어를 사용하여 아래 문장을 완성하라. 필요시 단어를 적절한 형태로 변형하라.

1. He jumped into the river and saved the _____ man.

2. It is not a(n) _____ but a real story.

3. The cheers[8] of their schoolmates _____ the players to try to win the game for the school.

4. He was very _____ when I said he had to stay at home on Sunday.

5. The little girl's joy was _____ when she saw the present her father had bought her.

---

8. cheer[tʃiər] *n.* 갈채, 환호, 격려

New Vocabulary -3

infamous
[ínfəməs]
adj. 악명 높은, 불명예스런
syn. notorious, disreputable
Everybody doesn't like him because he is an *infamous* liar.

introduce
[ìntrədjúːs]
v. 소개하다, 인사시키다
n. introduction
adj. introductory
The chairman *introduced* the speaker to the audience[9].

labor
[léibər]
n. 노동, 근로, 노고
syn. effort
adj. laborious
The majority of men earn their living by manual[10] *labor*.

lid
[lid]
n. 뚜껑, 덮개
syn. cover
Do not open the *lid* of the stove.

majority
[mədʒɔ́rəti]
n. 대다수, 대부분
ant. minority
The *majority* of people prefer[11] peace to war.

mercy
[mə́ːrsi]
n. 자비, 연민, 인정
adj. merciful
He showed *mercy* to his enemies and let them live.

moral
[mɔ́rəl]
adj. 도덕적인, 도덕의
syn. ethical
ant. immoral
n. morality
The teacher felt a *moral* responsibility for the student's crime.

nod
[nɔd]
v. (머리를) 끄덕이다, 묵례하다
The president *nodded* and everyone sat down around the table.

operate
[ɔ́pəreit]
v. 작동하다, 작용하다, 움직이다
n. operation
The machine *operates* day and night.

---

9. audience[ɔ́ːdiəns] *n.* 청중, 관중   10. manual[mǽnjuəl] *adj.* 손으로 하는   11. prefer A to B : A를 B보다 좋아하다

painful
[péinfəl]

adj. 아픈, 괴로운, 비통한
ant. pleasant
n. pain
He had a *painful* cut on his thumb[12].

Practice 3

위 단어를 사용하여 아래 문장을 완성하라. 필요시 단어를 적절한 형태로 변형하라.

1. He tried to _____ a sewing machine.[13]
2. Tobacco[14] was _____ into Europe from America.
3. To win an election, a candidate[15] must receive the _____ of the votes.
4. Land, _____ and capital are the three principal[16] factors of production.
5. They showed little _____ to their enemies.

New Vocabulary –4

pearl
[pəːrl]

n. 진주
The natural *pearl* is much more expensive than a cultured one[17].

pitch
[pitʃ]

v. 1. 던지다, 팽개치다
syn. throw
Every child likes to *pitch* stones into a lake.

2. 세우다, (천막을) 치다
syn. erect
We *pitched* our tent under the tree.

precious
[préʃəs]

adj. 귀중한, 값진, 가치 있는
syn. valuable
ant. cheap
Time is *precious*; do not waste it on worthless deeds[18].

property
[prápərti]

n. 재산, 자산, 소유물, 소유지
syn. possessions
The police found some stolen *property* hidden in the thief's house.

---

12. thumb[θʌm] *n.* 엄지손가락   13. sewing machine : 재봉틀   14. tobacco[təbǽkou] *n.* 담배   15. candidate[kǽndidit] *n.* 후보자
16. principal[prínsəpəl] *adj.* 주요한, 으뜸가는   17. cultured pearl : 양식(養殖) 진주   18. worthless deeds : 무가치한 행동

rage
[reidʒ]

n. 격노, 분노
syn. anger, fury
He flew into a *rage* when he found they had gone without him.

relieve
[rilí:v]

v. 1. 완화하다, 경감하다
n. relief
The medicine will soon *relieve* your headache.

2. 안심시키다, 위로하다
We were *relieved* to hear that you had arrived safely.

restless
[réstlis]

adj. 안절부절못하는, 참지 못하는
syn. uneasy
ant. calm
He couldn't sit still; he was very *restless*.

rug
[rʌg]

n. 융단, 까는 모피
syn. carpet
There were several small *rugs* in the living room.

scout
[skaut]

n. 척후, 정찰병
The *scouts* went out during the night.

shame
[ʃeim]

n. 수치, 의욕
syn. humiliation, dishonor
ant. boldness
She felt *shame* at having been so thoughtless[19].

Practice 4

위 단어를 사용하여 아래 문장을 완성하라. 필요시 단어를 적절한 형태로 변형하라.

1. In his _____ at being scolded, he broke the teacher's vase.
2. The child blushed[20] with _____ when he was caught stealing candy.
3. She was presented a beautiful necklace of _____ on her birthday.
4. The city is growing and _____ in the center is becoming more valuable.
5. The sick child passed a _____ night.

---

19. thoughtless[θɔ́:tlis] *adj.* 지각 없는, 조심성 없는   20. blush[blʌʃ] *v.* 얼굴을 붉히다

New Vocabulary -5

sketch
[sketʃ]

n. 스케치, 초안, 줄거리
syn. outline, plan
He gave me a *sketch* of his plans for the expedition[21].

sound
[saund]

adj. 건전한, 온건한, 흠 없는
syn. healthy
He had a *sound* body; he is in healthy condition.

n. 음, 소리, 음성
They heard the *sound* of the train whistle.

spy
[spai]

n. 염탐군, 간첩, 첩자
The *spy* reported the development of a new weapon.

v. 염탐하다, 몰래 조사하다
His job was to *spy* on the enemy.

storage
[stɔ́:ridʒ]

n. 저장(소), 보관(소)
A cold *storage* is used to keep eggs and meat from spoiling.

summon
[sʌ́mən]

v. 소환하다, 호출하다
syn. call
They were *summoned* to the bedside of their dying father.

tame
[teim]

adj. 길든, 유순한
syn. domesticated
ant. wild
It is not difficult to ride a *tame* horse.

v. 길들이다
He *tamed* the lions for the circus.

thrust
[θrʌst]

v. 밀어넣다, 찌르다, 찔러 박다
p., pp. thrust
Jack *thrust* his hands into his pockets.

trap
[træp]

n. 올가미, 함정, 덫
The police set a *trap* to catch the escaped prisoner[22].

---

21. expedition[ekspidíʃən] *n.* 탐험 여행, 원정   22. escaped prisoner : 탈옥수

vaccinate
[vǽksəneit]

v. 예방 주사를 놓다
He was *vaccinated* against several diseases at one time[23].

wage
[wéidʒ]

n. 임금(賃金), 급료
syn. salary, pay
His *wage* is $30 a week.

witness
[witnis]

v. 목격하다, 입증하다
The boy *witnessed* the accident.

n. 목격자, 증인
He made the remark[24] in the presence of several *witnesses*.

Practice 5

위 단어를 사용하여 아래 문장을 완성하라. 필요시 단어를 적절한 형태로 변형하라.

1. They were asking for a _____ increase of $5 a week.
2. She made a _____ of the landscape in pencil before painting it.
3. His furniture is in _____ while he finds a new house.
4. The birds are so _____ that they eat from our hands.
5. I was _____ against typhus[25] last month.

해답					
Practice 1	1. challenged	2. Congress	3. damp	4. academic	5. ahead
Practice 2	1. drowning	2. fable	3. encouraged	4. disappointed	5. evident
Practice 3	1. operate	2. introduced	3. majority	4. labor	5. mercy
Practice 4	1. rage	2. shame	3. pearls	4. property	5. restless
Practice 5	1. wage	2. sketch	3. storage	4. tame	5. vaccinated

23. at one time : 동시에, 한꺼번에   24. make the remark : 발언하다   25. typhus [táifəs] *n.* 발진 티푸스

종합 연습 문제 Lesson 3

1 네 개의 단어 중 다른 셋과 관련이 없는 것을 골라 공란에 그 번호를 써넣어라.

_____ 1.	(A) wet	(B) curious	(C) moist	(D) damp
_____ 2.	(A) sum	(B) wage	(C) salary	(D) pay
_____ 3.	(A) require	(B) demand	(C) claim	(D) desire
_____ 4.	(A) sketch	(B) bulk	(C) outline	(D) plan
_____ 5.	(A) dishonor	(B) shame	(C) shade	(D) humiliation
_____ 6.	(A) firm	(B) hard	(C) solid	(D) damp
_____ 7.	(A) notorious	(B) infamous	(C) horrible	(D) disreputable
_____ 8.	(A) rage	(B) fury	(C) anger	(D) scorn
_____ 9.	(A) common	(B) unusual	(C) numerous	(D) frequent
_____ 10.	(A) evident	(B) absolute	(C) clear	(D) obvious

2 왼쪽에 주어진 우리말과 같은 뜻을 가진 단어를 골라 그 번호를 공란에 써넣어라.

_____ 1. 길든, 유순한   (A) rude   (B) generous
                                    (C) tame   (D) fame

_____ 2. (머리를) 끄덕이다   (A) vanish   (B) spy
                                    (C) haul   (D) nod

_____ 3. 분노   (A) wage   (B) voyage
                                    (C) pitch   (D) rage

_____ 4. 죄를 범하다   (A) commit   (B) relieve
                                    (C) release   (D) scorn

_____ 5. 물에 빠지다   (A) wage   (B) drown
                                    (C) vaccinate   (D) trap

3 왼쪽에 주어진 단어와 반대되는 뜻을 가진 단어를 골라 그 번호를 공란에 써넣어라.

_____ 1. evident   (A) firm   (B) ambiguous
                              (C) excellent   (D) plain

_____ 2. demand   (A) direct   (B) command
                               (C) request   (D) grant

_____ 3. encourage   (A) disappear   (B) relieve
                                 (C) affect   (D) wither

_____ 4. frequent   (A) shallow   (B) evident
                              (C) rude   (D) rare

_____ 5. shame   (A) charm   (B) rug
                          (C) boldness   (D) challenge

Lesson 3

종합 연습 문제

4 괄호 속에 주어진 우리말과 같은 뜻을 가진 단어를 사용하여 문장을 완성하라.

1. He is the only W_____S of the accident. (증인, 목격자)
2. I saw him T____T the tent pole into the ground. (찔러 박다)
3. Aspirin will R_____E your headache. (완화하다)
4. Children usually like to read old F___ES. (우화들)
5. Einstein was a mathematical and physical G____S. (천재)

5 이탤릭체로 된 단어와 같은 뜻을 가진 단어를 골라 그 번호를 공란에 써넣어라.

_____ 1. We could see the *blaze* of a cheerful fire through the window.
    (A) pitch   (B) rage   (C) fury   (D) flame

_____ 2. My parents will be *disappointed* if I fail the examination again.
    (A) despaired (B) disappeared (C) vanished (D) released

_____ 3. They put meat in the *trap* to attract the lion.
    (A) rug   (B) rag   (C) snare   (D) freight

_____ 4. The church bells *summon* people to worship[26].
    (A) call   (B) commit   (C) pray   (D) attract

_____ 5. The dog seemed *restless* as if he sensed some danger.
    (A) shallow   (B) uneasy   (C) generous   (D) painful

_____ 6. Your friendship is most *precious* to me.
    (A) firm   (B) evident   (C) rude   (D) valuable

_____ 7. We heard a wolf *howl* near the house.
    (A) disappear (B) yell   (C) drown   (D) thrust

_____ 8. He refused to join the army[27], believing that he had no *moral* right to kill.
    (A) ethical   (B) normal   (C) sound   (D) bold

_____ 9. The car is my *property*; you can't use it without my permission.
    (A) faculty   (B) possessions   (C) resort   (D) responsibility

_____ 10. The doctor said that the patient's[28] heart was *sound*.
    (A) healthy   (B) curious   (C) candid   (D) neutral

---

26. worship [wə́ːrʃip] *n.* 예배, 참배   27. join the army : 군에 입대하다   28. patient [péiʃənt] *n.* 환자

1. 1. B 2. A 3. D 4. B 5. C 6. D 7. C 8. D 9. B 10. B
2. 1. C 2. D 3. D 4. A 5. B
3. 1. B 2. D 3. D 4. D 5. C
4. 1. WITNESS 2. THRUST 3. RELIEVE 4. FABLES 5. GENIUS
5. 1. D 2. A 3. C 4. A 5. B 6. D 7. B 8. A 9. B 10. A

LESSON 4

Self-test 4

적당한 단어를 골라 빈칸을 채우라.

1. Just before sunset the *peasant* stopped working in the _____.
   (A) factory   (B) field

2. Let's _____ now and *resume* working at 2 o'clock.
   (A) stop   (B) start

3. The little girl was *frightened* by the _____ dog.
   (A) horrible   (B) beautiful

4. He looked _____ as if he had seen a *ghost*.
   (A) happy   (B) pale

5. Your hair is so *tangled* that it looks as if _____.
   (A) it has not been combed[1] for a week.
   (B) it has been combed every day

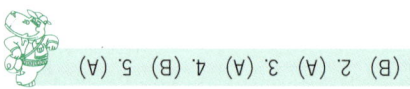

1. (B) 2. (A) 3. (A) 4. (B) 5. (A)

New Vocabulary -1

accentuate
[əkséntʃueit]
v. 두드러지게 하다, 강조하다
syn. emphasize, intensify
The dark frame *accentuates* the brightness of the picture.

aim
[eim]
v. 겨냥하다, 조준하다, 목표 삼다
He *aimed* at the lion, fired, and killed it.

n. 겨냥, 조준, 목적
The hunter took *aim* at the lion.

audience
[ɔ́ːdiəns]
n. 청중, 관객, 청취자
The *audience* were very excited by the show.

---

1. comb[koum] *v.* 빗다, 빗질하다

bless [bles]	*v.* 은총을 빌다, 은총을 내리다 **ant.** damn, curse They brought the children to church and the priest *blessed* them.
bundle [bʌ́ndl]	*n.* 묶음, 묶은 것 **syn.** bunch, parcel We sent her a large *bundle* of present of her birthday.
characteristic [kæriktərístik]	*n.* 특징, 특색 *v.* characterize What are the *characteristics* that distinguish[2] the Chinese from the Japanese?
communicate [kəmjúːnikeit]	*v.* 1. 의사를 서로 통하다 We can now *communicate* with people in Europe and America by telephone. 2. (사상, 지식, 정보 등을) 전달하다 *n.* communication Radio, television, and newspapers quickly *communicate* news to all parts of the world.
connect [kənékt]	*v.* 잇다, 연결하다, 접속시키다 **syn.** link *n.* connection The two towns are *connected* by a railway.
correspond [kɔrispɔ́nd]	*v.* 1. 편지 왕래를 하다, 통신하다 **syn.** communicate, write Janet and Bob *corresponded* for many years before they met. 2. 일치하다, 부합하다 **syn.** match, agree The house exactly *corresponds* with my needs.
darken [dáːrkən]	*v.* 어둡게 하다〔되다〕 **ant.** lighten **adj.** dark The sky quickly *darkened* after sunset.

Practice 1

위 단어를 사용하여 아래 문장을 완성하라. 필요시 단어를 적절한 형태로 변형하라.

1. The priest _____ the bread and wine in preparation for the ceremony.

---

2. distinguish [distíŋgwiʃ] *v.* 구별하다

2. His face was _____ with anger when he heard the bad news.

3. A popular television program may have a(n) _____ of several million people.

4. A useful _____ of the cat is its ability to catch and kill mice[3].

5. His expenses[4] do not _____ to his income.

New Vocabulary -2

deny
[dinái]

v. 부인(부정)하다, 거절하다
syn. reject
ant. affirm, admit
n. denial
Their employer *denied* them and increase of wage.

discharge
[distʃáːrdʒ]

v. 1. 배출하다, 배설하다
syn. eject
Factory chimneys *discharge* smoke into the atmosphere and make it dirty.

2. 해고시키다, 면직시키다
syn. dismiss
The servant was *discharged* for being dishonest.

dull
[dʌl]

adj. 무딘, 둔감한
syn. blunt, dim
ant. sharp, keen
The blade[5] of this knife is so *dull* that it will not cut a radish[6].

endeavor
[indévər]

n. 노력
syn. effort, attempt
He made an *endeavor* to save the drowning girl.

v. 노력하다
The sick man did not *endeavor* to get better.

excellence
[éksələns]

n. 탁월, 우수
syn. pre-eminence, superiority

---

3. mice[mais] *n.* 쥐(mouse의 복수)   4. expense[ikspéns] *n.* 지출, 비용   5. blade[bleid] *n.* 칼날   6. radish[rǽdiʃ] *n.* 무

adj. excellent
v. excel
His teacher praised him for the *excellence* of his report.

fade
[feid]
v. (꽃이) 시들다, (색깔이) 바래다
syn. wither, disappear, dim
The flowers in the garden *faded* at the end of summer.

fist
[fist]
n. 주먹
He raised his *fist* and threatened to hit me.

frighten
[fráitn]
v. 깜짝 놀라게 하다
syn. surprise, terrify
n. fright
She was *frightened* to look down from the top of the tall building.

ghost
[goust]
n. 유령, 망령
syn. apparition
They claim that the *ghost* of the murdered man appears every night.

hardship
[háːrdʃip]
n. 고난, 곤경, 고초
syn. suffering, difficulty
ant. comfort
Hunger, cold, and sickness were among the *hardship* of pioneer life.

Practice 2

위 단어를 사용하여 아래 문장을 완성하라. 필요시 단어를 적절한 형태로 변형하라.

1. The old man's hearing has become _____, and you must speak loudly to him.
2. The Han River _____ its water into the Yellow Sea.
3. Everything is clear; how can we _____ the truth of his statement?
4. All memories of her childhood had _____ from her mind.
5. Thunder and lightning[7] _____ most children and many adults[8].

---

7. lightning [láitniŋ] *n.* 번갯불   8. adult [ǽdʌlt/ədʌ́lt] *n.* 어른, 성인(成人)

New Vocabulary -3

huge
[hju:dʒ]
adj. 거대한, 막대한
syn. gigantic, enormous, immense
Samson was a man of *huge* physical strength.

inferior
[infíəriər]
adj. 하위의, 열등의, 아래의
ant. superior
n. inferiority
His grades are *inferior* to[9] mine this semester.

invent
[invént]
v. 발명하다, 창안하다, 고안하다
syn. discover, devise
n. invention
Alexander Graham Bell *invented* the telephone in 1876.

lighten
[laitn]
v. 밝게 하다, 밝히다, 비추다
syn. brighten
ant. darken
A candle *lightened* the darkness of the great hall.

male
[meil]
n. 남자, 사내, 수컷
ant. female
Boys and men are *males*; girls and women are females.

merit
[mérit]
n. 장점, 공적, 업적, 수훈
syn. worth
ant. demerit
Each child will get a mark according to the *merit* of his work.

mortal
[mɔ́:rtl]
adj. 1. 치명적인, 죽음의
syn. fatal
n. mortality
He received a *mortal* wound soon after the battle began.

2. 인간의, 인생의
It's beyond *mortal* power to bring a dead man back to life[10].

opportunity
[ɔpərtjú:nəti]
n. 기회, 호기(好機)
syn. chance
I am glad to have this *opportunity* of speaking to you.

---

9. be inferior to ~ : ~ 보다 열등한   10. bring ~ to life : ~을 소생시키다

palace
[pǽlis]
n. 궁전, 대궐
His home is a *palace* compared to our poor little house.

peasant
[pézənt]
n. 농부, 농민
syn. farmer
Many *peasants* were needed to help the farmer with the harvest[11].

Practice 3

위 단어를 사용하여 아래 문장을 완성하라. 필요시 단어를 적절한 형태로 변형하라.

1. They are building a new _____ for their king.
2. For most birds the _____ is bigger and more brightly colored than the female.
3. I have had no _____ to give him your message, because I have not seen him.
4. Edison didn't _____ many useful things for money.
5. Whales and elephants are _____ animals.

New Vocabulary -4

pity
[piti]
n. 동정, 불쌍함
syn. sympathy
adj. pitiful
I gave the beggar some money, feeling *pity* for him.

preface
[préfis]
n. 서문, 서언
syn. foreword
What did the writer say in the *preface* of the book?

proportion
[prəpɔ́ːrʃən]
n. 비율, 비
The *proportion* of sunny days to rainy days last month was four to one.

range
[reindʒ]
n. 범위, 한계, 구역
syn. scope, extent
The power of God is outside the *range* of human understanding.

religious
[rilídʒəs]
adj. 종교의, 신앙심이 깊은
n. religion
Religious services[12] are held here every Sunday.

---

11. harvest[háːrvist] *n.* (곡식의) 수확, 추수   12. service[sə́ːrvis] *n.* 예배, 식(式)

resume
[rizjú:m]

v. 다시 계속하다, 다시 차지하다
n. resumption
We *resumed* our journey after a short rest.

ruin
[rú:in]

n. 파멸, 황폐, 폐허
syn. destruction
Proper care protects our property from *ruin*.

v. 파멸시키다, 황폐시키다
syn. destroy, spoil
She poured water all over my painting and *ruined* it.

scrape
[skreip]

v. 문지르다, 닦다
syn. rub
The boy *scraped* the mud from his shoes.

sharp
[ʃɑːrp]

adj. 날카로운, 뾰족한
syn. keen
ant. blunt, dull
She cut the meat with a *sharp* knife.

adv. 정각에
syn. exactly
The meeting starts at two o'clock *sharp*; don't be late.

skill
[skil]

n. 재주, 기술, 숙련
syn. ability, talent
The teacher managed her pupils with wonderful *skill*.

Practice 4

위 단어를 사용하여 아래 문장을 완성하라. 필요시 단어를 적절한 형태로 변형하라.

1. Too much smoking and drinking will _____ your health.

2. Mix water and orange juice in the _____ of three to one.

3. After two weeks' vacation, he _____ his work.

4. The policeman felt _____ for the lost and crying child.

5. Everyone within the _____ of his voice heard the remark and laughed.

New Vocabulary -5

sour
[sáuər]
adj. 신, 시큼한
syn. acid
Some people do not like lemon juice; it tastes *sour*.

square
[skwɛər]
n. 정사각형, 정방형
A *square* has four equal sides and four 90-degree angles.

stout
[staut]
adj. 건장한, 뚱뚱한
syn. fat
ant. slender
He was too *stout* to fit into his old clothes.

superintendent
[sjuːpərinténdənt]
n. 교장, 감독자
v. superintend
He is the *superintendent* of this school.

tangle
[tǽŋgl]
v. 엉키다, 엉키게 하다, 얽히다
syn. entangle
ant. disentangle
I don't like to sew[13] with thread that *tangles* easily.

thumb
[θʌm]
n. 엄지 손가락, 엄지 부분
He accidentally[14] hit his *thumb* with the hammer.

treaty
[tríːti]
n. 조약, 협정
syn. agreement
The peace *treaty* was signed in Paris last summer.

vanish
[vǽniʃ]
v. 사라지다, 없어지다
syn. disappear
ant. appear
Their fear *vanished* when the storm ended.

warfare
[wɔ́ːrfɛər]
n. 전쟁 (행위), 교전
syn. war
Civilians as well as soldiers take part in[15] modern *warfare*.

---

13. sew [sou] *v.* 꿰매다, 재봉하다   14. accidentally [æksədéntəli] *adv.* 우연히, 우발적으로   15. take part in ~ : ~에 참가하다

witty
[wíti]

adj. 재치 있는, 기지 있는
syn. clever
A *witty* person makes *witty* remarks.

Practice 5

위 단어를 사용하여 아래 문장을 완성하라. 필요시 단어를 적절한 형태로 변형하라.

1. The thief ran into the crowd and _____.
2. That trade _____ was signed by five countries.
3. Most green grapes or apples taste _____.
4. Your glove has a hole in the _____.
5. The _____ of our school is responsible for[16] our education.

Practice 1	1. blessed	2. darkened	3. audience	4. characteristic	5. correspond
Practice 2	1. dull	2. discharges	3. deny	4. faded	5. frighten
Practice 3	1. palace	2. male	3. opportunity	4. invent	5. huge
Practice 4	1. ruin	2. proportion	3. resumed	4. pity	5. range
Practice 5	1. vanished	2. treaty	3. sour	4. thumb	5. superintendent

16. be responsible for ~ : ~을 책임지다

Lesson 4 종합 연습 문제

1 이탤릭체로 된 단어와 같은 뜻을 가진 단어를 골라 그 번호를 공란에 써넣어라.

_____ 1. a *bunch* of flowers
    (A) field   (B) sum   (C) bundle   (D) file

_____ 2. major *characteristics* of the animal
    (A) features   (B) realms   (C) knots   (D) testimonies

_____ 3. to *deny* one's offer
    (A) preach   (B) reject   (C) curse   (D) accept

_____ 4. a *dull* color
    (A) keen   (B) ghastly   (C) horrible   (D) dim

_____ 5. to make every *endeavor*
    (A) effort   (B) evidence   (C) incident   (D) skill

_____ 6. the *faded* flowers
    (A) rubbed   (B) vanished   (C) uttered   (D) withered

_____ 7. a limited *range* of ideas
    (A) charm   (B) scope   (C) snare   (D) aim

_____ 8. to *devise* a machine
    (A) bend   (B) hire   (C) invent   (D) repair

_____ 9. a certificate of *merit*
    (A) worth   (B) ceremony   (C) summit   (D) commerce

_____ 10. a peace *treaty*
    (A) testimony   (B) agreement   (C) trade   (D) peasant

2 왼쪽에 주어진 우리말과 같은 뜻을 가진 단어를 골라 그 번호를 공란에 써넣어라.

_____ 1. 해고하다   (A) deny   (B) frighten
                            (C) vanish   (D) discharge

_____ 2. 주먹   (A) bunch   (B) fist
                        (C) thumb   (D) finger

_____ 3. 치명적인   (A) keen   (B) sharp
                          (C) mortal   (D) huge

_____ 4. 폐허   (A) ruin   (B) despair
                        (C) cemetery   (D) curse

_____ 5. 교장   (A) excellence   (B) superintendent
                        (C) faculty   (D) palace

Lesson 4 종합 연습 문제

3 왼쪽에 주어진 단어와 반대되는 뜻을 가진 단어를 골라 그 번호를 공란에 써넣어라.

_____ 1. sharp   (A) huge   (B) shallow
                       (C) blunt   (D) lazy

_____ 2. slender (A) stout   (B) dull
                       (C) tame   (D) flimsy

_____ 3. vanish   (A) draw   (B) appear
                       (C) wither (D) deny

_____ 4. bless   (A) confuse (B) stoop
                       (C) sprinkle (D) damn

_____ 5. comfort (A) peak   (B) trap
                       (C) suffering (D) mercy

4 괄호 속에 주어진 우리말과 같은 뜻을 가진 단어를 사용하여 문장을 완성하라.

1. There was a large A_____E at the theater. (청중)
2. Would you like to C_____D with an English boy? (편지 왕래하다)
3. His E_____R to persuade her to go with him failed. (노력)
4. When he returns, he will R____E his previous job. (다시 계속하다)
5. You'd better use a ruler[17] to draw a S____E. (정사각형)

5 이탤릭체로 된 단어와 같은 뜻을 가진 단어를 골라 그 번호를 공란에 써넣어라.

_____ 1. She became *stout* as she grew older.
       (A) tall   (B) fat   (C) stiff   (D) rude

_____ 2. We *scraped* the old paint from the furniture.
       (A) rubbed   (B) resumed   (C) rejected   (D) released

_____ 3. He won a *huge* sum of money in the horse-race game.
       (A) generous (B) enormous (C) grand (D) splendid

_____ 4. Her white dress *accentuated* the redness of her sunburned[18] arms.
       (A) lightened (B) affirmed   (C) encouraged (D) emphasized

_____ 5. Most foods are not good to eat when they have gone *sour*.
       (A) sore   (B) rotten   (C) bitter   (D) acid

---

17. ruler(=rule)[rúːlər] ***n.*** 자   18. sunburned[sʌ́nbəːrnd] ***adj.*** 볕에 탄

Lesson 4

종합 연습 문제

6 왼쪽에 주어진 단어의 적당한 파생어를 사용하여 문장을 완성하라.

1. *invent*   Necessity is the mother of _____.
2. *deny*   The minister asked the newspaper to print a _____ of the true story.
3. *correspond*   The library bought all the _____ between Queen Victoria and her daughters.
4. *communicate*   Radio and television are important means of _____.
5. *mortal*   If this disease spreads in the country, the doctors fear that there'll be a high _____.

 **Answers**

1. 1. C   2. A   3. B   4. D   5. A   6. D   7. B   8. C   9. A   10. B
2. 1. D   2. B   3. C   4. A   5. B
3. 1. C   2. A   3. B   4. D   5. C
4. 1. AUDIENCE   2. CORRESPOND   3. ENDEAVOR   4. RESUME   5. SQUARE
5. 1. B   2. A   3. B   4. D   5. D
6. 1. invention   2. denial   3. correspondence   4. communication   5. mortality

LESSON 5

Self-test 5

적당한 단어를 골라 빈칸을 채우라.

1. The *blind* man _____ things clearly.
   (A) cannot see   (B) can see

2. There is some *deposit* at the _____ of this bottle.
   (A) top   (B) bottom

3. The President is *burdened* with _____ for decisions which may affect the whole country.
   (A) responsibility   (B) happiness

4. His mother _____ a box and *disclosed* what was in it.
   (A) opened   (B) hid

5. He has a *humble* job with very _____ wages.
   (A) high   (B) low

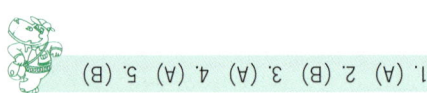

1. (A) 2. (B) 3. (A) 4. (A) 5. (B)

New Vocabulary -1

accept
[əksépt]
v. 받아들이다, 수락하다
syn. receive, approve
ant. reject, object, oppose
She asked me to go to the party and I *accepted* her invitation.

alarm
[əlá*r*m]
n. 놀람, 불안, 공포
syn. fear
Small earthquakes[1] are so common here that people don't feel much *alarm* at them.

author
[ɔ́:θə*r*]
n. 저자, 작가, 저술가
syn. writer
Do you know who the *author* of this novel is?

---

1. earthquake[ɜ́:*r*θkweik] *n.* 지진

blind
[blaind]

adj. 눈 먼, 장님의
syn. sightless
The deaf[2] and the *blind* deserve sympathy and help.

burden
[bə́:rdn]

v. 짐을 지우다, 부담시키다
syn. load
ant. unload
The mule[3] was *burdened* with the heavy loads.

n. 짐, 부담
She had too heavy a *burden* and became sick.

charitable
[tʃǽritəbl]

adj. 자비로운, 관대한, 자선의
syn. benevolent
ant. cruel
n. charity
He was a *charitable* man who used his wealth for the poor and sick men.

companion
[kəmpǽnjən]

n. 동반자, 동료
syn. colleague
John traveled around the world with me as my *companion*.

conquer
[kɔ́ŋkər]

v. 정복하다, 극복하다
syn. defeat, subjugate, vanquish
n. conquest
Scientists are seeking ways to *conquer* cancer[4].

costume
[kɔ́stjum]

n. 복장, 옷차림
syn. dress
The professor was in academic *costume* when I saw him yesterday.

dash
[dæʃ]

v. 내던지다, 때려부수다
syn. throw, hurl
In a moment of anger he *dashed* the glass against the door.

Practice 1

위 단어를 사용하여 아래 문장을 완성하라. 필요시 단어를 적절한 형태로 변형하라.

1. The Romans _____ much of the ancient world.

---

2. deaf [def] *adj.* 귀머거리의, 귀가 먼   3. mule [mju:l] *n.* 노새   4. cancer [kǽnsər] *n.* 암(癌)

2. The guides at the museum were dressed in Korean _____.

3. The design of the new car was not _____ by the public.

4. Tom helped the _____ man across the road.

5. A person who lives or travels with you as a friend and helper is your _____.

New Vocabulary -2

deposit
[dipózit]

n. 퇴적물, 침전물
There is often a *deposit* of sand and mud at the mouth of a river[5].

v. 예금하다, 맡기다, 침전시키다
He *deposited* quite a lot of money in the bank.

disclose
[disklóuz]

v. 노출시키다, 폭로하다, 드러내다
syn. reveal, show
ant. conceal
n. disclosure
The lifting of the curtain *disclosed* a beautiful painting.

dumb
[dʌm]

adj. 벙어리의, 멍청한, 말 없는
syn. mute
The class remained *dumb* when the teacher asked a difficult question.

endure
[indjúər]

v. 참다, 견디어내다
syn. bear, stand
n. endurance
Be quiet! I can't *endure* that noise any longer.

exception
[iksépʃən]

n. 예외, 제외
syn. exclusion
adj. exceptional
You all must take the examination; I can make no *exception*.

extreme
[ikstrí:m]

adj. 극도의, 극심한, 최후의
syn. utmost

5. mouth of a river : 강 하구

n. extremity
adv. extremely
The *extreme* penalty of the law is punishment by death[6].

flame
[fleim]
n. 불꽃, 화염
syn. blaze
The whole village was in *flames* when we got there.

glance
[glæns]
n. 얼핏 보기, 일견(一見)
syn. glimpse
He looked over the newspapers with a hasty *glance*.

v. 얼핏 보다, 힐끗 보다
I *glanced* out of the window to see if the rain had stopped.

hardware
[háːrdwɛər]
n. 철물, 쇠붙이
He bought a hammer and other *hardware* at the store.

humble
[hʌ́mbl]
adj. 1. 겸손한, 겸양하는, 삼가는
syn. modest
ant. proud, insolent
The vastness of the universe makes a person feel *humble*.

2. (신분 따위가) 천한, 초라한
syn. meek, lowly
Lincoln was born in a *humble* log cabin[7].

Practice 2

위 단어를 사용하여 아래 문장을 완성하라. 필요시 단어를 적절한 형태로 변형하라.

1. You must answer all the questions without _____.
2. Hellen Keller learned to speak; she was blind and deaf but not _____.
3. There are rich _____ of gold in those hills.
4. The _____ of the burning candle was yellow.
5. Locks[8], nails[9], screws, knives and tools are _____.

---

6. punishment by death : 사형   7. log cabin : 통나무 오두막집   8. lock [lɔk] *n.* 자물쇠   9. nail [neil] *n.* 못

New Vocabulary -3

influence
[ínfluəns]

n. 영향, 감화(력)
adj. influential
His *influence* made me a better man.

v. 영향을 끼치다, 감화시키다
syn. affect
Don't let me *influence* your decision.

investigate
[invéstigeit]

v. 조사하다, 취조하다
syn. examine
n. investigation
The police *investigated* the causes of a railway accident.

lack
[læk]

n. v. 부족(하다), 결핍(하다)
syn. shortage, want, need
The plants died for *lack* of water.

lightning
[láitniŋ]

n. 번갯불, 전광(電光)
Lightning is usually followed by thunder[10].

mammal
[mǽməl]

n. 포유 동물
A whale is not a fish, but a *mammal*.

motion
[móuʃən]

n. 동작, 운동, 몸짓
syn. movement
Avoid unnecessary *motion* of your hand while you are writing.

normal
[nɔ́ːrməl]

adj. 정상적인, 표준의, 정규의
syn. regular, standard
ant. abnormal, unusual
The *normal* temperature of the human body is 36.5 degrees.

oppose
[əpóuz]

v. 반대하다, 방해하다
syn. resist
ant. agree
I am very mush *opposed* to your going abroad.

---

10. thunder[θʌ́ndər] *n.* 천둥, 우레

palm
[pɑːm]
n. 손바닥, 뼘
She put a coin in the *palm* of the beggar's hand.

peck
[pek]
v. 부리로 쪼다, 쪼아 먹다
The bird *pecked* a hole in the tree.

Practice 3

위 단어를 사용하여 아래 문장을 완성하라. 필요시 단어를 적절한 형태로 변형하라.

1. A(n) _____ feeds[11] its young with milk from the breast[12].
2. Detectives[13] _____ crimes to find out who did them.
3. In the backyard I saw many hens _____ at the corn.
4. If a thing is in _____, it is not at rest.
5. Many people _____ building a new highway because of cost.

New Vocabulary -4

planet
[plǽnit]
n. 행성(行星), 유성(遊星)
The earth is one of the *planets* that move around the sun.

preparation
[prepəréiʃən]
n. 준비, 채비
v. prepare
We are getting things together in *preparation* for the trip.

proposal
[prəpóuzəl]
n. 신청, 제의, 건의
syn. suggestion
v. propose
He has made a *proposal* that she should take a rest for a while.

rapid
[rǽpid]
adj. 빠른, 급한, 신속한
syn. fast, swift, quick
The *rapid* development of Korea surprised all other countries.

remarkable
[rimάːrkəbl]
adj. 주목할 만한, 놀랄 만한, 뛰어난
syn. notable
She is *remarkable* for her sweet temper[14].

---

11. feed[fiːd] *n.* 먹이를 주다, 기르다   12. breast[brest] *n.* 가슴, 유방   13. detective[ditéktiv] *n.* 탐정, 형사
14. temper[témpər] *n.* 성미, 기질(disposition)

retain
[ritéin]

v. 보유하다, 유지하다, 존속시키다
syn. keep
ant. lose
She *retains* a clear memory of her schooldays.

rust
[rʌst]

n. (금속의) 녹
The unpainted metal tools were covered with *rust*.

scratch
[skrætʃ]

v. 긁다, 할퀴다
syn. rub, scrape
The man *scratched* a match on the wall.

n. 할퀴기, 할퀸 상처
He has a deep *scratch* on his face.

shave
[ʃeiv]

v. 면도하다, 털을 깎다
Do you *shave* yourself or go to the barber's?

slant
[slænt]

n. 경사, 비탈, 사면
syn. slope
The *slant* of the roof is too steep[15] to climb.

Practice 4

위 단어를 사용하여 아래 문장을 완성하라. 필요시 단어를 적절한 형태로 변형하라.

1. Many's landing on the moon is the most _____ event in all human history.
2. The champion has _____ his championship title longer than anyone else.
3. Plans for selling the new products are now in _____.
4. The _____ on your hand will soon be well.
5. Please rub the _____ of the old helmet.

---

15. steep[stiːp] ***adj.*** 가파른

New Vocabulary -5

sow
[sou]
v. (씨를) 뿌리다
ant. harvest
The farmer *sowed* the field with wheat.

squirrel
[skwə́:rəl]
n. 다람쥐
The *squirrels* were very busy gathering nuts[16] for the winter.

strain
[strein]
v. 팽팽하게 하다, 긴장시키다
He *strained* every muscle to lift the heavy rock.

supreme
[su:prí:m]
adj. 최고의, 최상의, 지고의
syn. highest, utmost
He showed *supreme* courage in his decision.

tap
[tæp]
v. 가볍게 두드리다, 톡톡 치다
He *tapped* me on the shoulder.

n. (수도)꼭지, 마개
Hot water flowed from the *tap*.

thunder
[θʌ́ndər]
v. 천둥, 우레
We have had a lot of *thunder* this summer.

tremble
[trémbl]
v. 떨다, 진동하다
syn. shake
She *trembled* when she heard the bad news.

vapor
[véipər]
n. 증기, 김
syn. steam
Strange *vapors* rose from the dark lake.

warrior
[wɔ́riər]
n. 군인, 무인
syn. soldier, fighter
The *warriors* couldn't defeat their enemy only with their spears[17].

woe
[wou]
n. 비애, 재앙, 불행
syn. grief, distress, trouble
Sickness and poverty are common *woes*.

---

16. nut[nʌt] *n.* 견과(堅果)(호두, 개암, 밤 따위)   17. spear[spiər] *n.* 창(槍)

Practice 5

위 단어를 사용하여 아래 문장을 완성하라. 필요시 단어를 적절한 형태로 변형하라.

1. The President is the _____ commander of the armed forces[18].
2. After the lightning came the _____.
3. The farmer will _____ the wheat next week.
4. The children _____ with fear when they saw the accident.
5. _____ can easily climb trees.

해답					
Practice 1	1. conquered	2. costumes	3. accepted	4. blind	5. companion
Practice 2	1. exception	2. dumb	3. deposits	4. flame	5. hardware
Practice 3	1. mammal	2. investigate	3. pecking	4. motion	5. oppose(d)
Practice 4	1. remarkable	2. retained	3. preparation	4. scratch	5. rust
Practice 5	1. supreme	2. thunder	3. sow	4. trembled	5. Squirrels

---

18. armed forces : (육 · 해 · 공군을 합친) 군대

Lesson 5 종합 연습 문제

1 네 개의 단어 중 다른 셋과 관련이 없는 것을 골라 공란에 그 번호를 써넣어라.

_____	1.	(A) soldier	(B) peasant	(C) warrior	(D) fighter
_____	2.	(A) lack	(B) shortage	(C) want	(D) ruin
_____	3.	(A) grief	(B) flame	(C) woe	(D) distress
_____	4.	(A) shake	(B) scratch	(C) rub	(D) scrape
_____	5.	(A) rapid	(B) slender	(C) swift	(D) quick
_____	6.	(A) subjugate	(B) conquer	(C) vanish	(D) vanquish
_____	7.	(A) reject	(B) object	(C) oppose	(D) defeat
_____	8.	(A) endure	(B) endeavor	(C) stand	(D) bear
_____	9.	(A) keep	(B) hold	(C) retain	(D) resume
_____	10.	(A) close	(B) show	(C) reveal	(D) disclose

2 왼쪽에 주어진 우리말과 같은 뜻을 가진 단어를 골라 그 번호를 공란에 써넣어라.

_____ 1. 벙어리의 (A) dull (B) dumb (C) dim (D) damp

_____ 2. 불꽃, 화염 (A) flame (B) fame (C) shame (D) tame

_____ 3. 포유 동물 (A) plant (B) squirrel (C) fable (D) mammal

_____ 4. 가볍게 두드리다 (A) nod (B) tap (C) tangle (D) rub

_____ 5. 증기 (A) rust (B) fist (C) vapor (D) feature

3 왼쪽에 주어진 단어와 반대되는 뜻을 가진 단어를 골라 그 번호를 공란에 써넣어라.

_____ 1. cruel (A) dull (B) religious (C) benevolent (D) restless

_____ 2. conceal (A) discharge (B) disclose (C) reject (D) vanish

_____ 3. humble (A) proud (B) cheap (C) huge (D) firm

_____ 4. burden (A) scrape (B) unload (C) tangle (D) connect

_____ 5. sow (A) harvest (B) plant (C) bless (D) strain

Lesson 5.

종합 연습 문제

4 괄호 속에 주어진 우리말과 같은 뜻을 가진 단어를 사용하여 문장을 완성하라.

1. Please don't leave the T_P running. (수도꼭지)
2. Two persons were killed by the L_____G last night. (번갯불)
3. The W_____RS agreed to defend their castle to the last man[19]. (군인)
4. The stars' I_____E on men has not been proved. (영향)
5. Before writing your check[20], you must D_____T some of your money in the bank. (예금하다)

5 이탤릭체로 된 단어와 같은 뜻을 가진 단어를 골라 그 번호를 공란에 써넣어라.

_____ 1. Grandfathers are usually *charitable* toward the mistakes of their grandchildren.
　(A) cruel　(B) benevolent　(C) enormous　(D) ambitious

_____ 2. She was gathering flowers with her *companions* in the valley.
　(A) challenges　(B) warriors　(C) trades　(D) colleagues

_____ 3. If you go to Scotland, you may see people in Highland *costume*.
　(A) dress　(B) parcel　(C) custom　(D) charm

_____ 4. The waves *dashed* the boat against the rocks.
　(A) pulled　(B) rejected　(C) hurled　(D) resumed

_____ 5. If help does not come, we must *endure* to the end[21].
　(A) bear　(B) endeavor　(C) retain　(D) strain

_____ 6. I could recognize the old car at a *glance*.
　(A) square　(B) feature　(C) flame　(D) glimpse

_____ 7. What *influenced* you to do it?
　(A) affirmed　(B) affected　(C) invited　(D) interested

_____ 8. They soon began to *investigate* the cause of the fire.
　(A) affirm　(B) invent　(C) examine　(D) deny

_____ 9. The farmers worried about the *lack* of rain.
　(A) shortage　(B) drift　(C) woe　(D) burden

_____ 10. Japan made a *proposal* to Korea for increasing trade between two countries.
　(A) preparation　(B) exception　(C) suggestion　(D) companion

---

19. to the last man : 마지막 한 사람이 남을 때까지　20. write one's check : 수표를 발행하다　21. to the end : 끝까지

TOEFL · TOEIC · TEPS 초급 Junior Vocabulary

Lesson 5

종합 연습 문제

Answers

1. 1. B 2. D 3. B 4. A 5. B 6. C 7. D 8. B 9. D 10. A

2. 1. B 2. A 3. D 4. B 5. C

3. 1. C 2. B 3. A 4. B 5. A

4. 1. TAP 2. LIGHTNING 3. WARRIORS 4. INFLUENCE 5. DEPOSIT

5. 1. B 2. D 3. A 4. C 5. A 6. D 7. B 8. C 9. A 10. C

LESSON 6

Self-test 6

적당한 단어를 골라 빈칸을 채우라.

1. We can see the _____ star at *dusk*.
   (A) evening   (B) morning

2. He has some *rare* stamps which are _____ available[1].
   (A) easily   (B) scarcely

3. She left her children at home with a *pang* of _____.
   (A) happiness   (B) sadness

4. A *cottage* is a small house used by people during holidays in the _____.
   (A) country   (B) city

5. He was *faint* with _____.
   (A) praise and encouragement (B) hunger and cold

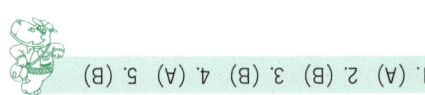

1. (A) 2. (B) 3. (B) 4. (A) 5. (B)

New Vocabulary -1

accidental　　*adj.* 우연의, 뜻하지 않은, 예측치 않은
[æksidéntl]　　*syn.* unexpected, casual
　　　　　　　　ant. intentional
　　　　　　　　We became friends after our *accidental* meeting at the Christmas party.

ambition　　*n.* 야심, 야망, 큰 뜻
[æmbíʃən]　　*adj.* ambitious
　　　　　　　　One of his *ambitions* is to become a famous politician.

authority　　*n.* 권위, 권력
[əːθɔ́rəti]　　*v.* authorize
　　　　　　　　A policeman has the *authority* to arrest[2] speeding drivers.

---

1. available [əvéiləbl] *adj.* 손에 넣을 수 있는　　2. arrest [ərést] *v.* 체포하다

blossom
[blɔ́səm]

v. (나무에) 꽃이 피다
syn. bloom, flower
All the orchards *blossom* in spring.

n. (특히 과수의) 꽃, 꽃 철
syn. bloom, flower
The cherry trees are in full *blossom*[3] now.

bureau
[bjúərou]

n. 사무국, 사무소, (관청의)국 및 부
syn. office
An information *bureau* collects and keeps various facts.

charm
[tʃɑːrm]

n. 매력, 아름다운 점
syn. attraction, allurement
ant. ugliness
His essays have a *charm* of style that cannot be found in other writers.

comparison
[kəmpǽrisn]

n. 비교, 대조
v. compare
adj. comparative
The buildings in Seoul are small in *comparison* with the skyscrapers[4] in New York.

conscience
[kɔ́nʃəns]

n. 양심, 도덕 의식, 도의심, 본심
adj. conscientious
Jean's got no *conscience*; she'd steal anything from anybody.

cottage
[kɔ́tidʒ]

n. 시골집, 작은집
syn. cabin
He lives in a *cottage* in the woods.

dawn
[dɔːn]

n. 새벽, 여명, 동틀 녘
syn. daybreak
ant. dusk
We started our trip at *dawn* in order to get there before noon.

Practice 1

위 단어를 사용하여 아래 문장을 완성하라. 필요시 단어를 적절한 형태로 변형하라.

1. If you have a guilty _____, you feel or know you have done wrong.

---

3. in full blossom : (꽃이) 만발하여   4. skyscraper[skaiskreipər] *n.* 마천루, 고층 빌딩

Lesson 6

2. They worked hard from _____ till dusk.

3. It was _____ that we arrived at the party at the same time.

4. Because he was filled with _____, he worked after school[5] and on Saturday.

5. The teacher's _____ of the heart to a pump helped the students to understand its action.

New Vocabulary -2

depress
[diprés]

v. 1. 우울하게 하다, 의기를 떨어뜨리다
syn. sadden, deject
n. depression
adj. depressive
The raining season always *depresses* me.

2. 경기를 나쁘게 만들다, 침체시키다
ant. boost
When business is *depressed*, many men lose their positions.

discourage
[diskə́ːridʒ]

v. 1. (계획, 사업 따위를) 말리다
syn. deter
We tried to *discourage* him from climbing the mountain without a guide[6].

2. 낙담시키다, 용기를 잃게 하다
syn. depress
ant. encourage
Try again! Don't let one failure *discourage* you.

dusk
[dʌsk]

n. 땅거미, 황혼, 어스름
syn. twilight
ant. dawn
The buildings over there are scarcely visible[7] in the *dusk*.

exchange
[ikstʃéindʒ]

n. 교환, 주고 받기
syn. interchange
Exchange of prisoners during a war is not very common.

extraordinary
[ikstrɔ́ːrdinəri]

adj. 보통이 아닌, 별난, 흔치 않은
syn. exceptional, unusual

---

5. after school : 방과 후, 수업이 끝난 후   6. guide[gaid] *n.* 안내자   7. visible[vízəbl] *adj.* 보이는, 눈에 띄는

	ant. usual, common
	Eight feet is an *extraordinary* height for a man.
faint [feint]	**adj.** 희미한, 힘없는, 어지러운
	syn. weak, dim
	ant. strong, sharp, vigorous, bright
	She called for help in a *faint* voice.
flash [flæʃ]	***v.*** 번쩍이다, 번쩍거리다
	syn. sparkle
	The lightning[8] *flashed* across the sky.
frost [frɔst]	***n.*** 서리
	adj. frosty
	Frost has killed several of our young plants.
gleam [gliːm]	***n.*** 번쩍임, 빛남, 섬광
	syn. flash, beam
	A *gleam* of light shone[9] through the partly opened door.
harness [háːrnis]	***n.*** 마구(馬具)
	The saddle[10] is a part of a horse's *harness*.
	v. (자연을) 이용하다, 동력화하다
	We can *harness* water in a river to produce electric power.

Practice 2

위 단어를 사용하여 아래 문장을 완성하라. 필요시 단어를 적절한 형태로 변형하라.

1. The scientist is a man of _____ genius.

2. The young buds[11] on the tree have been damaged by the late _____.

3. There have been numerous _____ of views between the two countries.

4. The wet weather _____ people from going to the sports meeting.

5. I was _____ after reading the newspaper that was filled with news of accidents.

---

8. lightning [láitniŋ] ***n.*** 번갯불   9. shone [ʃɔn] ***v.*** shine의 과거, 과거분사   10. saddle [sǽdl] ***n.*** 안장   11. bud [bʌd] ***n.*** 싹

New Vocabulary -3

hymn
[him]
n. 찬송가, 성가, 찬가
The people joined together in singing a *hymn*.

v. 찬송가를 부르다, 찬송하다
They *hymned* their thanks to God.

inform
[infɔ́:rm]
v. 알려주다, 알리다, 통지하다
syn. notify
n. information
Can you *inform* me where he lives right now?

invite
[inváit]
v. 초래하다, 초청하다
syn. request
n. invitation
She *invited* her friends to her birthday party.

ladder
[lǽdər]
n. 사닥다리
The boys climbed the *ladder* to get into their tree house.

limb
[lim]
n. 손발, 사지, 수족(手足)
That man with one arm lost his other *limb* in an airplane crash[12].

manage
[mǽnidʒ]
v. 1. (사람, 동물을) 다루다, 부리다
syn. handle
He couldn't *manage* his horse, and it threw him to the ground.

2. 경영하다, 운영하다, 관리하다
syn. control, conduct
They hired a young man to *manage* their business.

method
[méθəd]
n. 방법, 수법
syn. way
Jonas Salk found a new *method* of teaching music.

motive
[móutiv]
n. 동기, 동인(動因)
syn. cause
We despise[13] those who act from low or selfish *motive*.

nostril
[nɔ́stril]
n. 콧구멍
The Indian princess wore[14] a diamond in her right *nostril*.

---

12. crash[kræʃ] *n.* (비행기의) 추락   13. despise[dispáiz] *v.* 경멸하다   14. wore *v.* wear의 과거형

oral
[ɔ́:rəl]

adj. 구두의, 구술의
syn. spoken
ant. written
She gave us an *oral* report instead of a written report.

Practice 3

위 단어를 사용하여 아래 문장을 완성하라. 필요시 단어를 적절한 형태로 변형하라.

1. We were _____ that the prisoner had escaped[15].
2. We _____ all our relatives to my grandfather's sixtieth birthday party.
3. She knows how to _____ her husband when he is angry.
4. A(n) _____ agreement is not enough; we must have a written promise.
5. A rope _____ was hung over the ship's side.

New Vocabulary –4

pang
[pæŋ]

n. 고통, 격통, 쓰라림
syn. pain
It is hard to stand[16] the *pangs* of a toothache.

peculiar
[pikjú:ljər]

adj. 독특한, 고유의, 특유의
syn. unusual, strange, odd
ant. common, usual
n. peculiarity
All cultures seem to have *peculiar* customs.

plate
[pleit]

n. 접시, 접시류
syn. dish
In America food is usually served on *plates*.

preserve
[prizə́:rv]

v. 보존하다, 유지하다, 간수하다
syn. keep
n. preservation
The city decided to *preserve* the beautiful old building as a museum.

prospect
[prɔ́spekt]

n. 1. 조망, 전망, 경치
syn. view, scene
From the top of the hill there is a beautiful *prospect* over the hill.

---

15. escape [iskéip] *v.* 달아나다, 탈출하다   16. stand [stænd] *v.* 참다, 견디다

2. 가망, 기대, 희망
syn. expectation, hope
I see no *prospect* of his recovery[17] from the disease.

rare
[rɛər]

adj. 1. 보기 드문, 희귀한, 진귀한
syn. unusual, uncommon, scarce
ant. common
Today tigers are *rare* animals in Korea.

2. 설 구운, 덜 익은
I want my steak very *rare*, please.

remedy
[rémidi]

n. 치료, 의료, 치유
syn. cure
This pill[18] is a good *remedy* for a headache and toothache.

retire
[ritáiər]

v. 퇴직하다, 은퇴하다, 물러나다
ant. inaugurate
n. retirement
My father *retired* from his job at the age of 60.

scream
[skri:m]

n. (공포, 고통의) 절규, 외침
A *scream* for help came from inside the building.

shed
[ʃed]

n. 오두막, 헛간
syn. cottage, hut
The garden tools are in that *shed*.

v. (피, 눈물을) 흘리다 (*p., pp.* shed)
syn. pour
We *shed* our blood for our country.

Practice 4

위 단어를 사용하여 아래 문장을 완성하라. 필요시 단어를 적절한 형태로 변형하라.

1. That way of speaking is _____ to people in this part of the country.

2. They built a new school as a _____ for crowded classrooms.

3. Ancient Egyptians knew how to _____ dead bodies from decay[19].

4. She helped her mother wash the _____ in the kitchen.

5. Seeing no _____ of success, we quit[20] the attempt to climb the mountain.

---

17. recovery[rikʌ́vəri] *n.* 회복   18. pill[pil] *n.* 환약, 알약   19. decay[dikéi] *n.* 부식   20. quit[kwit] *v.* 그만두다

New Vocabulary -5

slavery [sléivəri]	***n.*** 노예 제도, 노예 신분 **ant.** liberty **cf.** slave Many men fought for the abolition[21] of *slavery*.
spacious [spéiʃəs]	***adj.*** 공간이 넓은, 널찍한 **syn.** roomy **ant.** narrow The rooms of the palace[22] were *spacious*.
staff [stæf]	***n.*** 직원, 부원, 요원 The teaching *staff* of the school is excellent.
straw [strɔː]	***n.*** 짚, 밀짚 The farmers covered the barn[23] floor with *straw*.
surface [sə́ːrfis]	***n.*** 표면, 외면 **ant.** bottom Leaves were floating on the *surface* of the pond.
tick [tik]	***n.*** 똑딱똑딱(하는 소리) The silence was broken only by the *tick* of the clock.
tremendous [triméndəs]	***adj.*** 엄청난, 막대한, 굉장한 **syn.** dreadful, immense The army suffered[24] a *tremendous* defeat in that battle.
variety [vəráiəti]	***n.*** 다양성, 다양한 종류, 변화 **syn.** diversity, variation **ant.** sameness, monotony The store over there has a great *variety* of toys.
waterfall [wɔ́ːtərfɔːl]	***n.*** 폭포 **syn.** falls The Niagara Falls is one of the most beautiful *waterfalls* in the world.
worm [wəːrm]	***n.*** 벌레, 연충 The *worm* turns the soil.

21. abolition[æbəlíʃən] ***n.*** 폐지   22. palace[pǽlis] ***n.*** 궁전, 관저   23. barn[bɑːrn] ***n.*** 헛간, 창고   24. suffer[sʌ́fər] ***v.*** 겪다, 당하다

Practice 5

위 단어를 사용하여 아래 문장을 완성하라. 필요시 단어를 적절한 형태로 변형하라.

1. A _____ hat protects us from hot sun.

2. On the _____ the two men seemed friendly[25].

3. The President has _____ responsibilities for the nation.

4. Many Africans were captured[26] and sold into _____.

5. We demanded more _____ in our food.

Practice 1	1. conscience	2. dawn	3. accidental	4. ambition	5. comparison
Practice 2	1. extraordinary	2. frost	3. exchange	4. discouraged	5. depressed
Practice 3	1. informed	2. invited	3. manage	4. oral	5. ladder
Practice 4	1. peculiar	2. remedy	3. preserve	4. plates	5. prospect
Practice 5	1. straw	2. surface	3. tremendous	4. slavery	5. variety

25. friendly [fréndli] *adj.* 친한   26. capture [kǽptʃər] *v.* 사로잡다

Lesson 6

종합 연습 문제

1 이탤릭체로 된 단어와 같은 뜻을 가진 단어를 골라 그 번호를 공란에 써넣어라.

_____ 1. her *method* of teaching children
(A) effort (B) way (C) ability (D) opinion

_____ 2. a *prospect* of victory
(A) proposal (B) hope (C) motive (D) woe

_____ 3. a humanistic *motive*
(A) suggestion (B) conscience (C) cause (D) mercy

_____ 4. to *shed* tears of sorrow
(A) wash (B) pour (C) hurl (D) retain

_____ 5. an *accidental* happening
(A) casual (B) unusual (C) usual (D) benevolent

_____ 6. a *spacious* hall
(A) roomy (B) tremendous (C) magnificent (D) special

_____ 7. an *extraordinary* power
(A) military (B) exceptional (C) foreign (D) human

_____ 8. a *remedy* for cancer
(A) harness (B) cause (C) cure (D) pang

_____ 9. a *gleam* of firelight
(A) blossom (B) bureau (C) flash (D) frost

_____ 10. at a *tremendous* speed
(A) normal (B) dreadful (C) slow (D) specified

2 왼쪽에 주어진 우리말과 같은 뜻을 가진 단어를 골라 그 번호를 공란에 써넣어라.

_____ 1. 표면
(A) deposit (B) surface
(C) planet (D) slant

_____ 2. 양심
(A) conscience (B) mammal
(C) motive (D) pang

_____ 3. 벌레
(A) straw (B) limb
(C) worm (D) dawn

_____ 4. 사지, 손발
(A) limb (B) tick
(C) fist (D) thumb

_____ 5. 매력
(A) prospect (B) charm
(C) cottage (D) palm

Lesson 6
종합 연습 문제

3 왼쪽에 주어진 단어와 반대되는 뜻을 가진 단어를 골라 그 번호를 공란에 써넣어라.

_____ 1. surface (A) bottom   (B) conscience
                       (C) bureau   (D) hymn

_____ 2. monotony (A) ambition   (B) hardship
                       (C) variety   (D) nonsense

_____ 3. dawn   (A) dusk   (B) daybreak
                       (C) authority   (D) blossom

_____ 4. scarce   (A) huge   (B) common
                       (C) religious   (D) humble

_____ 5. faint   (A) dumb   (B) notable
                       (C) rare   (D) strong

4 괄호 속에 주어진 우리말과 같은 뜻을 가진 단어를 사용하여 문장을 완성하라.

1. He explained the new policy to the editorial[27] S___F. (직원)

2. We heard someone S____M in fright[28]. (소리치다)

3. She didn't like the work, because it lacked V_____Y. (다양성)

4. The child put the watch to its ear and listened to its T__K. (똑딱똑딱하는 소리)

5. The doctor put some medicine in each N_____L. (콧구멍)

5 가장 적합한 단어를 골라 빈칸을 채우라.

1. I want to run away, but my _____ bothers[29] me.
   (A) pang   (B) remedy   (C) rust   (D) conscience

2. A boy who is filled with _____ always works hard.
   (A) vapor   (B) ambition (C) harness (D) burden

3. He doesn't work in the office any longer; he _____ from his job several years ago.
   (A) retired (B) retained (C) strained (D) resumed

4. Her letter _____ us how and when she expected to arrive.
   (A) faded   (B) blessed   (C) informed (D) managed

5. I gave him my old textbooks and received a dictionary in _____.
   (A) exchange (B) preparation (C) proposal (D) proportion

---

27. editorial [editɔ́:riəl] *adj.* 편집의   28. in fright [frait] : 놀라서   29. bother [bɔ́ðər] *v.* 괴롭히다

6 왼쪽에 주어진 단어의 적당한 파생어를 사용하여 문장을 완성하라.

1. *ambition*   Jack is an _____ boy; he wants to become as famous as Edison.
2. *authority* I have _____ him to act for me while I am abroad.
3. *inform*   Can you give me any _____ about this matter?
4. *retire*   There have been several _____ recently.
5. *invite*   I received an _____ card to her birthday party.

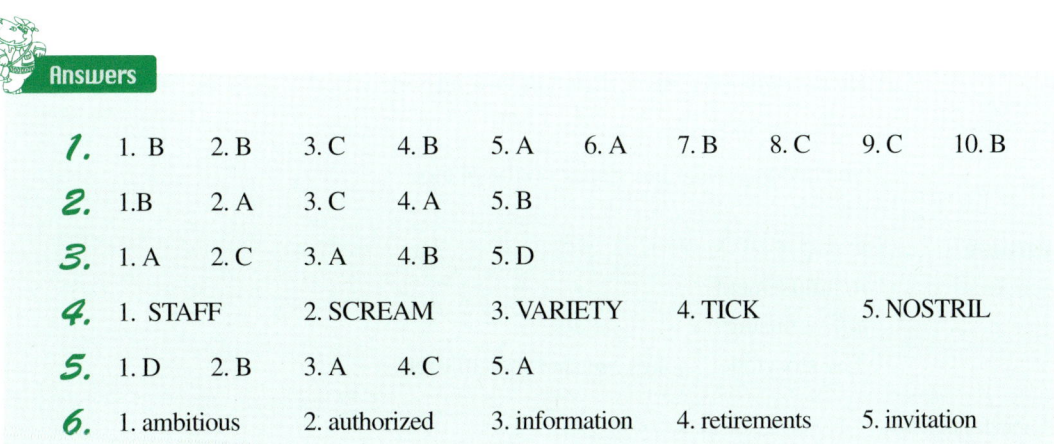

Answers

1. 1. B 2. B 3. C 4. B 5. A 6. A 7. B 8. C 9. C 10. B
2. 1. B 2. A 3. C 4. A 5. B
3. 1. A 2. C 3. A 4. B 5. D
4. 1. STAFF 2. SCREAM 3. VARIETY 4. TICK 5. NOSTRIL
5. 1. D 2. B 3. A 4. C 5. A
6. 1. ambitious 2. authorized 3. information 4. retirements 5. invitation

LESSON 7

Self-test 7

적당한 단어를 골라 빈칸을 채우라.

1. A hard blow on the _____ deafened him for life[1].
   (A) ear (B) eye

2. The _____ car on the dirt raised a great *dust*.
   (A) standing (B) speeding

3. An *energetic* effort on the part of all members will ensure[2] the _____ of our plan.
   (A) success (B) failure

4. We could see many *lambs* in the _____ on our way to school.
   (A) valley (B) river

5. The drunkard _____ a *pledge* never to drink again.
   (A) sold (B) signed

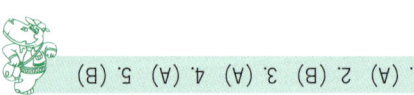
1. (A) 2. (B) 3. (A) 4. (A) 5. (B)

New Vocabulary -1

accompany
[əkʌ́mpəni]
v. 1. ~와 함께 가다, ~에 동반하다
syn. attend
He *accompanied* his girlfriend to the airport.

2. ~에 반주하다
She *accompanied* the singer on the piano.

amuse
[əmjúːz]
v. 즐겁게 하다, 재미나게 하다
n. amusement
adj. amusing
The storyteller's jokes *amused* the children.

---

1. for life : 평생토록   2. ensure [inʃúər] *v.* 확실하게 하다, 보장하다

avoid
[əvɔ́id]

v. 피하다, 회피하다
syn. escape
n. avoidance
Children should try to *avoid* crossing the road except when the policeman stops the traffic.

bomb
[bɔm]

n. 폭탄
A time *bomb* explodes[3] sometime after it is placed in position.

burial
[bériəl]

n. 매장, 매장식
v. bury
The *burial* of the dead sailor was performed[4] at sea.

chase
[tʃeis]

v. 쫓다, 추격하다
The old lady saw the thief running up the street and *chased* him on her bicycle.

compel
[kəmpél]

v. 억지로 ~시키다, 강제로 ~시키다
syn. force, impel
He was *compelled* by illness to give up[5] his studies.

consent
[kənsént]

v. 동의하다, 승낙하다, 승인하다
syn. agree, assent
ant. disagree
He asked the girl to marry him and she *consented*.

counterpart
[káuntərpɑːrt]

n. 1. 상대(대조)되는 사람(것)
The Korean Minister[6] met his Japanese *counterpart*.
   2. 짝진 것의 한쪽
Your right hand is the *counterpart* of your left hand.

deafen
[défən]

v. 귀머거리로 만들다, 멍멍하게 하다
adj. deaf
A sudden explosion[7] *deafened* us for a moment.

Practice 1

위 단어를 사용하여 아래 문장을 완성하라. 필요시 단어를 적절한 형태로 변형하라.

1. The rain _____ us to stop our ball game.
2. As soon as we saw the enemy ship, we began to _____ it.

---

3. explode [iksplóud] *v.* 폭발하다   4. perform [pərfɔ́ːrm] *v.* 이행하다, 실행하다   5. give up : 포기하다
6. minister [mínistər] *n.* 대신, 장관   7. explosion *n.* explode의 명사형

3. _____ may be filled with chemical substance[8] and sometimes dropped from aircraft.

4. The children _____ themselves by playing games while their parents talked.

5. The warships _____ the merchant ships through the Mediterranean[9].

New Vocabulary -2

derive
[diráiv]

v. 1. (다른 물건, 근원에서) 끌어내다
We have *derived* benefit[10] from the new method of generating electricity.

2. ~에서 유래하다
The word 'deride' is *derived* from the Latin 'de' (down) and 'riddere' (to laugh).

display
[displéi]

v. 전시하다, 진열하다, 보이다
syn. show, reveal
Department stores *display* their goods in the windows.

dust
[dʌst]

n. 먼지
adj. dusty
There was half an inch of *dust* on the books before I cleaned them.

energetic
[enərdʒétik]

adj. 정력적인, 원기 왕성한
syn. vigorous, active
ant. faint
Cool autumn days make us feel *energetic*.

extent
[ikstént]

n. 범위, 폭
syn. range, scope
I was amazed[11] at the *extent* of his knowledge.

fairy
[fɛ́əri]

n. 요정(妖精)
syn. nymph
The *fairy* promised to grant the child's wish.

flatter
[flǽtər]

v. 아첨하다, 알랑거리다
n. flattery

---

8. chemical substance : 화학 물질   9. the Mediterranean[meditəréiniən] *n.* 지중해   10. benefit[bénifit] *n.* 이익, 이득
11. amaze[əméiz] *v.* 몹시 놀라게 하다

	adj. flattering
	He *flattered* her with flowers and expensive gifts.
frown [fraun]	*v.* 눈살을 찌푸리다, 얼굴을 찡그리다 syn. scowl ant. smile Mary wanted to go to Europe by herself, but her parents *frowned* on the idea.
glimpse [glimps]	*n.* 힐끗 보기, 일견(一見), 일별 syn. glance I caught a *glimpse* of the falls[12] as our train went by.
harvest [há:rvist]	*n.* 수확, 추수 syn. crop Many men were needed to help the farmer with the *harvest*.

Practice 2

위 단어를 사용하여 아래 문장을 완성하라. 필요시 단어를 적절한 형태로 변형하라.

1. He _____ much pleasure from reading adventure stories[13].

2. The motor car raised a terrible _____ as it passed us.

3. I agree with your plans, but only to a certain _____.

4. He was only _____ her when he said that she sang well; he didn't really mean it.

5. My grandmother always _____ when she's putting thread into a needle.

New Vocabulary -3

inhabit [inhǽbit]	*v.* (∼에) 살다, (∼에) 거주하다 syn. dwell, live *n.* inhabitant *adj.* inhabitable The earth we *inhabit* is a point in space.
involve [inv́ɔlv]	*v.* 포함하다, 수반하다, 끌어들이다 syn. include

---

12. fall : (보통 *pl.*) 폭포.   13. adventure story : 모험 소설.

ant. exempt, exclude
Housekeeping *involves* cooking, washing dishes, sweeping, cleaning.

lamb
[læm]

n. 새끼 양, 어린 양(고기)
The *lambs* were playing on the hillside.

liquid
[líkwid]

n. 액체
ant. solid
Water, oil, and milk are *liquids*.

adj. 액체의
The sick man could eat only *liquid* foods.

mighty
[máiti]

adj. 막강한, 강대한, 힘센
syn. powerful
n. might
The *mighty* battleship[14] was so badly damaged that it could not be used again.

mount
[máunt]

v. 1. 오르다, 올라가다
syn. climb, ascend
ant. descend
He *mounted* the bicycle and rode away.

2. (말에) 타다, (말에) 태우다
The soldiers *mounted* on fine black horses.

notify
[nóutifai]

v. 통지하다, 통보하다
syn. inform
Our teacher *notified* us that there would be a test on Monday.

orbit
[ɔ́ːrbit]

n. 궤도, 행로
The moon travels in an *orbit* around the earth.

paradise
[pǽrədais]

n. 천국, 극락, 낙원
syn. heaven
ant. hell
The island was a *paradise* of birds and flowers.

peer
[piər]

v. 응시하다, 자세히 보다
syn. stare
She *peered* through the mist, trying to find the right way.

---

14. battleship[bǽtlʃip] *n.* 전(투)함

Practice 3

위 단어를 사용하여 아래 문장을 완성하라. 필요시 단어를 적절한 형태로 변형하라.

1. A person as good as he deserves[15] to go to _____.
2. He lifted up his little son, and _____ him on the donkey[16].
3. Jelly is not _____ but solid[17].
4. When my guest arrives, please _____ me.
5. The United States of America is one of the _____ nations in the world.

New Vocabulary -4

pledge
[pledʒ]

n. 맹세, 서약
I give my *pledge* that I will continue to help you.

v. 서약하다, 맹세하다
syn. promise, vow
They *pledged* themselves never to tell the secrets.

pressure
[préʃər]

n. 압력, 압축, 압박
v. press
The air *pressure* at sea level is nearly 15 pounds for each square inch[18].

prosper
[práspər]

v. 번영하다, 번창하다
syn. succeed
n. prosperity
adj. prosperous
His business *prospered* at its new location.

raw
[rɔː]

adj. 날것의, 가공하지 않은
syn. unripe, uncooked
Children like to eat *raw* fruits.

remind
[rimáind]

v. 상기시키다, 생각나게 하다
This picture *reminds* me of the story I heard before.

retreat
[ritríːt]

v. 후퇴하다, 퇴각하다
syn. withdraw

---

15. deserve[dizə́ːrv] *v.* ~을 할 가치가 있다   16. donkey[dáŋki] *n.* 당나귀   17. solid[sálid] *n.* 고체   18. square inch : 평방 인치

ant. advance
The enemy *retreated* before the advance of our soldiers.

sacred
[séikrid]
adj. 신성한, 성스러운
syn. holy, solemn
ant. secular, profane
The Bible and the Koran[19] are *sacred* writings.

screen
[skri:n]
n. 차폐물, 발, 가리개
We have *screens* at the windows to keep out flies[20].

shelf
[ʃelf]
n. 1. 암붕(岩棚), 암초
The wrecked ship[21] rested on a *shelf* at the bottom of the sea.

2. 선반, 서가(書架)
I kept that book on the bottom *shelf*.

sleeve
[sli:v]
n. 소매, 소맷자락
The *sleeves* of his coat were too long.

Practice 4

위 단어를 사용하여 아래 문장을 완성하라. 필요시 단어를 적절한 형태로 변형하라.

1. I've forgotten what you said; will you _____ me of it?
2. The defeated[22] army had to _____ hastily from the battlefield.
3. In India, the cow is a _____ animal.
4. The tailor shortend the _____ of his shirt.
5. The windows were covered with _____ to keep out insects[23].

---

19. the Koran[kərǽn] *n.* 회교의 경전   20. fly[flai] *n.* 파리   21. wrecked ship : 난파선   22. defeat[difí:t] *v.* 패배시키다
23. insect[ínsekt] *n.* 곤충, 벌레

New Vocabulary -5

spare
[spɛər]

v. 목숨을 살려주다
Take my money but *spare* my life!

adj. 여분의
syn. extra
She is looking for something to read in her *spare* time.

stability
[stəbíləti]

n. 안정성, 안정
ant. fluctuation
adj. stable
A concrete wall has more *stability* than a wooden fence.

strawberry
[strɔ́:bəri]

n. 딸기, 양딸기
We had *strawberries* and ice cream for dessert[24].

surgeon
[sə́:rdʒən]

n. 외과 의사
ant. physician
der. surgery
A *surgeon* took out Fred's tonsils[25].

task
[tæsk]

n. 직무, 임무, 과업
syn. assignment, job
The President has to perform many *tasks*.

tide
[taid]

n. 조수(潮水), 조류(潮流)
cf. ebb
They liked to walk along the beach at low *tide*.

trial
[tráiəl]

n. 1. 시도, 시험
syn. testing
v. try
She learned to cook by *trial* and error.

   2. 재판, 공판
In the *trial*, she changed her previous statement.

vast
[væst]

adj. 광대한, 방대한
syn. immense, huge

---

24. dessert[dizə́:rt] *n.* 디저트, 후식   25. tonsil[tɑ́nsil] *n.* 편도선

Lesson 7   85

	ant. tiny, small	
	Texas and Alaska cover *vast* territories.	
waterproof [wɔ́tərpruːf]	***n. adj.*** 방수(의) Put on[26] your *waterproof* coat before you go out in the rain. ***v.*** 방수 처리하다 These hiking shoes have been *waterproofed*.	
worsen [wɔ́ːrsn]	***v.*** 악화시키다, 악화되다 **ant.** improve ***adj.*** worse The rain *worsened* our difficulties.	

Practice 5

위 단어를 사용하여 아래 문장을 완성하라. 필요시 단어를 적절한 형태로 변형하라.

1. The prisoner asked the judge to _____ his life.
2. The political situation of the country has _____ since its independence.
3. A billion dollars is a _____ amount of money.
4. Many thieves were caught and brought to _____.
5. The _____ of the government is required to overcome[27] the present hardship.

해답					
Practice 1	1. compelled	2. chase	3. Bombs	4. amused	5. accompanied
Practice 2	1. derives	2. dust	3. extent	4. flattering	5. frowns
Practice 3	1. paradise	2. mounted	3. liquid	4. notify	5. mightiest
Practice 4	1. remind	2. retreat	3. sacred	4. sleeves	5. screens
Practice 5	1. spare	2. worsened	3. vast	4. trial	5. stability

---

26. put on : 입다   27. overcome [ouvərkʌ́m] ***v.*** 극복하다

Lesson 7

종합 연습 문제

1 네 개의 단어 중 다른 셋과 관련이 없는 것을 골라 공란에 그 번호를 써넣어라.

_____ 1. (A) live (B) inhabit (C) dwell (D) reject
_____ 2. (A) display (B) discourage (C) show (D) reveal
_____ 3. (A) defeat (B) consent (C) agree (D) assent
_____ 4. (A) compel (B) force (C) impel (D) reject
_____ 5. (A) vast (B) immense (C) stable (D) huge
_____ 6. (A) pledge (B) promise (C) preserve (D) vow
_____ 7. (A) energetic (B) swift (C) active (D) vigorous
_____ 8. (A) job (B) task (C) assignment (D) bureau
_____ 9. (A) extent (B) range (C) burial (D) scope
_____ 10. (A) raw (B) solemn (C) sacred (D) holy

2 왼쪽에 주어진 우리말과 같은 뜻을 가진 단어를 골라 그 번호를 공란에 써넣어라.

_____ 1. 요정(妖精) (A) twilight (B) charm (C) fairy (D) squirrel
_____ 2. 소맷자락 (A) staff (B) sleeve (C) straw (D) slant
_____ 3. 외과 의사 (A) surgeon (B) physician (C) suggestion (D) colleague
_____ 4. 여분의 (A) sour (B) stout (C) spacious (D) spare
_____ 5. 즐겁게 하다 (A) amuse (B) prosper (C) tap (D) peck

3 왼쪽에 주어진 단어와 반대되는 뜻을 가진 단어를 골라 그 번호를 공란에 써넣어라.

_____ 1. profane (A) secular (B) sacred (C) peculiar (D) extreme
_____ 2. flee (A) chase (B) discharge (C) lose (D) vanish
_____ 3. exempt (A) retire (B) notify (C) involve (D) faint
_____ 4. advance (A) ensure (B) retreat (C) affect (D) reveal
_____ 5. tiny (A) vast (B) witty (C) dumb (D) dim

Lesson 7 종합 연습 문제

4 괄호 속에 주어진 우리말과 같은 뜻을 가진 단어를 사용하여 문장을 완성하라.

1. The air is a fluid[28] but not a L____D. (액체)
2. The B____L ceremony of the late[29] President was held yesterday. (매장)
3. Please R____D me to take my medicine in the morning. (상기시키다)
4. Don't try to F_____R her with praises. (아첨하다)
5. I only caught a G_____E of the parcel[30], so I can't guess what was inside it. (힐끗 보기)

5 이탤릭체로 된 단어와 같은 뜻을 가진 단어를 골라 그 번호를 공란에 써넣어라.

_____ 1. John likes to have *raw* vegetables.
   (A) soft   (B) cheap   (C) rotten   (D) unripe

_____ 2. He *pledged* to marry her when he returned from England.
   (A) devised   (B) denied   (C) vowed   (D) flattered

_____ 3. Our soldiers *displayed* no fear under the enemy's fire.
   (A) revealed   (B) vanquished   (C) discharged   (D) informed

_____ 4. This year's wheat *harvest* was very small because of bad weather.
   (A) peasant   (B) crop   (C) deposit   (D) bunch

_____ 5. We will *notify* you when the books arrive.
   (A) inform   (B) reveal   (C) request   (D) guess

_____ 6. When I asked him a question, the old man *peered* at me over his glasses.
   (A) pecked   (B) stared   (C) screamed   (D) scratched

_____ 7. The soldiers stood beside their horses, waiting for the order to *mount*.
   (A) relieve   (B) run   (C) dismiss   (D) climb

_____ 8. Seeing the big dog, the boys *retreated* rapidly[31].
   (A) advanced   (B) screamed   (C) withdrew   (D) vanished

_____ 9. He gave the machine another *trial* to see if it would work[32].
   (A) motion   (B) testing   (C) pressure   (D) flame

_____ 10. Jane's *task* is to set the table[33].
   (A) assignment   (B) distress   (C) tide   (D) rust

---

28. fluid[flú(:)id] *n.* 유체(流體)   29. late : 최근에 죽은, 고(故)…   30. parcel[pɑ́ːrsl] *n.* 소포, 꾸러미
31. rapidly[rǽpidli] *adv.* 신속하게   32. work *v.* 작동하다   33. set the table : 식탁을 차리다, 상을 보다

Lesson 7

Answers

1. 1. D 2. B 3. A 4. D 5. C 6. C 7. B 8. D 9. C 10. A
2. 1. C 2. B 3. A 4. D 5. A
3. 1. B 2. A 3. C 4. B 5. A
4. 1. LIQUID 2. BURIAL 3. REMIND 4. FLATTER 5. GLIMPSE
5. 1. D 2. C 3. A 4. B 5. A 6. B 7. D 8. C 9. B 10. A

LESSON 8

Self-test 8

적당한 단어를 골라 빈칸을 채우라.

1. The *lame* boy could not _____ fast.
   (A) speak   (B) walk

2. A _____ lowered the *anchor* easily.
   (A) sailor   (B) surgeon

3. The whole nation *mourned* the _____ of the much-loved king.
   (A) birth   (B) death

4. He *pretended* to like the meal so that he _____ offend[1] his wife.
   (A) wouldn't   (B) would

5. The little girl was so _____ that she *blushed* every time she was spoken to.
   (A) vigorous   (B) shy

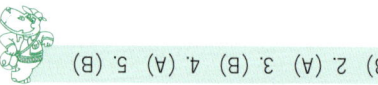
1. (B) 2. (A) 3. (B) 4. (A) 5. (B)

New Vocabulary -1

accomplish
[əkɔ́mpliʃ]
v. 달성하다, 성취하다
syn. achieve, perform
n. accomplishment
How many years did it take to *accomplish* your purpose?

anchor
[ǽŋkər]
n. 닻
The *anchor* caught in the mud[2] of the lake bottom and kept the boat from moving.

awaken
[əwéikən]
v. 눈을 뜨다, 깨어나다
syn. awake
The sun was shining when I *awakened* this morning.

1. offend[əfénd] *v.* ~의 감정을 상하게 하다   2. mud[mʌd] *n.* 진흙, 진창

blush
[blʌʃ]

v. 얼굴을 붉히다, 얼굴이 붉어지다
She *blushed* as red as a rose with shame[3].

bush
[buʃ]

n. 관목, 수풀, 덤불
He came out of the shadow of the *bush* and blinked[4] in the sun.

cheat
[tʃiːt]

v. 속이다, 부정 행위를 하다
syn. deceive
The boy doesn't study hard, and he always *cheats* in examinations.

compete
[kəmpíːt]

v. 겨루다, 경쟁하다, 서로 맞서다
syn. contend
n. competition
The rival schools *competed* for the football trophy.

consequence
[kɔ́nsikwəns]

n. 결과, 결말
syn. result, effect, outcome
ant. cause
adj. consequent
He fell ill[5] and the *consequence* was that he lost his position.

courage
[kʌ́ridʒ]

n. 용기, 용맹, 용감성
syn. bravery
ant. cowardice
adj. courageous
Courage is the ability to control fear, not the absence of fear.

debate
[dibéit]

v. 논쟁하다, 토론하다
syn. discuss, argue
The question of whether war can be abolished[6] has often been *debated*.

Practice 1

위 단어를 사용하여 아래 문장을 완성하라. 필요시 단어를 적절한 형태로 변형하라.

1. He _____ the old woman by making her sign a paper she didn't understand.

2. The man was highly praised for having the _____ to go into the burring house to save the little girl.

3. We were _____ whether to go to the mountain or to the seaside our summer holidays.

---

3. shame[ʃeim] *n.* 수치   4. blink[bliŋk] *v.* (눈을) 깜박거리다   5. fall ill : 병에 걸리다   6. abolish[əbɔ́liʃ] *v.* 폐지하다

4. The horse was _____ against many fine horses for the first prize.

5. The _____ of the heavy rain was the flooding[7] of large areas of the nation.

New Vocabulary -2

descend
[disénd]

v. 내려가다, 하강하다
ant. ascend
der. descendant
The sun slowly *descended* over the western hills.

dispose
[dispóuz]

v. 1. 배열하다, 배치하다
syn. arrange
The general *disposed* soldiers for the coming battle.

2. 처리하다, 처분하다
n. disposal
You'd better *dispose* of rubbish[8] before you go out.

earnest
[ə́ːrnist]

adj. 진지한, 성실한
syn. sincere, diligent
He made an *earnest* attempt to persuade[9] her.

enforce
[infɔ́ːrs]

v. 시행하다, 실시하다
syn. execute
n. enforcement
Policemen and judges will *enforce* the laws of the city.

extend
[iksténd]

v. 1. 뻗다, 펴다, 내밀다
syn. stretch, reach
He refused to take the hand I *extended* in friendship.

2. (범위, 영토, 권력 따위를) 넓히다, 확장하다
syn. enlarge
n. extension
An imperialistic[10] country *extends* its power and influence into neighboring countries.

---

7. flood [flʌd] *v.* 범람하다   8. rubbish [rʌ́biʃ] *n.* 쓰레기   9. persuade [pə(ː)rswéid] *v.* 설득하다   10. imperialistic [impìəriəlístik] *adj.* 제국주의의

faithful
[féiθfəl]

adj. 성실한, 충실한
syn. loyal, trustworthy
ant. unfaithful, insincere
Dogs are always *faithful* to their masters.

flavor
[fléivər]

n. 맛, 풍미
syn. taste
Chocolate and vanilla[11] have different *flavors*.

frustrate
[frʌ́streit]

v. 좌절시키다, 실망시키다
syn. disappoint, defeat
n. frustration
His indifference[12] *frustrated* the teacher's efforts.

glorious
[glɔ́:riəs]

adj. 영광스러운, 명예로운
syn. honorable, splendid
n. glory
A *glorious* victory could be attained[13] only by effort and patience.

haste
[heist]

n. 서두름, 신속, 급속
syn. hurry
ant. deliberation
adj. hasty
Make *haste* or you will miss the train again.

Practice 2

위 단어를 사용하여 아래 문장을 완성하라. 필요시 단어를 적절한 형태로 변형하라.

1. All his _____ was of no use; he missed the last train.
2. The sun _____ behind the hills and it was dark everywhere.
3. The _____ student tried very hard to do his best[14].
4. A _____ friend is reliable[15] and can be depended on to do his work.
5. The bad weather _____ our plans for a picnic.

---

11. vanilla[vənílə] *n.* 바닐라 (열대 아메리카산 덩굴식물)   12. indifference[indífərəns] *n.* 무관심, 냉담
13. attain[ətéin] *v.* 섭취하다, 달성하다   14. do one's best : 최선을 다하다   15. reliable[riláiəbl] *adj.* 믿을 수 있는

New Vocabulary -3

identify
[aidéntifai]

v. 확인하다, 감정하다
syn. recognize
n. identification
Can you *identify* a composer by listening to his music?

injure
[índʒər]

v. 상처를 입히다, 손상하다
syn. harm
ant. aid, help, benefit
She was *injured* badly in the car accident yesterday.

irregular
[irégjulər]

adj. 불규칙한, 고르지 못한
syn. unusual
ant. regular
Train schedules were *irregular* during the flood.

lame
[leim]

adj. 절름발이의, 다리를 저는
syn. crippled, disabled
The soldier is not able to walk normally because he is *lame* from an old wound.

liquor
[líkər]

n. 술, 주류(酒類)
Does this restaurant have a license[16] to serve *liquor*?

manly
[mǽnli]

adj. 남자다운, 씩씩한, 용맹스러운
ant. womanly, womanish
My aunt was a lady of strong mind and great resolution[17]; she was a very *manly* woman.

mild
[maild]

adj. 부드러운, 온화한, 관대한
syn. gentle, kind, moderate
The thief was given a *milder* punishment than he deserved.

mourn
[mɔ:rn]

v. 슬퍼하다, 애도하다, 비탄하다
syn. lament, grieve
All the people *mourned* the loss of their President.

notion
[nóuʃən]

n. 관념, 생각, 의견
syn. idea, opinion
Your head is full of silly[18] *notions*.

---

16. license [láisəns] *n.* 면허장, 인가서   17. resolution [rezəljú:ʃən] *n.* 결의, 결심   18. silly [síli] *adj.* 어리석은

order	***n. v.*** 명령(하다), 지시(하다)
[ɔ́:rdər]	**syn.** command
	He gave *orders* that the work should be done at once.

Practice 3

위 단어를 사용하여 아래 문장을 완성하라. 필요시 단어를 적절한 형태로 변형하라.

1. John could easily _____ his own son among many boys.
2. A soldier who doesn't obey _____ will be in serious trouble[19].
3. He _____ his leg when he fell over[20] the big stone.
4. It was her _____ that planes were safer than trains.
5. He was _____ over the loss of his best friend.

New Vocabulary -4

paragraph	***n.*** 문단, 절(節)
[pǽrəgrɑ:f]	A new *paragraph* always begins on a new line.

penalty	***n.*** 형벌, 벌칙, 응징
[pénəlti]	**syn.** punishment
	The *penalty* for his offense[21] was five years in prison.

pluck	***v.*** 뜯다, 따다, 뽑다
[plʌk]	**syn.** pick
	Do not *pluck* the flowers in the garden, please.

pretend	***v.*** ~인 체하다, 가장하다
[priténd]	**syn.** assume
	n. pretence, pretension
	He *pretended* to be asleep when his mother called him.

protect	***v.*** 보호하다, 지키다, 방호하다
[prətékt]	**syn.** guard
	n. protection
	We keep our army to *protect* our country from the enemy.

19. be in trouble : 곤란한 상황에 처하다, 벌받다   20. fall over : ~에 걸려 넘어지다   21. offense[əféns] ***n.*** 위반, 반칙

realize
[ríːəlaiz]

v. 1. 깨닫다, 이해하다, 실감하다
syn. understand
He didn't *realize* how cold it was until he went outside.

　2. 실현하다
n. realization
He *realized* his dreams when he became a doctor.

remove
[rimúːv]

v. 1. 옮기다, 이전하다
n. removal
Our office has *removed* from New York to Chicago.

　2. 제거하다, 떼어내다
syn. eliminate
She could not *remove* the spot[22] from the carpet.

reveal
[rivíːl]

v. 폭로하다, 밝히다, 드러내다
syn. show, disclose
ant. conceal
n. revelation
Can you promise never to *reveal* my secret?

sacrifice
[sǽkrəfais]

v. 희생하다
A mother will *sacrifice* her life for her children.

n. 희생, 손실
Success is not worth the *sacrifice* of your health.

screw
[skruː]

n. 나사, 나사못
Turn the *screw* to the right to tighten it.

v. 나사로 죄다, 나사로 고정시키다
The carpenter[23] *screwed* a lock[24] on the door.

Practice 4

위 단어를 사용하여 아래 문장을 완성하라. 필요시 단어를 적절한 형태로 변형하라.

1. She suddenly _____ the fact that she was not married.
2. Please _____ mud from your shoes before you get into the hall.
3. She _____ her dream of becoming an actress[25].
4. He raised his arm in order to _____ his face from the blow[26].
5. She wasn't really crying; she was only _____.

---

22. spot[spɔt] *n.* 얼룩　23. carpenter[káːrpintər] *n.* 목수　24. lock[lɔk] *n.* 자물쇠　25. actress[ǽktris] *n.* 여배우
26. blow[blou] *n.* 강타, 구타

New Vocabulary -5

shell
[ʃel]

n. 껍질, 외피(外皮)
ant. core
The cook[27] broke the *shell* of an egg.

slender
[sléndər]

adj. 날씬한, 호리호리한, 가냘픈
syn. thin
ant. fat
She is a very *slender* blonde[28].

sparkle
[spá:rkl]

v. 번쩍이다, 번득이다
The lake *sparkled* in the sunshine.

stain
[stein]

n. 얼룩, 더러운 점
syn. spot
He has ink *stains* on his shirt.

v. 더럽히다, 얼룩이 지다
The tablecloth is *stained* where food has been spilled.

stream
[strí:m]

n. 개울, 시내
They walked along the bank of the *stream*.

surrender
[səréndər]

v. 항복하다, 굴복하다
syn. yield, abandon
We advised the bandits[29] to *surrender* themselves to the police.

tasty
[téisti]

adj. 맛 좋은, 맛있는
n. taste
All of us had a very *tasty* meal yesterday.

tight
[tait]

adj. 꽉 죄는, 탄탄한, 야무진
ant. loose
v. tighten
The drawer[30] is so *tight* that I can't open it.

tribe
[traib]

n. 부족, 종족
America was once the home of many Indian *tribes*.

---

27. cook[kuk] *n.* 요리사   28. blonde[blɔnd] *n.* 금발의 여인   29. bandit[bǽndit] *n.* 산적, 노상 강도   30. drawer[drɔːr] *n.* 서랍

weapon
[wépən]

n. 무기, 병기
syn. arms
The soldiers were cleaning their *weapons*.

wreck
[rek]

v. 파괴하다, 부수다
syn. destroy
der. wreckage
n. 난파, 조난
The *wreck* of the ship was reported last night.

Practice 5

위 단어를 사용하여 아래 문장을 완성하라. 필요시 단어를 적절한 형태로 변형하라.

1. There were blood _____ at the scene of the murder[31].
2. We will never _____ to the enemy.
3. Pack[32] the cases as _____ as possible.
4. Guns are of little value[33] against modern _____ in war.
5. Most girls want to be _____.

Practice 1	1. cheated	2. courage	3. debating	4. competing	5. consequence
Practice 2	1. haste	2. descended	3. earnest	4. faithful	5. frustrated
Practice 3	1. identify	2. orders	3. injured	4. notion	5. mourning
Practice 4	1. revealed	2. remove	3. realized	4. protect	5. pretending
Practice 5	1. stains	2. surrender	3. tight	4. weapons	5. slender

---

31. murder[mə́rdər] *n.* 살인   32. pack[pæk] *v.* 짐을 꾸리다   33. be of little value : 가치가 거의 없다

Lesson 8 종합 연습 문제

1 이탤릭체로 된 단어와 같은 뜻을 가진 단어를 골라 그 번호를 공란에 써넣어라.

_____ 1. a *slender* girl   (A) thin   (B) faint
                                                     (C) tiny   (D) small

_____ 2. a sweet *flavor*   (A) blossom   (B) flower
                                                     (C) taste   (D) pledge

_____ 3. to *compete* for prize   (A) spare   (B) contend
                                                     (C) impel   (D) amuse

_____ 4. to *surrender* unconditionally   (A) conquer   (B) love
                                                     (C) escape   (D) yield

_____ 5. to *identify* the coat at once   (A) notify   (B) display
                                                     (C) disclose   (D) recognize

_____ 6. to be *frustrated* by rain   (A) cheated   (B) disappointed
                                                     (C) removed   (D) compelled

_____ 7. to *injure* one's feelings   (A) harm   (B) control
                                                     (C) reveal   (D) flatter

_____ 8. the *consequence* of war   (A) escape   (B) outcome
                                                     (C) trial   (D) prospect

_____ 9. an *earnest* man   (A) sincere   (B) rich
                                                     (C) strong   (D) unusual

_____ 10. to *reveal* secrets   (A) identify   (B) conceal
                                                     (C) disclose   (D) inform

2 왼쪽에 주어진 우리말과 같은 뜻을 가진 단어를 골라 그 번호를 공란에 써넣어라.

_____ 1. 얼룩   (A) clan   (B) veil
                              (C) stain   (D) blush

_____ 2. 희생하다   (A) sacrifice   (B) stare
                              (C) deserve   (D) derive

_____ 3. 처분하다   (A) compete   (B) dispose
                              (C) perform   (D) worsen

_____ 4. 실현하다   (A) identify   (B) awaken
                              (C) realize   (D) stretch

_____ 5. 난파, 조난   (A) woe   (B) screw
                              (C) shell   (D) wreck

Lesson 1 종합 연습 문제

3 왼쪽에 주어진 단어와 반대되는 뜻을 가진 단어를 골라 그 번호를 공란에 써넣어라.

_____ 1. courage   (A) punishment   (B) cowardice
                           (C) injury   (D) unstability

_____ 2. conceal   (A) avoid   (B) debate
                           (C) deceive   (D) reveal

_____ 3. consequence (A) haste   (B) result
                           (C) cause   (D) conscience

_____ 4. insincere   (A) faithful   (B) mighty
                           (C) extensive   (D) profane

_____ 5. ascend   (A) frustrate   (B) descend
                           (C) protect   (D) debate

4 괄호 속에 주어진 우리말과 같은 뜻을 가진 단어를 사용하여 문장을 완성하라.

1. For the moment he did not R____E his eyes from the face of the little girl. (옮기다)
2. Many children were swimming in the S____M. (개울)
3. She saw the diamonds S_____E in the bright light. (번쩍이다)
4. He has too M__D a nature to get angry, even if he has good cause. (온화한)
5. It took three years to A_____H his ambition. (성취하다)

5 가장 적합한 단어를 골라 빈칸을 채워라.

1. In his attempt to escape, the prisoner was _____ by a watchful guard[34].
   (A) amused   (B) frustrated   (C) wrecked   (D) plucked

2. Government makes laws and the police _____ them.
   (A) enforce   (B) stretch   (C) dispose   (D) chase

3. The city _____ the road to the next town.
   (A) yielded   (B) guarded   (C) disposed   (D) extended

4. A _____ friend keeps his promises.
   (A) solemn   (B) splendid   (C) faithful   (D) lame

5. The sick man's heartbeat[35] was _____.
   (A) irregular (B) raw   (C) spare   (D) tiny

---

34. guard[gɑːrd] *n.* 간수   35. heartbeat[hάːrtbiːt] *n.* 심장의 고동

6 왼쪽에 주어진 단어의 적당한 파생어를 사용하여 문장을 완성하라.

1. *haste*   His _____ decisions caused many mistakes.
2. *frustrate*   Life is full of _____ for most people.
3. *accomplish*   She is known for her _____ in improving the country's hospitals.
4. *pretend*   He often uses my car without my permission under the _____ of friendship.
5. *courage*   It was _____ of you to try and save the drawning man.

Answers

1. 1. A   2. C   3. B   4. D   5. D   6. B   7. A   8. B   9. A   10. C
2. 1. C   2. A   3. B   4. C   5. D
3. 1. B   2. D   3. C   4. A   5. B
4. 1. REMOVE   2. STREAM   3. SPARKLE   4. MILD   5. ACCOMPLISH
5. 1. B   2. A   3. D   4. C   5. A
6. 1. hasty   2. frustration   3. accomplishment   4. pretence   5. courageous

Lesson 8 ▶ 101

LESSON 9

Self-test 9

적당한 단어를 골라 빈칸을 채우라.

1. When a man is *innocent*, he is _____.
   (A) ignorant[1]   (B) guiltless

2. He *boasts* that he is the _____ billiard[2]-player in the town.
   (A) best   (B) worst

3. A *peninsula* is surrounded on three sides by _____.
   (A) islands   (B) water

4. The person whose work is _____ animals for food is called a *butcher*.
   (A) killing   (B) protecting

5. The man put a *saddle* on the _____ and ran away.
   (A) horse   (B) bicycle

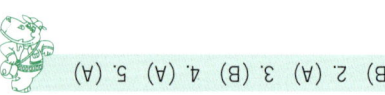
1. (B) 2. (A) 3. (B) 4. (A) 5. (A)

New Vocabulary -1

accord
[əkɔ́:rd]
v. 일치하다, 부합하다
syn. concur, harmonize
ant. discord
What you have just said does not *accord* with what you told us yesterday.

award
[əwɔ́:rd]
v. 상을 주다, 수여하다
He was *awarded* the first prize in the speech contest[3].

boast
[boust]
v. 자랑하다, 뽐내다
He *boasted* about the big fish he had caught.

butcher
[bútʃər]
n. 푸주한, 도살자, 백정
You can buy meat at the *butcher*'s shop.

---

1. ignorant [ígnərənt] *adj.* 무식한   2. billiards [bíljərdz] *n. (pl.)* 당구   3. speech contest : 웅변 대회

grace
[greis]

n. 우아, 우미, 기품
adj. graceful
The ballet[12] dancer danced with much *grace*.

haunt
[hɔ:nt]

v. (유령 따위가) 종종 나타나다
People say that the old house is *haunted* by a ghost[13].

innocent
[ínəsnt]

adj. 죄없는, 결백한
syn. guiltless
ant. guilty
Is he guilty or *innocent* of the crime?

Practice 2

위 단어를 사용하여 아래 문장을 완성하라. 필요시 단어를 적절한 형태로 변형하라.

1. The robbers tried to _____ but they were caught soon.
2. The old woman _____ a maid servant[14] to clean her house.
3. His speech was full of _____ and wit.
4. A nurse has many duties to _____ in caring for[15] the sick.
5. They were still _____ the rights and wrongs of the case at midnight.

New Vocabulary -3

issue
[íʃu:]

v. 1. 발행하다, 발하다
The government *issues* money and stamps.

2. 출판하다, 간행하다
syn. publish
This book was *issued* in New York in 1972.

3. 분출하다, 유출하다
A lot of blood was *issuing* from the wound.

landlord
[lǽndlɔ:rd]

n. (하숙집, 여관의) 주인
syn. host, innkeeper
The *landlord* put a new stove in my room.

---

12. ballet[bǽlei] *n.* 발레, 무용극   13. ghost[goust] *n.* 유령   14. maid servant : 하녀   15. care for ~ : ~을 돌보다

literature
[lítərətʃər]

n. 문학
adj. literary
Many foreigners are studying Korean *literature*.

manufacture
[mænjufǽktʃər]

n. 제조, 제작
The *manufacture* of watches[16] is the chief business of Switzerland.

v. 제조하다, 제작하다
syn. make, produce
The factory *manufactures* automobiles in large quantity[17] by using machines.

military
[mílitèri]

adj. 군대의, 군사의
ant. civilian
In some countries every healthy young man must do 2 or 3 years' *military* service[18].

multiply
[mʌ́ltiplai]

v. 증가하다, 증가시키다
syn. increase
adj. multiple
The population of the city is *multiplying* rapidly.

numerous
[njúːmərəs]

adj. 다수의, 엄청난 수의
syn. many, plentiful
Children often ask *numerous* questions about the universe[19].

ordinary
[ɔ́ːrdinèri]

adj. 통상의, 보통의, 정규의
syn. common, average
ant. extraordinary
His *ordinary* lunch consists of soup, a sandwich and milk.

pardon
[páːrdn]

n. 용서
I beg your *pardon* for being late.

v. 용서하다, 관대히 봐주다
syn. excuse, forgive
We must *pardon* him for his little faults.

peninsula
[pinínsjulə]

n. 반도(半島)
Korea or Italy is a *peninsula*.

---

16. watch [wɔtʃ] *n.* 손목 시계　　17. in large quantity : 대량으로　　18. military service : 군복무　　19. universe [júːnivəːrs] *n.* 우주

Practice 3

위 단어를 사용하여 아래 문장을 완성하라. 필요시 단어를 적절한 형태로 변형하라.

1. The chimney[20] _____ smoke from the fireplace[21].

2. As we climbed up the mountain the dangers and difficulties _____.

3. At night we can see _____ stars in the sky.

4. Shakespeare is a great name in English _____.

5. I beg your _____, but I didn't hear you.

New Vocabulary –4

plunge
[plʌndʒ]
v. 뛰어들다, 돌입하다
syn. dive
He *plunged* into the river and saved the boy.

prevent
[privént]
v. 막다, 못하게 하다, 예방하다
syn. stop
ant. enable
n. prevention
A heavy rain *prevented* us from going on a picnic.

protest
[prətést]
v. 항의하다, 이의를 제기하다
syn. object
ant. agree
Most of them *protested* against the new, heavy tax.

rear
[riər]
n. 뒤, 후미
syn. back
ant. front
The people in the *rear* of the room could not hear the speaker.

rent
[rent]
n. 임대료
Rent for that three-bedroom apartment is $500 a month.
v. 빌리다, 세들다, 임대하다
We don't own our house, we *rent* it from Mr. Gay.

revenge
[rivéndʒ]
n. 복수, 보복
His mind was filled with *revenge*.

---

20. chimney [tʃímni] *n.* 굴뚝   21. fireplace [fáiərpleis] *n.* 난로, 벽난로

saddle [sǽdl]	***n.*** 안장 It is difficult to ride a horse without a *saddle*.
seal [siːl]	***n.*** 인장, 날인, 봉인 The paper had been stamped[22] with the required official *seal*[23]. ***v.*** 날인하다, 조인하다 The treaty was signed and *sealed* by both governments.
shelter [ʃéltər]	***n.*** 피난처, 숨을 곳 **syn.** refuge, protection The cave provided a good *shelter* for the ancient[24] people. ***v.*** 보호하다, (비·바람을) 막아주다 The abandoned[25] car *sheltered* them from the rain.
slice [slais]	***n.*** 얇은 조각 He ate two *slices* of bread for his breakfast.

Practice 4

위 단어를 사용하여 아래 문장을 완성하라. 필요시 단어를 적절한 형태로 변형하라.

1. The _____ for the house was more than they could afford[26].
2. The garage[27] is usually at the _____ of a house.
3. There was a large crowd in the street, _____ against the war.
4. Illness _____ him from taking the examination.
5. The fireman _____ into the burning house to rescue[28] the baby in it.

---

22. stamp[stæmp] ***v.*** (도장 따위)로 찍다   23. official seal : 관인   24. ancient[éinʃənt] ***adj.*** 옛날의   25. abandoned[əbǽndənd] ***adj.*** 버려진
26. afford[əfɔ́ːrd] ***v.*** ~할 (돈의) 여유가 있다   27. garage[gərάːdʒ] ***n.*** 자동차 차고   28. rescue[réskjuː] ***v.*** 구출하다

New Vocabulary -5

spear
[spiər]

n. 창(槍)
ant. shield
In Africa *spears* are still used in hunting or fishing.

stake
[steik]

n. 1. 말뚝, 막대기
Stakes mark the boundary of his ranch[29].

2. 이해 관계
As a partner, he has a *stake* in that business.

v. 내기에 (돈을) 걸다
syn. bet
He *staked* all his money on the black horse.

stretch
[stretʃ]

v. 쭉 펴다, 뻗다
syn. extend
The beggar *stretched* out his hand for the money.

surround
[səráund]

v. 둘러 싸다, 에워 싸다
syn. enclose
n. surrounding
The field is *surrounded* by a high fence.

tavern
[tǽvərn]

n. 선술집
They met at the *tavern* for a drink.

timber
[tímbər]

n. 재목, 목재, 입목(立木)
syn. lumber
The fire destroyed thousands of acres of *timber*.

trick
[trik]

n. 속임수, 계교, 요술
The *tricks* of the magician delighted the children.

v. 속이다, 협잡하다
syn. cheat
We were *tricked* into buying a poor car.

---

29. ranch[ræntʃ] *n.* 목장

vein
[vein]

n. 정맥
ant. artery
Blood poured[30] from the cut *vein*.

weaken
[wíːkən]

v. 약화시키다, 약화되다
ant. strengthen
adj. weak
The illness *weakened* her heart.

wring
[riŋ]

v. 비틀다, 짜다
syn. twist, squeeze
I'll *wring* your neck if you don't behave[31] well.

Practice 5

위 단어를 사용하여 아래 문장을 완성하라. 필요시 단어를 적절한 형태로 변형하라.

1. The bird _____ its wings when it wants to fly.

2. The soldiers _____ the enemy in the town.

3. The _____ carries the blood to the heart from all parts of the body.

4. She _____ as her illness grew worse[32].

5. _____ the water from your bathing suit[33].

해답					
Practice 1	1. debt	2. accord	3. boast	4. awarded	5. consists
Practice 2	1. flee	2. engaged	3. grace	4. fulfil	5. disputing
Practice 3	1. issues	2. multiplied	3. numerous	4. literature	5. pardon
Practice 4	1.rent	2. rear	3. protesting	4. prevented	5. plunged
Practice 5	1. stretches	2. surrounded	3. vein	4. weakened	5. Wring

30. pour[pɔːr] *v.* 흘러나오다   31. behave[bihéiv] *v.* 처신하다   32. grow worse : 악화되다   33. bathing suit : 수영복

종합 연습 문제

1 네 개의 단어 중 다른 셋과 관련이 없는 것을 골라 공란에 그 번호를 써넣어라.

_____ 1. (A) accomplish (B) perform (C) stretch (D) fulfil
_____ 2. (A) make (B) manufacture (C) produce (D) wring
_____ 3. (A) defeat (B) express (C) reveal (D) represent
_____ 4. (A) twist (B) squeeze (C) yield (D) wring
_____ 5. (A) protection (B) revenge (C) refuge (D) shelter
_____ 6. (A) many (B) plentiful (C) numerous (D) extensive
_____ 7. (A) concur (B) harmonize (C) achieve (D) accord
_____ 8. (A) flee (B) fly (C) escape (D) chase
_____ 9. (A) ordinary (B) useful (C) common (D) average
_____ 10. (A) landlord (B) host (C) rent (D) innkeeper

2 왼쪽에 주어진 우리말과 같은 뜻을 가진 단어를 골라 그 번호를 공란에 써넣어라.

_____ 1. 우아함 (A) reverse (B) grace (C) blush (D) clean
_____ 2. 비틀다, 짜다 (A) wing (B) ring (C) wring (D) seal
_____ 3. (유령이) 종종 나타나다 (A) haunt (B) flee (C) multiply (D) enclose
_____ 4. 쭉 펴다 (A) pretend (B) fulfil (C) spare (D) stretch
_____ 5. 속임수 (A) seal (B) trick (C) screw (D) stain

3 왼쪽에 주어진 단어와 반대되는 뜻을 가진 단어를 골라 그 번호를 공란에 써넣어라.

_____ 1. chase (A) assume (B) flee (C) wreck (D) conceal
_____ 2. artery (A) vein (B) veil (C) manufacture (D) literature
_____ 3. front (A) revenge (B) opposite (C) sleeve (D) rear
_____ 4. discord (A) baffle (B) mourn (C) haunt (D) harmonize
_____ 5. dismiss (A) discharge (B) engage (C) disclose (D) find

Lesson 9 종합 연습 문제

4 괄호 속에 주어진 우리말과 같은 뜻을 가진 단어를 사용하여 문장을 완성하라.

1. Hamlet wanted R_____E for his father's murder. (복수)
2. He found a room for the night at a T____N. (선술집)
3. His peaceful words and violent[34] actions do not A____D. (일치하다)
4. What kind of T____R was used for the frame of the house? (재목)
5. You can W____N tea by adding water. (약하게 하다)

5 이탤릭체로 된 단어와 같은 뜻을 가진 단어를 골라 그 번호를 공란에 써넣어라.

_____ 1. He threw the mirror on the floor, but there was not a *crack* in it.
(A) sound   (B) crevice   (C) stake   (D) trick

_____ 2. That magazine is *issued* once a month.
(A) sold   (B) bought   (C) published   (D) shown

_____ 3. If you want to learn German, you must first find a *competent* teacher.
(A) capable   (B) faithful   (C) honorable   (D) sacred

_____ 4. Some husbands and wives are always *disputing*.
(A) discharging   (B) disposing   (C) competing   (D) arguing

_____ 5. Water *consists* of hydrogen[35] and oxygen[36].
(A) disposes   (B) comprises   (C) derives   (D) revenged

_____ 6. The children *protested* loudly when they were told to go to bed.
(A) objected   (B) protected   (C) discorded   (D) revenged

_____ 7. They *engaged* a man to paint their new house.
(A) employed   (B) forced   (C) dismissed   (D) pardoned

_____ 8. Did I really hear someone come in or was it only a *fancy*?
(A) notion   (B) flavor   (C) grace   (D) illusion

_____ 9. The old house is *enclosed* with trees.
(A) protected   (B) prevented   (C) disclosed   (D) surrounded

_____ 10. *Forgive* my mistakes. I'll try not to make the same mistakes.
(A) mourn   (B) deter   (C) pardon   (D) forget

---

34. violent[vaiələnt] ***adj.*** 격렬한   35. hydrogen[haidridʒən] ***n.*** 수소   36. oxygen[ɔ́ksidʒən] ***n.*** 산소

Lesson 9

종합 연습 문제

Answers

1. 1. C 2. D 3. A 4. C 5. B 6. D 7. C 8. D 9. B 10. C

2. 1. B 2. C 3. A 4. D 5. B

3. 1. B 2. A 3. D 4. D 5. B

4. 1. REVENGE 2. TAVERN 3. ACCORD 4. TIMBER 5. WEAKEN

5. 1. B 2. C 3. A 4. D 5. B 6. A 7. A 8. D 9. D 10. C

LESSON 10

Self-test 10

적당한 단어를 골라 빈칸을 채우라.

1. The *fleet* has a lot of _____.
   (A) warships   (B) cars

2. Make *hay* while _____.
   (A) it is raining   (B) the sun shines

3. When a person is _____, he is *ignorant*.
   (A) guiltless   (B) uneducated

4. John is guilty of *murder*; he _____.
   (A) killed someone   (B) stole something

5. A _____ citizen *obeys* the laws of his country.
   (A) good   (B) bad

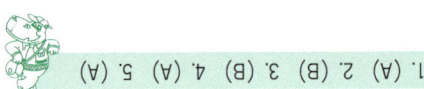
1. (A) 2. (B) 3. (B) 4. (A) 5. (A)

New Vocabulary -1

account
[əkáunt]
n. 설명, 기술(記述)
syn. story
The boy gave his father an *account* of the ball game.

angle
[ǽŋgl]
n. 각(角), 각도(角度)
An *angle* of 90 degrees is called a right angle[1].

aware
[əwέər]
adj. 의식하는, 깨닫는
syn. conscious
n. awareness
I was too sleepy to *aware* how cold it was.

1. right angle : 직각

bold [bould]	***adj.*** 대담한, 담력이 있는 **syn.** brave, courageous, fearless **ant.** cowardly Climbing the steep[2] mountain is a *bold* act.
cabin [kǽbin]	***n.*** 오두막 **syn.** hut The pioneers[3] lived in a *cabin* in the wood.
cheer [tʃiər]	***v.*** 격려하다, 갈채를 보내다, 성원하다 **syn.** acclaim, applaud Everyone was *cheered* by the news that peace had come.
complain [kəmpléin]	***v.*** 불평하다, 불만을 호소하다 ***n.*** complaint She *complained* to the police about the barking[4] of her neighbor's dog.
consolation [kànsəléiʃən]	***n.*** 위로, 위안 **syn.** comfort ***v.*** console I got many letters of *consolation* when my mother died.
crash [kræʃ]	***n.*** 1. (물건이 무너질 때, 부딪칠 때 나는) 요란한 소리 The bottles fell on the floor with a *crash*. 2. 추락, 충돌 He was killed in an aircraft *crash*.
decay [dikéi]	***v.*** 썩다, 부패하다 **syn.** deteriorate, decline, rot Her teeth *decayed* because the ate too many sweets[5].

Practice 1

위 단어를 사용하여 아래 문장을 완성하라. 필요시 단어를 적절한 형태로 변형하라.

1. The two roads lie at a(n) _____ of 45 degrees.
2. When your teeth begin to _____ you should go to see a dentist[6] at once.

---

2. steep[stiːp] ***adj.*** 가파른   3. pioneer[paiəníər] ***n.*** 개척자, 선구자   4. bark[bɑːrk] ***v.*** (개, 여우가) 짖다
5. sweet[swiːt] ***n.*** 단 것, (특히) 과자   6. dentist[déntist] ***n.*** 치과 의사

3. Every time an American runner won a race, the crowd _____.

4. Are you _____ that you are sitting on my hat?

5. Please give a(n) _____ of everything as it happened.

New Vocabulary -2

deserve
[dizə́:rv]
v. ~할 가치가 있다, ~을 받아 마땅하다
If you do wrong, you *deserve* severe punishment.

distinction
[distíŋkʃən]
n. 구별, 차별
syn. discrimination
v. distinguish
adj. distinct
She treated all the children alike without *distinction*.

echo
[ékou]
v. 메아리 치다, 반향하다, 울리다
Their voices *echoed* in the big hall.

enormous
[inɔ́:rməs]
adj. 거대한, 막대한, 방대한
syn. huge, immense
ant. trivial, tiny, ordinary
The war cost an *enormous* sum of money.

expose
[ikspóuz]
v. 1. 노출시키다, 드러내다
syn. uncover
n. exposure
Soldiers in an open field are *exposed* to the enemy's fire[7].

   2. (비밀 등을) 폭로하다
syn. disclose, reveal
He threatened to *expose* the secret to the police.

farewell
[fɛərwél]
n. 작별, 이별
syn. good-bye
We shall have a *farewell* party before we leave.

fleet
[fli:t]
n. 함대
The Sixth *Fleet* in the harbor is moving toward our coast.

---

7. fire [fáiər] *n.* 사격

function	***n.*** 기능, 작용
[fʌ́ŋkʃən]	**syn.** operation
	adj. functional
	v. function
	The brain performs a very important *function*; it controls the nervous system[8] of the body.

gradual	***adj.*** 점진적인
[grǽdjuəl]	**ant.** swift
	A child's growth into an adult[9] is *gradual*.

hay	***n.*** 건초(乾草)
[hei]	They usually keep the *hay* in the barn[10].

Practice 2

위 단어를 사용하여 아래 문장을 완성하라. 필요시 단어를 적절한 형태로 변형하라.

1. The murderer was hanged[11]; he _____ his fate.

2. He gave all his servants the same wages, without making any _____.

3. The change was _____, but now it looks completely different.

4. The hill _____ back the noise of the gunshot[12].

5. During the last ten years, he has made a(n) _____ amount of money to become a millionaire.

New Vocabulary -3

ignorant	***adj.*** 무식한, 무지한, 모르는
[ígnərənt]	**syn.** illiterate, uneducated
	ant. learned, educated
	He is quite *ignorant*; he can't even read or write.

inquire	***v.*** 문의하다, 묻다, 질문하다
[inkwáiər]	**syn.** ask
	ant. reply, answer
	n. inquiry
	I *inquired* of him what he wanted.

---

8. nervous system : 신경 계통, 신경 조직   9. adult[ǽdʌlt] ***n.*** 성인   10. barn[bɑːrn] ***n.*** (농가의) 헛간
11. hang[hæŋ] ***v.*** 목매달다, 교수형에 처하다   12. the noise of the gunshot : 총성(銃聲)

item
[áitəm]

n. 항목, 세목
Meat, salad, and potatoes were three of the *items* on her shopping list.

landscape
[lǽndskeip]

n. 경치, 풍경, 전망, 조망
From the church tower, we can overlook the beautiful *landscape* of the valley.

liver
[lívər]

n. 간, 간장(肝臟)
He was sent to hospital because of his bad *liver*.

manuscript
[mǽnjuskript]

n. (저자의) 원고, 고본(稿本)
He sent the *manuscript* to the printer[13] yesterday.

millionaire
[miljənɛ́ər]

n. 백만 장자, 대부호
The man is a *millionaire*; he is a very rich man.

murder
[mə́:rdər]

n. 살인
syn. killing
The man was guilty of *murder*; he killed someone.

obey
[oubéi]

v. 준수하다, 따르다
n. obedience
Obey the law or you will be punished.

organization
[ɔ̀:rgənaizéiʃən]

n. 조직, 구성
The human body has a very complex *organization*.

Practice 3

위 단어를 사용하여 아래 문장을 완성하라. 필요시 단어를 적절한 형태로 변형하라.

1. We could see the beautiful _____ of the English Lakes through the train window.

2. An army without _____ would be useless.

3. Soldiers should _____ orders immediately[14].

4. That _____ owns his own ship and helicopter.

5. A person who has not had much chance to learn may be _____.

---

13. printer [príntər] *n.* 출판업자, 인쇄업자   14. immediately [imí:diətli] *adv.* 즉각적으로, 즉시

New Vocabulary -4

parliament
[pá:rləmənt]
n. 의회, 국회
syn. congress, assembly
Parliament is the lawmaking group in Great Britain.

pepper
[pépər]
n. 후추
Pepper is used for making food taste better.

poetry
[póuitri]
n. 시(詩), 운문(韻文)
der. poem, poet
The teacher praised her great efforts at *poetry*.

preview
[prí:vju]
n. (연극, 영화의) 시사(試寫), 시연(試演)
Before the movie was shown to the students, there was a *preview* for the teachers.

provide
[prəváid]
v. 공급하다, 제공하다
syn. supply, furnish
The farm *provided* them with all the food they needed.

reckless
[réklis]
adj. 무모한, 앞뒤를 가리지 않는
syn. careless
Two children were killed by a *reckless* driving.

repair
[ripɛ́ər]
v. 수리하다, 고치다
syn. mend, fix
We'd better *repair* the house before we move into it.

saint
[seint]
n. 성자, 성인, 성현
They named their child after[15] the *saint*.

search
[sə:rtʃ]
v. 수색하다, 찾다
We *searched* all day for the lost cat.

sheriff
[ʃérif]
n. (美) 보안관
The *sheriff* brought the captured criminal[16] before the judge.

---

15. name after ~ : ~의 이름을 따서 명명하다   16. criminal [kríminəl] *n.* 범인

Practice 4

위 단어를 사용하여 아래 문장을 완성하라. 필요시 단어를 적절한 형태로 변형하라.

1. The _____ in the United Kingdom is made up of the Queen, the Lords[17], and the elected representatives of the people.
2. Shakespeare and Milton were masters[18] of English _____.
3. _____ driving causes many automobile accidents.
4. The _____ pursued[19] the man who robbed the bank.
5. They will _____ the school building during the summer vacation.

New Vocabulary -5

specialist
[spéʃəlist]
n. 전문가, 전문 의사
The patient[20] was advised to see a heart *specialist*.

stalk
[stɔːk]
v. 1. ~에 살금 살금 다가서다, ~에 몰래 접근하다
The hunter *stalked* the lion.

2. 거드름 피우며 걷다, 활보하다
With her head in the air, she *stalked* out of the room.

n. 줄기, 대
syn. stem
The trunk[21] of a tree and the *stalks* of corn are stems.

strict
[strikt]
adj. 엄한, 엄격한
They are very *strict* with their children.

survey
[sə(ː)rvéi]
v. 조망하다, 살펴보다, 조사하다
He stood on the hill and *surveyed* the surrounding country.

temper
[témpər]
n. 기분, 성질, 기질
syn. disposition
He was in a good *temper* yesterday and smiled all day.

tin
[tin]
n. 주석, 양철
The house over there has a *tin* roof.

---

17. lord[lɔːrd] *n.* (英) 귀족   18. master : 대가(大家)   19. pursue[pərsjúː] *v.* 추적하다   20. patient[péiʃənt] *n.* 환자
21. trunk[trʌŋk] *n.* (나무) 줄기

trim
[trim]

v. 다듬다, 정돈하다, 손질하다
The student had his hair *trimmed*.
adj. 말쑥한, 정돈된
The new house has a *trim* appearance.

venture
[véntʃər]

n. 모험, 투기
syn. adventure, speculation
If his business *venture* succeeds, he will be wealthy.
v. (생명, 재산 따위를) 걸다, 모험하다
syn. risk
He *ventured* his life to save her from drowning.

wealthy
[wélθi]

adj. 부유한, 넉넉한
syn. rich
ant. poor, miserable
Mr. Johnson is a very *wealthy* man.

wrist
[rist]

n. 손목
He took the girl by the *wrist*[22].

Practice 5

위 단어를 사용하여 아래 문장을 완성하라. 필요시 단어를 적절한 형태로 변형하라.

1. The carpenter[23] _____ the lumber with a plane[24].
2. This can[25] is made of steel protected by a coating[26] of _____.
3. She is in a bad _____ because she missed the bus and had to walk to work[27].
4. Dr. White is a(n) _____ in diseases of the nose and throat.
5. The buyers _____ the goods[20] offered for sale.

해답

Practice 1	1. angle	2. decay	3. cheered	4. aware	5. account
Practice 2	1. deserved	2. distinctions	3. gradual	4. echoed	5. enormous
Practice 3	1. landscape	2. organization	3. obey	4. millionaire	5. ignorant
Practice 4	1. Parliament	2. poetry	3. Reckless	4. sheriff	5. repair
Practice 5	1. trimmed	2. tin	3. temper	4. specialist	5. surveyed

---

22. take one by the wrist : ~의 손목을 잡다   23. carpenter[káːrpintər] *n.* 목수, 목공   24. plane[plein] *n.* 대패
25. can[kæn] *n.* 깡통   26. coat[kout] *v.* 칠하다, 씌우다   27. work[wəːrk] *n.* 직장, 일터   28. goods[gudz] *n.* (*pl.*) 상품, 물품

Lesson 10
종합 연습 문제

1 이탤릭체로 된 단어와 같은 뜻을 가진 단어를 골라 그 번호를 공란에 써넣어라.

_____ 1. *bold* behavior (A) common (B) brave
(C) lazy (D) military

_____ 2. in a good *temper* (A) speed (B) stake
(C) disposition (D) temperature

_____ 3. to *repair* shoes (A) stretch (B) accord
(C) mend (D) make

_____ 4. to *inquire* something (A) ask (B) identify
(C) require (D) protest

_____ 5. to *expose* one's secret (A) forgive (B) conceal
(C) object (D) disclose

_____ 6. *reckless* behavior (A) safe (B) careless
(C) innocent (D) earnest

_____ 7. a *farewell* speech (A) goodbye (B) competent
(C) powerful (D) honorable

_____ 8. to get treated without *distinction* of rank
(A) consolation (B) discrimination
(C) function (D) disposition

_____ 9. the *decayed* teeth (A) repaired (B) golden
(C) rotten (D) shaking

_____ 10. to *applaud* the singer (A) account (B) complain
(C) accord (D) cheer

2 왼쪽에 주어진 우리말과 같은 뜻을 가진 단어를 골라 그 번호를 공란에 써넣어라.

_____ 1. 전문가 (A) literature (B) saint
(C) host (D) specialist

_____ 2. 살인 (A) liver (B) destruction
(C) murder (D) stalk

_____ 3. 불평하다 (A) complain (B) deteriorate
(C) acclaim (D) furnish

_____ 4. 말쑥한 (A) swift (B) trim
(C) trivial (D) mild

_____ 5. 충돌 (A) rent (B) crack
(C) crash (D) stake

종합 연습 문제

3 왼쪽에 주어진 단어와 반대되는 뜻을 가진 단어를 골라 그 번호를 공란에 써넣어라.

_____ 1. swift   (A) huge   (B) strict
    (C) gradual   (D) trivial

_____ 2. cowardly   (A) average   (B) miserable
    (C) innocent   (D) bold

_____ 3. reply   (A) inquire   (B) award
    (C) deserve   (D) uncover

_____ 4. trivial   (A) reckless   (B) immense
    (C) gradual   (D) wealthy

_____ 5. illiterate   (A) tiny   (B) ignorant
    (C) learned   (D) daring

4 괄호 속에 주어진 우리말과 같은 뜻을 가진 단어를 사용하여 문장을 완성하라.

1. I remember that our English teacher was very S____T. (엄격한)
2. The author's M_____T was accepted for publication[29]. (원고)
3. You work very hard; you D_____E good pay. (~할 가치가 있다)
4. She broke her right W___T by falling on the ice. (손목)
5. A father must P_____E food and clothes for his children. (공급하다)

5 가장 적합한 단어를 골라 빈칸을 채워라.

1. Your presence[30] was a _____ to me at such a sad time.
   (A) discrimination   (B) consolation   (C) crash   (D) stalk

2. The lightning was followed by a(n) _____ of thunder.
   (A) crash   (B) echo   (C) stake   (D) trick

3. The film which has been _____ to light is no longer usable.
   (A) provided   (B) decayed   (C) expressed   (D) exposed

4. A person who is _____ can't write his own name.
   (A) lame   (B) ignorant   (C) idle   (D) innocent

5. The gardener[31] _____ the dead branches from the trees.
   (A) deserved   (B) protected   (C) trimmed   (D) repaired

---

29. publication [pʌblikéiʃən] ***n.*** 출판, 발간   30. presence [prézns] ***n.*** 출석, 참석   31. gardener [gɑ́ːrdnər] ***n.*** 정원사

Lesson 10 종합 연습 문제

6 왼쪽에 주어진 단어의 적당한 파생어를 사용하여 문장을 완성하라.

1. *inquire*   My _____ about his health was never answered.
2. *complain*   The children were full of _____ about their food.
3. *obey*   Soldiers act in _____ to the orders of their superior officers.
4. *distinction* The twins were so much alike that it was impossible to _____ one from the other.
5. *expose*   _____ of the body to strong sunlight may be harmful.

Answers

1. 1. B   2. C   3. C   4. A   5. D   6. B   7. A   8. B   9. C   10. D
2. 1. D   2. C   3. A   4. B   5. C
3. 1. C   2. D   3. A   4. B   5. C
4. 1. STRICT   2. MANUSCRIPT   3. DESERVE   4. WRIST   5. PROVIDE
5. 1. B   2. A   3. D   4. B   5. C
6. 1. inquiry   2. complaints   3. obedience   4. distinguish   5. Exposure

124 TOEFL · TOEIC · TEPS 초급 Junior Vocabulary

LESSON 11

Self-test 11

적당한 단어를 골라 빈칸을 채우라.

1. A baby *crawls* before it _____.
   (A) walks   (B) sleeps

2. A _____ for receiving or entertaining¹ guests is called a *parlor*.
   (A) woman   (B) room

3. *Poisonous* medicine is _____ to our body.
   (A) harmful   (B) foot

4. An *ankle* is the joint² that connects the _____ and the leg.
   (A) hip   (B) foot

5. A *bachelor* is an unmarried _____.
   (A) man   (B) woman

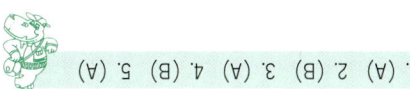
1. (A) 2. (B) 3. (A) 4. (B) 5. (A)

New Vocabulary -1

accustom
[əkʌ́stəm]
v. 익숙케 하다, 습관들게 하다
syn. habituate, familiarize
She could not *accustom* herself to a hot climate in Africa.

ankle
[ǽŋkl]
n. 발목
Human beings and all other animals that have feet and legs have *ankles*.

bachelor
[bǽtʃələr]
n. 독신 남자
ant. spinster
The young *bachelor* will soon be taking a wife³.

---

1. entertain [entərtéin] *v.* (손님을) 대접하다   2. joint [dʒɔint] *n.* 관절   3. take a wife : 아내를 맞아들이다

border
[bɔ́:rdər]

n. 가장자리, 변두리, 경계 지역
syn. frontier
When we went camping, we put up[4] our tents on the *border* of the lake.

calm
[kɑ:m]

adj. 조용한, 고요한, 온화한
syn. quiet
Mother's *calm* behavior made the frightened child quiet.

chew
[tʃu:]

v. 씹다, 깨물어 부수다
You should always *chew* your food before you swallow[5] it.

complex
[kɔ́mpleks]

adj. 복잡한, 어려운
syn. complicated
ant. simple
n. complexity
The instructions[6] for building the radio were so *complex* that we could not follow them.

consolidate
[kənsɔ́lideit]

v. (지위를) 강화하다, 굳게 하다
syn. solidify
Britain is trying to *consolidate* her position in the North Atlantic.

crawl
[krɔ:l]

v. 기다, 기어가다
syn. creep
The wounded soldier tried to *crawl* back to the tent.

decent
[dí:snt]

adj. 품위있는, 점잖은, 꽤 좋은
n. decency
You need *decent* clothes when you go to church.

Practice 1

위 단어를 사용하여 아래 문장을 완성하라. 필요시 단어를 적절한 형태로 변형하라.

1. You can get quite a(n) _____ meal there without spending too much money.

2. The presidential candidate _____ his reputation[7] by winning several primary elections[8].

3. He _____ a mouthful[9] of meat but it was too much to swallow.

---

4. put up : (텐트 등을) 가설하다, 치다   5. swallow[swɔ́lou] *v.* 삼키다   6. instruction[instrʌ́kʃən] *n.* 설명서
7. reputation[repjutéiʃən] *n.* 평판, 명성   8. primary election : 대통령 후보 예선   9. mouthful[máuθful] *n.* 한 입 가득

4. The Rio Grande River is the _____ between the United States and Mexico.

5. Hunting dogs are _____ to the noise of a gun.

New Vocabulary -2

despair
[dispέər]
- *n.* 실망, 자포 자기
- **syn.** desperation
- **ant.** hope
- A feeling of *despair* came to him as the boat sank deeper in the water.

distress
[distrés]
- *n.* 비탄, 근심, 걱정
- **syn.** worry
- **ant.** comfort, relief
- Her husband has just died and she is in great *distress*.

edge
[edʒ]
- *n.* 끝머리, 가장자리, 변두리
- **syn.** margin, border
- **ant.** center
- Don't put the glass on the *edge* of the table; it may get knocked off[10].

enterprise
[éntərpraiz]
- *n.* 사업, 기업, 모험심
- **syn.** business
- Building the steel manufacturing company is a great *enterprise*.

export
[ékspɔːrt]
- *n.* 수출
- **ant.** import
- Last year our *exports* exceeded[11] our imports in value.

fasten
[fǽsn]
- *v.* 잡아 매다, 고정시키다, 잠그다
- **syn.** fix, tie
- **ant.** unfasten, untie, loosen
- He *fastened* the pages together with a pin.

flesh
[fleʃ]
- *n.* 살, 살코기
- A fat man has much more *flesh* than a thin man.

---

10. knock off : 부딪쳐 떨어지다   11. exceed[iksíːd] *v.* 초과하다

fund
[fʌnd]
n. 자금, 기금, 재원
syn. capital
That *fund* will be used for the expenses of the poor people.

graduate
[grǽdjueit]
v. 졸업하다
n. graduation
Her brother *graduated* from Harvard University last year.

heal
[hi:l]
v. 낫게 하다, 고치다, 낫다
syn. cure
The medicine and rest will soon *heal* your wound.

Practice 2

위 단어를 사용하여 아래 문장을 완성하라. 필요시 단어를 적절한 형태로 변형하라.

1. He was filled with _____ as his enemies crowded[12] around him.
2. The high cost of living is a(n) _____ to most people.
3. Shipbuilding is one of the biggest _____ in this country.
4. Wood is one of the chief _____ of Australia.
5. The sharp knife cut into the _____ of his arm.

New Vocabulary -3

illustrate
[íləstreit]
v. 설명하다, 예증하다
syn. explain
n. illustration
The teacher compared the heart to a pump to *illustrate* its function[13].

insist
[insíst]
v. 주장하다, 우기다
She *insisted* that she was right.

jar
[dʒɑ:r]
n. 단지, (아가리가 넓은) 병
A *jar* has a wide mouth and sometimes has two handles.

lane
[lein]
n. 좁은 길, 골목길, 차선(車線)
syn. passage
He was driving his car down the narrow *lane* between buildings in a town.

---

12. crowd[kraud] *v.* 밀어 닥치다   13. function[fʌ́ŋkʃən] *n.* 기능

loan
[loun]

n. 대부(貸付)

He asked his brother for a small *loan* to buy a house.

maple
[méipl]

n. 단풍나무

We have a *maple* in our yard.

mingle
[míŋgl]

v. 섞이다, 어울리다
syn. mix, blend

It is not easy for him to *mingle* with people because he is very shy.

muscle
[mʌ́sl]

n. 근육
adj. muscular

You can develop your arm *muscle* by playing tennis.

object
[ɔ́bdʒikt]

[əbdʒékt]

n. 물건, 사물

A dark *object* moved between me and the door.

v. 반대하다
syn. oppose
n. objection

He stood up and *objected* in strong language.

origin
[ɔ́ridʒin]

n. 기원, 시초, 근원
syn. source, beginning

Ancient Greece is often called the *origin* of Western civilization.

Practice 3

위 단어를 사용하여 아래 문장을 완성하라. 필요시 단어를 적절한 형태로 변형하라.

1. I _____ to being treated like a child.

2. He injured[14] the _____ of his arm by throwing the heavy weight.

3. The king often left his palace at night, and _____ with the unknown people in the streets.

4. He asked me for a(n) _____ of five hundred dollars.

5. The _____ of this river is a stream[15] in the mountains.

---

14. injure [índʒər] *v.* 상처를 입히다   15. stream [striːm] *n.* 시내, 개울

New Vocabulary -4

parlor
[pá:rlər]
n. 응접실, 객실
The *parlor* was crowded with many people during the party.

perceive
[pərsí:v]
v. 지각(知覺)하다, 알아차리다
n. perception
I soon *perceived* that I could not change his mind.

poisonous
[pɔ́izənəs]
adj. 유독한, 유해한
n. poison
Some plants have *poisonous* roots or fruits.

previous
[prí:vjəs]
adj. 먼저의, 이전의, 앞의
syn. earlier
ant. later, following
I can't go, for I have a *previous* engagement[16].

province
[prɔ́vins]
n. 지방, 지역
Most countries are divided into several *provinces*.

recommend
[rekəménd]
v. 추천하다, 권하다
n. recommendation
The doctor *recommended* that she should stay in bed for a week.

replace
[ripléis]
v. 교체하다, 대치하다, 갈다
n. replacement
Most telephone operators[17] have been *replaced* by dial telephones.

ridiculous
[ridíkjuləs]
adj. 어리석은, 웃음거리의
syn. silly, absurd
ant. wise
It would be *ridiculous* to speak ill of[18] one's parents in public.

shift
[ʃift]
v. 바뀌다, 바꾸다
syn. change
ant. persist
The wind *shifted* from east to west.

---

16. engagement[ingéidʒmənt] *n.* 약속   17. telephone operator[ɔ́pəreitər] *n.* 교환수   18. speak ill of ~ : ~을 헐뜯다, ~을 흉보다

slip
[slip]

v. 미끄러지다, 미끄러 넘어지다
syn. slide
She *slipped* on the ice and hurt her hand.

n. 전표, 종이 쪽지
He inserted[19] a *slip* marking his place in the book.

Practice 4

위 단어를 사용하여 아래 문장을 완성하라. 필요시 단어를 적절한 형태로 변형하라.

1. He _____ on the icy road and broke his leg.
2. You look very _____ in that old hat.
3. His former employer _____ Miss Kim as a good typist.
4. Have you had any _____ experience, or is this kind of work new to you?
5. The _____ of their house is nicely decorated[20].

New Vocabulary -5

sphere
[sfiər]

n. 구(球), 구형
All points on the surface[21] of a *sphere* are equally distant from the center.

startle
[stá:rtl]

v. 깜짝 놀라게 하다, 소스라치게 하다
syn. surprise, frighten
ant. pacify, calm
I was *startled* at the news of his death.

stroke
[strouk]

n. 타격, 치기
syn. blow
The *strokes* of the church bell awakened us.

suspicion
[səspíʃən]

n. 용의, 혐의, 의심
syn. accusation
adj. suspicious
The young man is under *suspicion* of murder.

temple
[témpl]

n. 1. 신전, 사원, 절
The people went to the *temple* to pray.

---

19. insert[insə́:rt] *v.* 끼워 넣다   20. decorate[dékəreit] *v.* 장식하다   21. surface[sə́:rfis] *n.* 표면

2. 관자놀이
He had a cut on his right *temple*.

toad
[toud]

n. 두꺼비
Toads have shorter legs and are generally clumsier[22] than frogs.

troublesome
[trʌ́blsəm]

adj. 골칫거리인, 성가신, 까다로운
syn. annoying
n. trouble
He is the most *troublesome* person in our class.

vessel
[vésl]

n. 1. 용기, 그릇
syn. container
Empty *vessels* make the most sound.

2. 관, 도관(導管)
The mark on her skin was caused by broken blood *vessels*.

3. 배, 선박
syn. ship, boat
The port of London is filled with *vessels* of all kinds.

web
[web]

n. 거미줄
A spider captures small insects with its *web*.

yell
[jel]

n. 고함 소리, 외침
syn. shout
His *yell* of anger could be heard in the next room.

v. 외치다, 고함치다
During the game the students often *yelled* with cheers.

Practice 5

위 단어를 사용하여 아래 문장을 완성하라. 필요시 단어를 적절한 형태로 변형하라.

1. Bowls[23] and cups were among the anicent _____ they found.

2. She was _____ to see him looking so ill.

3. She can't swim yet, but has made a few _____ with her arms.

---

22. clumsy [klʌ́mzi] *adj.* 서투른, 어둔한   23. bowl [boul] *n.* 사발

4. The real thief tried to turn _____ toward others.

5. Ancient Greek _____ were beautifully built.

Practice 1	1. decent	2. consolidated	3. chewed	4. border	5. accustomed
Practice 2	1. despair	2. distress	3. enterprises	4. exports	5. flesh
Practice 3	1. object	2. muscles	3. mingled	4. loan	5. origin
Practice 4	1. slipped	2. ridiculous	3. recommended	4. previous	5. parlor
Practice 5	1. vessels	2. startled	3. strokes	4. suspicion	5. temples

Lesson 11 종합 연습 문제

1 네 개의 단어 중 다른 셋과 관련이 없는 것을 골라 공란에 그 번호를 써넣어라.

_____ 1. (A) surprise (B) frighten (C) flee (D) startle
_____ 2. (A) province (B) margin (C) edge (D) border
_____ 3. (A) ridiculous (B) absurd (C) silly (D) reckless
_____ 4. (A) blend (B) replace (C) mingle (D) mix
_____ 5. (A) vessel (B) ship (C) boat (D) cabin
_____ 6. (A) accustom (B) consolidate (C) habituate (D) familiarize
_____ 7. (A) margin (B) source (C) beginning (D) origin

2 왼쪽에 주어진 우리말과 같은 뜻을 가진 단어를 골라 그 번호를 공란에 써넣어라.

_____ 1. 혐의, 의심　(A) disposition　(B) suspicion
　　　　　　　　　　　(C) venture　　　(D) province

_____ 2. 졸업하다　　(A) graduate　　(B) illuminate
　　　　　　　　　　　(C) perceive　　 (D) shift

_____ 3. 기어가다　　(A) heal　　　　(B) slip
　　　　　　　　　　　(C) stalk　　　　(D) crawl

_____ 4. 씹다　　　　(A) shift　　　　(B) slip
　　　　　　　　　　　(C) chew　　　　(D) creep

_____ 5. 주장하다　　(A) perceive　　 (B) insist
　　　　　　　　　　　(C) object　　　 (D) consolidate

3 왼쪽에 주어진 단어와 반대되는 뜻을 가진 단어를 골라 그 번호를 공란에 써넣어라.

_____ 1. loosen　　(A) enrich　　　(B) fasten
　　　　　　　　　　(C) fold　　　　(D) untie

_____ 2. relief　　 (A) suspicion　　(B) border
　　　　　　　　　　(C) operation　　(D) distress

_____ 3. import　 (A) edge　　　　(B) object
　　　　　　　　　　(C) export　　　 (D) report

_____ 4. silly　　　(A) wise　　　　(B) calm
　　　　　　　　　　(C) troublesome　(D) careless

_____ 5. edge　　 (A) margin　　　(B) center
　　　　　　　　　　(C) sphere　　　 (D) temple

4 괄호 속에 주어진 우리말과 같은 뜻을 가진 단어를 사용하여 문장을 완성하라.

1. I tell you that D____T people just don't do things like that. (품위있는)
2. Some people believe in private E_____E, while others believe in government ownership of industry[24]. (기업, 사업)
3. His political ideas were too C_____X to get support from ordinary people. (복잡한)
4. A good traveler can A_____M himself to almost any kind of food. (익숙케 하다)
5. He could not P_____E any difference between the twins. (알아보다, 인지하다)

5 이탤릭체로 된 단어와 같은 뜻을 가진 단어를 골라 그 번호를 공란에 써넣어라.

_____ 1. His cut finger *healed* in a few days.
  (A) cured   (B) decayed   (C) weakened   (D) deteriorated

_____ 2. The teacher cut an apple into four equal pieces to *illustrate* what 1/4 means.
  (A) familiarize (B) replace   (C) perceive   (D) explain

_____ 3. Although she was frightened, she answered with a *calm* voice.
  (A) silly   (B) simple   (C) quiet   (D) humble

_____ 4. She did better in the *previous* lesson.
  (A) troublesome (B) earlier   (C) following   (D) gradual

_____ 5. The unexpected noise *startled* the audience[25].
  (A) mingled   (B) frightened (C) started   (D) exposed

_____ 6. He broke the lock with one *stroke* of the hammer.
  (A) crack   (B) crash   (C) wrist   (D) blow

_____ 7. He *shifted* the suitcase from one hand to another.
  (A) changed   (B) replaced   (C) mended   (D) stalked

_____ 8. The President walked down a *lane* formed by two lines of soldiers.
  (A) edge   (B) passage   (C) loan   (D) sphere

_____ 9. Part of the school sports *fund* will be used to improve the condition of the football field.
  (A) capital   (B) loan   (C) ground   (D) equipment

_____ 10. The failure of the rice harvest will cause great *distress* among the farmers.
  (A) worry   (B) debt   (C) yell   (D) damage

---

24. industry [índəstri] ***n.*** 산업   25. audience [ɔ́ːdjəns] ***n.*** 청중

Lesson 11 종합 연습 문제

Answers

1. 1. C 2. A 3. D 4. B 5. D 6. B 7. A

2. 1. B 2. A 3. D 4. C 5. B

3. 1. B 2. D 3. C 4. A 5. B

4. 1. DECENT 2. ENTERPRISE 3. COMPLEX 4. ACCUSTOM 5. PERCEIVE

5. 1. A 2. D 3. C 4. B 5. B 6. D 7. A 8. B 9. A 10. A

LESSON 12

Self-test 12

적당한 단어를 골라 빈칸을 채우라.

1. Many museums have collections of *priceless* paintings by _____ artists.
   (A) famous   (B) poor

2. There wasn't enough _____ to *float* the wood.
   (A) water   (B) fire

3. Those _____ over there are not *edible*.
   (A) books   (B) fruits

4. He was *jealous* of his neighbor's _____.
   (A) failure   (B) success

5. His long speech *bored* me so that I heard all his stories with _____ interest.
   (A) little   (B) great

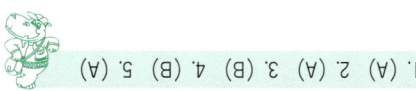
1. (A) 2. (A) 3. (B) 4. (B) 5. (A)

New Vocabulary -1

ache
[eik]

n. 아픔
syn. pain
The boy is trying to forget the *ache* in his back[1].

apparent
[əpǽrənt]

adj. 명백한, 분명한
syn. plain, obvious, clear
ant. unclear
It is *apparent* that you dislike your job.

barn
[bɑːrn]

n. 헛간, 광
A farmer keeps his crops[2] in the *barn*.

---

1. back[bæk] *n.* 등   2. crop[krɔp] *n.* 농작물, 수확물

bore
[bɔːr]

v. 싫증나게 하다, 지루하게 하다
syn. tire, weary
n. boredom
The man *bores* me; I've heard all his stories before.

canal
[kənǽl]

n. 운하, 수로(水路)
Canals have been built to take water to the desert[3].

chilly
[tʃili]

adj. 차가운, 쌀쌀한, 냉랭한
ant. warm
n. chill
You will feel *chilly* if you don't wear a coat in a cold day.

compose
[kəmpóuz]

v. 구성하다, 짜맞추다
syn. form, constitute
n. composition
The chemistry teacher asked the students what water is *composed* of.

constant
[kɔ́nstənt]

adj. 끊임없이 계속되는, 부단한
syn. continual, unceasing
ant. variable
He was tired of his wife's *constant* complaint[4].

create
[kriéit]

v. 창조하다, 만들다
ant. imitate
n. creation
adj. creative
The Bible says that God *created* this world in seven days.

decisive
[disáisiv]

adj. 결정적인
syn. conclusive
v. decide
Our air force[5] was *decisive* in winning the war.

Practice 1

위 단어를 사용하여 아래 문장을 완성하라. 필요시 단어를 적절한 형태로 변형하라.

1. Crops and food for animals are usually stored[6] in the _____.

---

3. desert[dézərt] *n.* 사막   4. complaint[kəmpléint] *n.* 불평   5. air force : 공군   6. store[stɔːr] *v.* 저장하다

138   TOEFL · TOEIC · TEPS 초급 Junior Vocabulary

2. _____ are used for ships or for carrying water to places that need it.

3. I hope you are not getting _____ listening to me.

4. The king was given a(n) _____ welcome when he arrived on the island.

5. Three days of _____ rain made the river overflow its bank[7].

New Vocabulary -2

desperate
[déspərit]

adj. 1. 필사적인, 목숨을 걸고 있는
The prisoners[8] became *desperate* in their attempts to get free.
　2. 자포자기의, 절망적인
syn. hopeless
She became so *desperate* that we feared for her sanity[9].

district
[dístrikt]

n. 지역, 구역, 지방
syn. region, area
The farming *district* of the United States is in the Middle West.

edible
[édəbl]

adj. 먹을 수 있는, 식용의
syn. eatable
This apple is rotten and no longer *edible*.

entertain
[entərtéin]

v. 즐겁게 하다, 접대하다
syn. amuse
n. entertainment
The circus *entertained* the children.

explore
[iksplɔ́:r]

v. 탐험하다, 답사하다
syn. search, investigate
Columbus discovered America but did not *explore* the new continent.

fate
[feit]

n. 숙명, 운명
syn. destiny
It was their *fate* to meet and marry.

float
[flout]

v. (물에) 뜨다, 표류하다
ant. sink
Wood *floats* on water and dust floats in the air.

---

7. bank[bæŋk] *n.* 강둑　8. prisoner[prízṇər] *n.* 죄수　9. we feared for her sanity : 우리는 그녀가 제정신인지 염려했다

Lesson 12　139

fundamental [fʌndəméntl]	***adj.*** 기본의, 기초의, 근본적인 **syn.** essential Freedom of speech is one of the *fundamental* human rights.
grand [græ(:)nd]	***adj.*** 웅장한, 장엄한 **syn.** magnificent, splendid The *grand* sight of the Niagra Falls cannot be forgotten for a long time.
healthy [hélθi]	***adj.*** 건강한, 튼튼한 **syn.** wholesome The children are quite *healthy* although they all have slight colds at the moment.

Practice 2

위 단어를 사용하여 아래 문장을 완성하라. 필요시 단어를 적절한 형태로 변형하라.

1. There is a(n) _____ difference between your proposal and mine.

2. The boat was _____ down the river when I saw it.

3. Many people blame[10] _____ for their failure in life.

4. Can you distinguish the _____ and the poisonous mushrooms[11]?

5. His failure made him _____ and he resolved[12] to succeed next time or die in the attempt.

New Vocabulary -3

imagine [imædʒin]	***v.*** 상상하다, 추측하다 **syn.** conceive ***adj.*** imaginative ***n.*** imagination I can *imagine* the scene clearly in my mind.
inspire [inspáiə]	***v.*** (사상, 감정을) 고취시키다 ***n.*** inspiration His brother's success *inspired* the boy to work harder.
jealous [dʒéləs]	***adj.*** 질투가 많은, 시샘하는 **syn.** envious ***n.*** jealousy He was *jealous* when he discovered that she loved someone else.

10. blame[bleim] ***v.*** ~의 탓으로 돌리다   11. mushroom[mʌ́ʃrum] ***n.*** 버섯   12. resolve[rizɔ́lv] ***v.*** 결심하다

lantern
[læntərn]

n. 초롱, 등
My wife bought a beautiful Chinese *lantern* for the living room.

local
[lóukəl]

adj. 지방의, 지방적인
syn. provincial
ant. national
We have a small *local* broadcasting station[13] in our town.

marble
[máːrbl]

n. 대리석
He was buried in a *marble* tomb.

minor
[máinər]

adj. 작은 쪽의, 중요치 않은
ant. major
n. minority
The young actress was given a *minor* part in the new play.

mutual
[mjúːtjuəl]

adj. 서로 관계 있는, 상호간의
syn. reciprocal
We were happy to have him as our *mutual* friend.

objective
[obdʒéktiv]

n. 목표, 목적
syn. goal, aim
She always wanted to own[14] her own house, and now she had obtained her *objective*.

ornament
[ɔ́ːrnəmənt]

n. 장식, 장식품
syn. decoration
adj. ornamental
There were carved *ornaments* on the cabinet door.

Practice 3

위 단어를 사용하여 아래 문장을 완성하라. 필요시 단어를 적절한 형태로 변형하라.

1. When my little brother sees mother holding the new baby, he becomes _____.
2. The front of the building was covered with _____.
3. He left most of his money to his sons; his daughter received only a(n) _____ part of his wealth.
4. Can you _____ life without gas, electricity, radio, and other modern conveniences[15]?
5. We must bring a(n) _____ to stay overnight in the mountain.

---

13. broadcasting station : 방송국   14. own[oun] *v.* 소유하다   15. modern conveniences : 현대 문명의 이기(利器)

New Vocabulary –4

partial
[páːrʃəl]

adj. 1. 부분적인, 일부분의
syn. incomplete
ant. complete
The play was only a *partial* success.

2. 편파적인, 불공평한
syn. biased
ant. fair
A parent should not be *partial* to any one of his children.

perform
[pərfɔ́ːrm]

v. 1. 수행하다, 실행하다
n. performance
He always *performs* his work with great care[16].

2. 공연하다
What kind of play will be *performed* in the theater tonight?

polish
[pɔ́liʃ]

v. 광을 내다, 빛나게 하다
We *polished* the furniture on the day the guest arrived.

priceless
[práislis]

adj. 매우 귀중한, 값으로 따질 수 없는
syn. invaluable
ant. worthless
Only a very rich man could afford to[17] buy these *priceless* paintings.

publish
[pʌ́bliʃ]

v. 출판하다, 발행하다
n. publication
It is a good story, but we can't *publish* it; it would offend[18] too many people.

recognize
[rékəgnaiz]

v. 알아보다, 인정하다
n. recognition
Honesty and sincerity[19] in students are easily *recognized* by teachers.

repeat
[ripíːt]

v. 반복하다, 되풀이하다
n. repetition
If you *repeat* that mistake, you will be punished.

---

16. with great care : 아주 조심스럽게   17. can afford to ~ : ~할 능력이 있다, ~할 여유가 있다
18. offend[əfénd] v. ~의 감정을 상하게 하다   19. sincerity[sinsérəti] n. 성실

reward
[riwɔ́ːrd]

n. 보상, 보답

As a *reward* for his bravery, the soldier was given a gold medal.

sake
[seik]

n. 위함, 목적, 이익
syn. benefit

If you won't do it for your own *sake*, then do it for my sake.

secret
[síːkrit]

adj. 비밀의, 은밀한

He kept some money in a *secret* place.

n. 비밀, 기밀

The old man had learned many of the *secrets* of nature.

Practice 4

위 단어를 사용하여 아래 문장을 완성하라. 필요시 단어를 적절한 형태로 변형하라.

1. You can easily _____ silverware[20] with this special cloth.
2. These plans must be kept _____ from the enemy.
3. He fought the war for the _____ of his country's freedom.
4. To buy books for your children is a _____ investment[21] for them.
5. He received a title as a _____ for his services.

New Vocabulary -5

shield
[ʃiːld]

n. 방패
ant. spear

The *shield* protected him from the blows[22] of his enemy.

v. 보호하다
syn. protect

Her wide hat *shielded* her eyes from the sun.

slight
[slait]

adj. 적은, 대수롭지 않은
syn. insignificant
ant. important

He stayed home for a day because of a *slight* illness.

---

20. silverware [sílvərwɛər] *n.* 은그릇, 은제품   21. investment [invéstmənt] *n.* 투자   22. blow [blou] *n.* 강타, 공격

spell
[spel]

n. 1. 주문(呪文), 마력
syn. enchantment, charm
He is under my *spell* and will do as I say.

2. 한동안, 한차례
We had a long *spell* of hot weather last summer.

stare
[stɛər]

v. 응시하다, 빤히 쳐다보다
syn. gaze
The little girl *stared* at the strange man at the store.

string
[striŋ]

n. 끈, 줄, 현(弦)
syn. thread, cord
The package was tied with red *strings*.

suspect
[səspékt]

v. 알아채다, ~아닌가하고 생각하다
syn. surmise, doubt
The mouse *suspected* danger and did not touch the trap[23].

[sʌ́spekt]

n. 용의자
The police have arrested two *suspects* in connection with[24] the bank robbery.

temperature
[témpərətʃər]

n. 온도, 기온
What's the average *temperature* in Seoul on a summer day?

tissue
[tíʃu:]

n. 조직, 직물
The teacher showed pictures of muscle *tissues* and brain *tissues*.

troop
[tru:p]

n. 1. 무리, 대(隊), 단(團)
syn. crowd, throng
A *troop* of children gathered around the teacher.

2. (*pl.*) 군대
syn. forces
The soldiers are preparing to attack enemy *troops*.

verse
[vəːrs]

n. 운문, 시가
syn. poetry
ant. prose
A collection of his *verse* has just been published.

---

23. trap[træp] *n.* 덫   24. in connection with ~ : ~와 관련해서

weary
[wíəri]

adj. 피곤한, 지친
syn. tired
He felt *weary* after playing tennis for two hours.

v. 지치게 하다, 싫증나게 하다
The boy *wearies* me with constant questions.

Practice 5

위 단어를 사용하여 아래 문장을 완성하라. 필요시 단어를 적절한 형태로 변형하라.

1. We were under the _____ of the beautiful music.

2. He got a _____ wound on his back but is all right now.

3. She often wears a _____ of pearls[25] around her neck.

4. The nurse took the _____ of the patient—it was 38.5℃.

5. The long hours of work have _____ me a lot.

해답					
Practice 1	1. barn	2. Canals	3. bored	4. chilly	5. constant
Practice 2	1. fundamental	2. floating	3. fate	4. edible	5. desperate
Practice 3	1. jealous	2. marble	3. minor	4. imagine	5. lantern
Practice 4	1. polish	2. secret	3. sake	4. priceless	5. reward
Practice 5	1. spell	2. slight	3. string	4. temperature	5. wearied

25. pearl [pəːrl] *n.* 진주

Lesson 12 종합 연습 문제

1 이탤릭체로 된 단어와 같은 뜻을 가진 단어를 골라 그 번호를 공란에 써넣어라.

_____ 1. *weary* in mind and body
    (A) healthy   (B) sound   (C) tired   (D) warm

_____ 2. to cast a *spell* over someone
    (A) marble   (B) enchantment   (C) stroke   (D) spear

_____ 3. to *stare* at someone
    (A) gaze   (B) yell   (C) inspire   (D) surmise

_____ 4. *constant* practice
    (A) apparent   (B) hard   (C) decisive   (D) unceasing

_____ 5. *desperate* attempts
    (A) careless   (B) decisive   (C) hopeless   (D) fundamental

_____ 6. *edible* fish
    (A) trivial   (B) audible   (C) eatable   (D) tiny

_____ 7. to *entertain* someone
    (A) amuse   (B) frighten   (C) encourage   (D) suspect

_____ 8. to *explore* an unknown world
    (A) destroy   (B) search   (C) perceive   (D) inquire

_____ 9. wonderful *ornament*
    (A) decoration   (B) enchantment   (C) string   (D) organization

_____ 10. living in a *grand* style
    (A) splendid   (B) huge   (C) gradual   (D) miserable

2 왼쪽에 주어진 우리말과 같은 뜻을 가진 단어를 골라 그 번호를 공란에 써넣어라.

_____ 1. 숙명   (A) destiny   (B) sake
                  (C) saint   (D) marble

_____ 2. 질투심이 많은   (A) wholesome   (B) obvious
                           (C) conclusive   (D) jealous

_____ 3. 대리석   (A) tissue   (B) canal
                  (C) marble   (D) tin

_____ 4. 목표   (A) operation   (B) objective
                (C) item   (D) protection

_____ 5. 보상   (A) reward   (B) verse
                (C) benefit   (D) spear

Lesson 12

3 왼쪽에 주어진 단어와 반대되는 뜻을 가진 단어를 골라 그 번호를 공란에 써넣어라.

_____ 1. insignificant   (A) slight   (B) vigorous
                                   (C) trivial   (D) important

_____ 2. biased   (A) reciprocal   (B) partial
                                (C) fair   (D) wholesome

_____ 3. verse   (A) tired   (B) prose
                               (C) plain   (D) chilly

_____ 4. apparent   (A) unclear   (B) constant
                               (C) calm   (D) local

_____ 5. sink   (A) wholesome   (B) float
                               (C) healthy   (d) partial

4 괄호 속에 주어진 우리말과 같은 뜻을 가진 단어를 사용하여 문장을 완성하라.

1. Doctors should P_____M their operations[26] with great care. (수행하다)

2. P____H your shoes with a brush. (광을 내다)

3. Dogs R_____E people by their smell. (알아 보다)

4. The continuous A__E in his head worried him. (아픔)

5. It is A_____T that the days become longer in June and July. (분명한)

5 가장 적합한 단어를 골라 빈칸을 채우라.

1. It is not polite to _____ at other people.
   (A) nod   (B) stare   (C) look   (D) inspire

2. You have to present a _____ evidence in the court.
   (A) decisive   (B) weary   (C) silly   (D) decent

3. We were all anxious about the _____ of the missing fisherman.
   (A) secret   (B) ache   (C) fate   (D) reward

4. He has a _____ appearance even though he is not well.
   (A) weary   (B) apparent   (C) grand   (D) wholesome

5. A family has _____ affection when each person likes the others and is liked by them.
   (A) mutual   (B) provincial   (C) slight   (D) desperate

---

26. operation[ɔpəréiʃən] *n.* 수술

Lesson 12 종합 연습 문제

6 왼쪽에 주어진 단어의 적당한 파생어를 사용하여 문장을 완성하라.

1. *bore*   The patient spent long days of _____ in the hospital.
2. *entertain* The city offers all kinds of _____ for young and old.
3. *repeat*   The play was a _____ of a theme used twenty years ago.
4. *minor*   The nation wants peace; only a _____ want the war to continue.
5. *chilly*   There is a _____ in the air this morning.

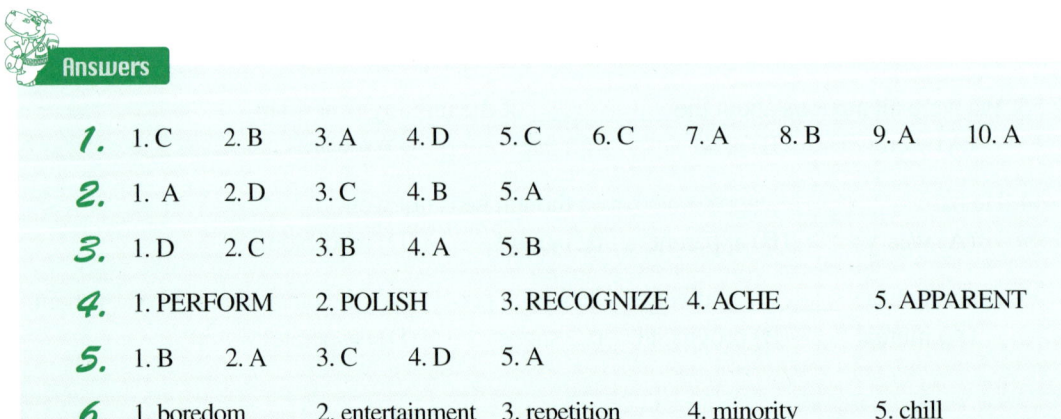

Answers

1. 1. C 2. B 3. A 4. D 5. C 6. C 7. A 8. B 9. A 10. A
2. 1. A 2. D 3. C 4. B 5. A
3. 1. D 2. C 3. B 4. A 5. B
4. 1. PERFORM 2. POLISH 3. RECOGNIZE 4. ACHE 5. APPARENT
5. 1. B 2. A 3. C 4. D 5. A
6. 1. boredom 2. entertainment 3. repetition 4. minority 5. chill

LESSON 13

Self-test 13

적당한 단어를 골라 빈칸을 채우라.

1. The boy *smashed* the window with _____.
   (A) a piece of cloth   (B) a stone

2. The _____ caused a serious *flood*.
   (A) heavy rains   (B) desperate battles

3. There were some people standing on the *deck* of the _____.
   (A) house   (B) ship

4. she gave her son some _____ for the *purchase* of his school books.
   (A) money   (B) time

5. Being a _____ is a *perilous* profession[1].
   (A) businessman   (B) fireman

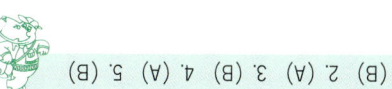

1. (B) 2. (A) 3. (B) 4. (A) 5. (B)

New Vocabulary −1

achieve
[ətʃíːv]
v. 성취하다, 달성하다
syn. perform, accomplish
The soldiers fought bravely and finally *achieved* victory.

appreciate
[əpríːʃieit]
v. 1. 감상하다, 평가하다
syn. understand, appraise
You can't *appreciate* English poetry unless you have a good knowledge of how English is spoken.

2. (호의를) 고맙게 여기다
Thank you very much for your help; I *appreciate* it.

---

1. profession[prəféʃən] *n.* 직업

basis
[béisis]
n. 기초, 근거, 기반
syn. foundation, base
We judge a worker on the *basis* of his performance[2].

bother
[bɔ́ðər]
v. 괴롭히다, 귀찮게 하다
syn. annoy, worry, trouble
Don't *bother* me with such foolish questions.

candle
[kǽndl]
n. (양)초
There are ten *candles* on his birthday cake.

choice
[tʃɔis]
n. 선택, 선정
syn. selection
v. choose
I don't like her, but if she's the peoples's *choice* I will obey her.

compound
[kəmpáund]
v. 혼합하다, 합성하다
syn. mix
He *compounded* various substances[3] into an effective medicine.

constitute
[kɔ́nstitjuːt]
v. 구성하다, 합성하다
syn. compose, comprise
Government should be *constituted* by the will[4] of the people.

deck
[dek]
n. 갑판
It's very hot in the cabinet[5]; let's go on the *deck*.

despise
[dispáiz]
v. 경멸하다, 깔보다, 업신여기다
syn. scorn, condemn, hate
ant. admire, esteem, appreciate
Fools *despise* wisdom and instruction.

Practice 1

위 단어를 사용하여 아래 문장을 완성하라. 필요시 단어를 적절한 형태로 변형하라.

1. Einstein's knowledge is so specialized[6] that I cannot _____ it.

2. I am sorry to _____ you, but can you tell me the time?

3. The _____ light is not as strong as the sunlight.

---

2. performance[pərfɔ́ːrməns] *n.* 공적, 업적   3. substance[sʌ́bstəns] *n.* 물질   4. will[wil] *n.* 의사(意思)
5. cabinet[kǽbinit] *n.* 선실   6. specialize[spéʃəlaiz] *v.* 전문화하다

4. Boys who tell lies and cheat at examinations are _____ by their classmates.

5. Seven specialists _____ the committee to investigate the accident.

New Vocabulary -2

distribute
[distríbju(ː)t]

v. 분배하다, 배부하다
ant. gather, assemble, accumulate
n. distribution
The teacher *distributed* the examination papers to each student of the class.

educate
[édju(ː)keit]

v. 교육하다, 육성하다
syn. teach, instruct
n. education
He was *educated* at a very good school when he was young.

enthusiastic
[inθjuːziǽstik]

adj. 열성적인, 열심인
syn. eager, anxious
ant. negligent
n. enthusiasm
My little brother is very *enthusiastic* about going to kindergarten[7].

explode
[iksplóud]

v. 폭발하다
n. explosion
adj. explosive
The bomb fell on a field and *exploded* harmlessly.

fault
[fɔːlt]

n. 결점, 흠, 단점
syn. defect, shortcoming
ant. merit
She loves him in spite of his *faults*.

flood
[flʌd]

n. 홍수
syn. inundation
ant. drought
The rainstorms[8] caused *floods* in the low-lying[9] parts of the town.

---

7. kindergarten [kíndərgɑːrtn] *n.* 유치원   8. rainstorm *n.* 폭풍우   9. low-lying [lóulaiiŋ] *adj.* 지대가 낮은, 저지대의

funeral
[fjúːnərəl]
n. 장례식
syn. burial
Many friends attended the old lady's *funeral*.

grant
[grænt]
v. 허가하다, 허용하다
syn. allow, give
He was *granted* admission[10] from Harvard University for the next fall semester.

heap
[hiːp]
v. 쌓다, 쌓아 올리다
syn. pile
The mother *heaped* the child's plate[11] with food.

immediate
[imíːdʒət]
adj. 즉시의, 즉각적인
syn. instant, direct
When there is a fire, it is necessary to take an *immediate* action[12].

Practice 2

위 단어를 사용하여 아래 문장을 완성하라. 필요시 단어를 적절한 형태로 변형하라.

1. Our requests for financial assistance[13] were _____ by the committee.
2. Please send a(n) _____ reply to my letter.
3. He is always finding _____ with the way I do my hair[14].
4. The boiler _____ and many people were injured by the hot steam.
5. The postman had thirty letters to be _____ at houses all over the town.

New Vocabulary -3

instance
[ínstəns]
n. 보기, 예(例), 실증
syn. example, case
Lincoln is an *instance* of a poor boy who became famous.

jewel
[dʒúːəl]
n. 보석
syn. gem
The *jewel* in her ring is a diamond.

lap
[læp]
n. 무릎
Mother holds the baby on her *lap*.

---

10. admission [ədmíʃən] *n.* 입학   11. plate [pleit] *n.* (큰) 접시   12. take an action : 조치를 취하다
13. financial assistance : 재정 지원   14. do one's hair : 머리 손질하다

locate
[lóukeit]

v. 위치시키다, 설립하다
syn. settle, situate, place
Where shall we *locate* our new office?

marvel
[máːrvəl]

n. 놀랄 만한 일〔사람, 것〕
syn. wonder
adj. marvelous
Space trip[15] is one of *marvels* of our time.

minute
[mainjúːt]

adj. 상세한, 미세한
syn. tiny, precise
ant. tremendous
He gave me *minute* descriptions of the structure of the building.

mysterious
[mistíəriəs]

adj. 신비로운, 불가사의한
syn. secret, hidden
She had a *mysterious* telephone call last night.

oblige
[əbláidʒ]

v. 강제로 ~하게 하다, 의무를 지우다
syn. compel
n. obligation
The students were *obliged* to do what the teacher had asked.

outbreak
[áutbreik]

n. 발발, 발생
The *outbreak* of disorder[16] was put down by the police in two hours.

participate
[paːrtísipeit]

v. 참가하다, 참여하다
Most of the students *participated* in the discussion.

Practice 3

위 단어를 사용하여 아래 문장을 완성하라. 필요시 단어를 적절한 형태로 변형하라.

1. He gave me _____ instructions[17] about how to do my work.

2. The airplane and television are among the _____ of science.

3. Television is a(n) _____ of improved communication facilities[18].

4. They were _____ to sell their house in order to pay their debts[19].

5. The disappearance of the ship still remains _____.

---

15. space trip : 우주 여행   16. disorder[disɔ́ːrdər] *n.* 혼란 (사태)   17. instruction[instrʌ́kʃən] *n.* (*pl.*) 지시 사항, 지침
18. communication facilities : 통신 설비   19. debt[det] *n.* 빚, 부채

New Vocabulary -4

perilous
[périlǝs]

adj. 위험한, 모험적인
syn. dangerous, risky, unsafe
n. peril
It is always *perilous* to neglect[20] our national defense.

polite
[pǝláit]

adj. 공손한, 예의바른
syn. courteous
He was *polite* to everyone he met at the party.

priest
[priːst]

n. 성직자, 목사, 사제(司祭)
syn. clergyman, minister
The *priest* will lead the church ceremony.

purchase
[pə́ːrtʃǝs]

v. 사다, 구입하다
syn. buy
ant. sell
They've just *purchased* a new house near Incheon.

n. 매입, 구입
They saved their money for the *purchase* of a house.

reference
[réfǝrǝns]

n. 참고, 참조
The journalist kept a card file[21] of information on his desk for easy *reference*.

request
[rikwést]

v. 요청하다, 부탁하다
syn. ask, beg
He *requested* her to go fishing with him.

n. 요청, 부탁
Your *request* for a ticket was made too late.

ripe
[raip]

adj. 무르익은, 익은
ant. raw, unripe
Ripe fruits taste good; unripe fruits usually taste bad.

satisfy
[sǽtisfai]

v. 만족시키다, 뜻을 충족시키다
syn. please, fulfill
Nothing *satisfies* him; he is always complaining[22].

---

20. neglect[niglékt] *v.* 등한시하다   21. keep a file : 철하여 두다   22. complain[kǝmpléin] *v.* 불평을 말하다

security [sikjúərəti]	***n.*** 안전, 무사 **syn.** safety, protection ***adj.*** secure I helped the old lady cross the street in *security*.
shortcoming [ʃɔ́ːrtkʌ́miŋ]	***n.* (*pl.*)** 결점, 단점 **syn.** fault, weakness, defect He is a good man, but he has many *shortcomings*.

Practice 4

위 단어를 사용하여 아래 문장을 완성하라. 필요시 단어를 적절한 형태로 변형하라.

1. Keep the dictionary on your desk for easy _____.

2. We _____ a loan[23] from the First National Bank.

3. The apples are not _____ enough to eat.

4. In spite of all my friend's _____, I still like him.

5. He _____ his hunger with bread and milk.

New Vocabulary -5

smash [smæʃ]	***v.*** 부서지다, 부수다 **syn.** crush The cup *smashed* when the girl dropped it. ***n.*** 부서지는 소리 We heard a *smash* in the kitchen.
spin [spin]	***v.*** 1. (실을) 잣다, 방적하다 There were hundreds of machines *spinning* cotton into thread[24]. 2. 돌다, 회전하다 **syn.** rotate The earth *spins* as it moves around the sun.
steady [stédi]	***adj.*** 꾸준한, 한결같은 **syn.** constant **ant.** changing He is making *steady* progress at school.

---

23. loan [loun] ***n.*** 대부(貸付)   24. thread [θred] ***n.*** 실

stuff [stʌf]	***n.*** 재료, 물질 syn. substance The shoes were made of some *stuff* that looked like leather[25]. ***v.*** ~에 채우다 syn. fill ant. empty She *stuffed* the pillow[26] with feathers[27].
sweat [swet]	***n.*** 땀 The old farmer wiped[28] the *sweat* off his brow. ***v.*** 땀을 흘리다 We *sweat* when it is very hot.
terrible [térəbl]	***adj.*** 무서운, 겁나는 The *terrible* storm destroyed many houses in the town.
torch [tɔːrtʃ]	***n.*** 횃불 The Statue of Liberty[29] holds a *torch* in her right hand.
turtle [tə́ːrtl]	***n.*** 거북 *Turtles* live in fresh or salt water or on land.
victim [víktim]	***n.*** 희생자, 피해자 They were the *victims* of a dishonest merchant.
welfare [wélfɛər]	***n.*** 행복, 복지, 번영 syn. happiness, well-being They did everything for the *welfare* of their children.

Practice 5

위 단어를 사용하여 아래 문장을 완성하라. 필요시 단어를 적절한 형태로 변형하라.

1. She _____ the trunk with old clothing.

2. He kept up a _____ speed on the road.

3. Climbing up the hill made us _____ much.

4. The _____ fire filled the sky with flames[30].

5. Admiral Lee built _____ ships almost 400 years ago.

---

25. leather[léðər] ***n.*** 가죽   26. pillow[pílou] ***n.*** 베개   27. feather[féðər] ***n.*** 깃, 깃털   28. wipe[waip] ***v.*** 닦다, 씻다
29. the Statue of Liberty : 자유의 여신상   30. flame[fleim] ***n.*** (때로 ***pl.***) 불꽃, 화염

Practice 1	1. appreciate	2. bother	3. candle	4. despised	5. constituted
Practice 2	1. granted	2. immediate	3. fault	4. exploded	5. distributed
Practice 3	1. minute	2. marvels	3. instance	4. obliged	5. mysterious
Practice 4	1. reference	2. requested	3. ripe	4. shortcomings	5. satisfied
Practice 5	1. stuffed	2. steady	3. sweat	4. terrible	5. turtle

Lesson 13

종합 연습 문제

1 네 개의 단어 중 다른 셋과 관련이 없는 것을 골라 공란에 그 번호를 써넣어라.

_____ 1.   (A) safety   (B) protection   (C) security   (D) victim
_____ 2.   (A) shortcoming (B) defect   (C) victim   (D) weakness
_____ 3.   (A) perilous   (B) risky   (C) dangerous   (D) steep
_____ 4.   (A) ripe   (B) enthusiastic (C) eager   (D) anxious
_____ 5.   (A) instance   (B) fault   (C) example   (D) case
_____ 6.   (A) grant   (B) grand   (C) allow   (D) give
_____ 7.   (A) study   (B) teach   (C) instruct   (D) educate
_____ 8.   (A) assemble   (B) gather   (C) participate (D) accumulate
_____ 9.   (A) achieve   (B) participate (C) perform   (D) accomplish
_____ 10. (A) welfare   (B) well-being   (C) happiness   (D) outbreak

2 왼쪽에 주어진 우리말과 같은 뜻을 가진 단어를 골라 그 번호를 공란에 써넣어라.

_____ 1. 안전   (A) decoration   (B) foundation
                         (C) substance   (D) security

_____ 2. 땀   (A) instance   (B) sweat
                         (C) spell   (D) flood

_____ 3. 분배하다 (A) distribute   (B) participate
                         (C) smash   (D) accumulate

_____ 4. 분쇄하다 (A) explode   (B) spin
                         (C) smash   (D) heap

_____ 5. 횃불   (A) marvel   (B) torch
                         (C) stuff   (D) turtle

3 왼쪽에 주어진 단어와 반대되는 뜻을 가진 단어를 골라 그 번호를 공란에 써넣어라.

_____ 1. esteem   (A) admire   (B) comprise
                         (C) despise   (D) annoy

_____ 2. merit   (A) benefit   (B) defect
                         (C) wonder   (D) victim

_____ 3. ripe   (A) safe   (B) fault
                         (C) direct   (D) raw

_____ 4. drought   (A) flood   (B) outbreak
                         (C) sweat   (D) well-being

_____ 5. perilous (A) dull   (B) safe
                         (C) terrible   (D) changing

Lesson 13

종합 연습 문제

4 괄호 속에 주어진 우리말과 같은 뜻을 가진 단어를 사용하여 문장을 완성하라.

1. We took the V____MS of the storm into our house for the night. (희생자들)
2. He has worked for the W_____E of the nation throughout his life. (복지)
3. The band is playing this song by R_____T of the Queen. (요청)
4. You will never A_____E anything if you don't work hard. (성취하다)
5. She was very careful in her C____E of friends. (선택)

5 이탤릭체로 된 단어와 같은 뜻을 가진 단어를 골라 그 번호를 공란에 써넣어라.

_____ 1. The problem *bothered* the scientists for many years.
　　(A) annoyed　(B) bored　(C) amused　(D) consolidated

_____ 2. He gave me *minute* descriptions of the inside of his house.
　　(A) important　(B) precise　(C) splendid　(D) fundamental

_____ 3. The operation was a *marvel* of medical skill.
　　(A) success　(B) jewel　(C) merit　(D) wonder

_____ 4. He has many *shortcomings*, but I still love him.
　　(A) pains　(B) destiny　(C) defects　(D) outbreaks

_____ 5. His office is *located* on the ground floor[31].
　　(A) compounded　(B) situated　(C) floated　(D) constituted

_____ 6. She *heaped* the dirty clothes next to the washing machine[32].
　　(A) placed　(B) smashed　(C) piled　(D) achieved

_____ 7. All the teachers *took part in* the children's game.
　　(A) participated　(B) discussed　(C) requested　(D) wanted

_____ 8. A *gem* is a precious[33] stone.
　　(A) spell　(B) marble　(C) stuff　(D) jewel

_____ 9. She *purchased* a new dress in her friend's shop.
　　(A) ordered　(B) bought　(C) sold　(D) requested

_____ 10. The *courteous* boy gave the lady his seat on the bus.
　　(A) tired　(B) polite　(C) wholesome　(D) jealous

---

31. ground floor : 일층　　32. washing machine : 세탁기　　33. precious [préʃəs] ***adj.*** 귀중한, 귀한

Lesson 13 종합 연습 문제

Answers

1. 1. D 2. C 3. D 4. A 5. B 6. B 7. A 8. C 9. B 10. D
2. 1. D 2. B 3. A 4. C 5. B
3. 1. C 2. B 3. D 4. A 5. B
4. 1. VICTIMS 2. WELFARE 3. REQUEST 4. ACHIEVE 5. CHOICE
5. 1. A 2. B 3. D 4. C 5. B 6. C 7. A 8. D 9. B 10. B

LESSON 14

Self-test 14

적당한 단어를 골라 빈칸을 채우라.

1. A *greedy* person wants to have everything as _____ as possible.
   (A) much   (B) little

2. The boy took the _____ to the *pasture* every morning.
   (A) cats   (B) cows

3. A *carpenter* makes things with _____.
   (A) wood   (B) stones

4. The hill is so *steep* that it is very _____ to climb.
   (A) easy   (B) difficult

5. He was sent to _____ for his *crimes*.
   (A) hospital   (B) prison

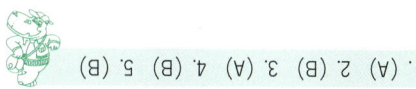
1. (A) 2. (B) 3. (A) 4. (B) 5. (B)

New Vocabulary -1

actual
[ǽktʃuəl]

adj. 실제의, 사실의
syn. true, real, genuine
The *actual* amount of money was not known although they knew it was large.

ash
[æʃ]

n. 재
Don't drop your cigarette *ash* on the carpet; use an ashtray[1].

beat
[biːt]

v. 치다, 두드리다
syn. strike, hit
The rain was *beating* against the windows.

---

1. ashtray [ǽʃtrei] *n.* 재떨이

bowl [boul]	***n.*** 사발, 공기 He ate only one *bowl* of rice and drank a glass of milk.
carpenter [ká:*r*pintə*r*]	***n.*** 목수, 목공 A *carpenter* builds and repairs the wooden parts of houses, barns, or ships.
circumstance [sə́:*r*kəmstæns]	***n.*** (보통 ***pl.***) 상황, 환경 **syn.** surroundings In no *circumstance* must a soldier leave his post[2] without permission[3].
conceive [kənsí:v]	***v.*** 상상하다, 생각하다, 마음에 품다 **syn.** think, imagine ***n.*** conception Young children like to watch television; they cannot *conceive* of life without it.
contain [kəntéin]	***v.*** 포함하다, 함유하다 **syn.** include **ant.** exclude The book *contains* all the information you need.
crime [kraim]	***n.*** 죄, 범죄 **syn.** offense He was found guilty of committing[4] a serious *crime*.
decorate [dékəreit]	***v.*** 장식하다, 꾸미다 **syn.** adorn, ornament ***n.*** decoration The streets were *decorated* with flags for the King's visit.

Practice 1

위 단어를 사용하여 아래 문장을 완성하라. 필요시 단어를 적절한 형태로 변형하라.

1. The boy _____ the girl with a stick.

2. The book _____ a good deal of[5] useful information.

3. I can't _____ of your allowing a child of five[6] to go such a long journey alone.

4. We _____ the Christmas tree with shining balls and bells last year.

5. If you commit a _____ you must expect to be punished.

---

2. post[poust] ***n.*** 초소   3. permission[pə(:)*r*míʃən] ***n.*** 허가   4. commit[kəmít] ***v.*** (죄를) 범하다   5. a good deal of : 다량의, 많은
6. a child of five : 다섯 살짜리의 어린이

New Vocabulary -2

determine
[ditə́:rmin]

v. 결정하다, 결심하다
syn. decide
n. determination
The size of your shoes is *determined* by the size of your feet.

divide
[diváid]

v. 나누다, 쪼개다, 분리하다
syn. separate, distribute
n. division
The small river *divides* my land from his.

elbow
[élbou]

n. 팔꿈치
He was watching television with his *elbows* bent, his chin[7] in his hands.

entrance
[éntrəns]

n. 입구
syn. gate, opening
ant. exit
v. enter
The *entrance* to the cave had been blocked[8] up.

expense
[ikspéns]

n. 지출, 비용
syn. expenditure
adj. expensive
v. expend
Most children are educated at public *expense*.

feast
[fi:st]

n. 향연, 잔치, 연회
syn. banquet
The king invited them to a *feast* last night.

fog
[fɔg]

n. 안개, 연무
syn. mist
adj. foggy
We often have bad *fogs* on the southern coast[9] during winter.

furnish
[fə́:rniʃ]

v. 1. 주다, 제공하다
syn. supply, give
No one in the class could *furnish* the right answer to the question.

---

7. chin [tʃin] *n.* 턱   8. block [blɔk] *v.* 봉쇄하다, 차단하다   9. coast [koust] *n.* 해안

Lesson 14 ▶ 163

2. (집, 방에) 가구를 설비하다
syn. equip
The new hotel is finished, but it is not yet *furnished*.

greedy
[gríːdi]

adj. 욕심 많은, 탐욕스러운
n. greed
Don't be so *greedy*! There is enough for everyone.

hesitate
[héziteit]

v. 망설이다, 주저하다
syn. falter, waver
n. hesitation
He *hesitated* to take such a big risk[10] in his business.

Practice 2

위 단어를 사용하여 아래 문장을 완성하라. 필요시 단어를 적절한 형태로 변형하라.

1. He got a deep wound on his right _____.

2. The _____ is the sailor's greatest enemy.

3. The _____ to the hotel was blocked with baggage so that no one could enter or leave.

4. I _____ to take his side[11] until I knew the whole story.

5. This hotel _____ clean sheets and towels every day.

New Vocabulary -3

impossible
[impásəbl]

adj. 불가능한
syn. impracticable
ant. practicable
Today it is *impossible* to cure[12] cancer[13] completely.

institution
[institjúːʃən]

n. 공공 기관, (학교 따위의) 공공 건물
Colleges and universities are educational *institutions*.

journal
[dʒə́ːrnl]

n. (신문, 잡지 따위의) 정기 간행물
Both he and his wife write for a business *journal*.

---

10. take a risk : 모험을 해보다   11. take one's side : ~의 편을 들다   12. cure [kjuər] *v.* 치료하다   13. cancer [kǽnsər] *n.* 암

launch
[lɔ:ntʃ]
v. 발사하다, 진수(進水)시키다
The United States *launched* a new spaceship[14] yesterday.

loss
[lɔs]
n. 상실, 유실
ant. gain
v. lose
Loss of health is more serious than loss of wealth.

match
[mætʃ]
v. 1. 필적하다, 상대하다
You can't *match* him in knowledge of wild plants.
2. 어울리다, 조화하다
syn. become
The drapes[15] of the room *match* the rug of the floor.

misfortune
[misfɔ́:rtʃən]
n. 불운, 불행
syn. unhappiness
ant. luck
His failure in business was due not to[16] *misfortune*, but to his mistakes.

native
[néitiv]
adj. 출생지의, 자국의
The politician was never popular in his *native* country.

obvious
[ɔ́bviəs]
adj. 분명한, 명백한
syn. evident, clear
It is *obvious* that two and two makes four.

outstanding
[autstǽndiŋ]
adj. 두드러진, 특출한
syn. prominent, eminent
He is an *outstanding* pitcher because of his ball control.

Practice 3

위 단어를 사용하여 아래 문장을 완성하라. 필요시 단어를 적절한 형태로 변형하라.

1. One of the _____ animals of India is the tiger.
2. She always thought that the greatest of her _____ was that she'd never had any children.
3. The carpets should _____ the wallpaper[17].
4. The _____ of so many ships worried the admiral[18].
5. The new ship was _____ as the crowd cheered.

---

14. spaceship[spéisʃip] *n.* 우주선   15. drape[dreip] *n.* (美) 커튼   16. due to~ : 때문이다   17. wallpaper[wɔ́:lpeipər] *n.* 벽지
18. admiral[ǽdmərəl] *n.* 해군 제독

New Vocabulary -4

pasture
[pǽstʃər]
n. 목장, 목초
syn. grassland
I saw many horses grazing[19] on the *pasture*.

personality
[pə:rsnǽləti]
n. 개성, 인품, 성격
syn. character
She was elected class president[20] because of her good *personality*.

port
[pɔ:rt]
n. 항구
syn. harbor
New York and San Francisco are important *ports* of the United States.

privilege
[prívilidʒ]
n. 특권, 특전
The members of the club have the *privilege* of buying the football ticket at special rates[21].

puzzle
[pʌ́zl]
n. 난문(難問), 수수께끼
syn. riddle
No one has yet succeeded in explaining the *puzzle* of how life first began.

region
[rí:dʒən]
n. 지방, 지역
syn. area
New York is one of the *regions* of the United States.

resemble
[rizémbl]
v. ~을 닮다, ~와 유사하다
They *resemble* each other in shape but not in color.

roast
[roust]
v. 굽다, 그슬리다
We need an oven[22] to *roast* meat and potatoes.

savage
[sǽvidʒ]
adj. 야만의, 미개한
syn. barbarous, wild
ant. civilized
They carried guns to protect themselves from the *savage* tribes[23].

sentiment
[séntimənt]
n. 감정, 감상(感傷), 정취
syn. feeling
The young girls preferred stories full of *sentiments*.

---

19. graze[greiz] *v.* (가축이) 풀을 뜯어먹다   20. class president : 학급 반장   21. rate[reit] *n.* 값, 요금
22. oven[ʌ́vən] *n.* 솥, 오븐   23. tribe[traib] *n.* 종족, 야만인 사회

Practice 4

위 단어를 사용하여 아래 문장을 완성하라. 필요시 단어를 적절한 형태로 변형하라.

1. In modern times there is less _____ and more of an equal chance in life for everyone.

2. There is only one _____ along this rocky[24] coast.

3. She _____ her sister in appearance but not in character.

4. Instead of frying, she likes to _____ the meat.

5. How to get all my clothes into one suitcase was a _____.

New Vocabulary -5

silence
[sáiləns]
n. 침묵, 정숙
syn. quietness
ant. noise
Students are required to maintain *silence* in the library.

sob
[sɔb]
v. 흐느껴 울다, 흐느끼며 말하다
syn. weep
ant. laugh
She *sobbed* when she heard the bad news.

spit
[spit]
v. 내뱉다, 침을 뱉다
Please *spit* your gum before you come into the classroom.

steep
[sti:p]
adj. 가파른, 급경사진
ant. flat
The hill was too *steep* for them to climb.

substantial
[səbstǽnʃəl]
adj. 실질적인, 본질적인, 실속있는
syn. real, actual
John has made a *substantial* improvement[25] in his health.

swift
[swift]
adj. 빠른, 신속한
syn. quick, speedy
ant. slow
Be careful not to fall down; the current[26] of the river is *swift*.

---

24. rocky[rɔ́ki] *adj.* 바위가 많은   25. improvement[imprúvmənt] *n.* 진보, 향상   26. current[kʌ́rənt] *n.* 흐름, 조류

thermometer
[θərmɔ́mitər]

n. 온도계

The doctor used a clinical[27] *thermometer* to measure the patient's temperature.

tower
[táuər]

n. 탑

You should visit the *Tower* of London when you have a chance to visit England.

typical
[típikəl]

adj. 전형적인, 대표적인
syn. representative
v. typify
Turkey is a *typical* food for the Thanksgiving Day dinner.

virgin
[və́:rdʒin]

n. 처녀, 동정녀

The man decided to marry a *virgin* who lives in the house next to his uncle.

whisper
[hwíspər]

v. 속삭이다, 귓속말하다

She *whispered* a few words at the corner.

Practice 5

위 단어를 사용하여 아래 문장을 완성하라. 필요시 단어를 적절한 형태로 변형하라.

1. If you _____ in the classroom, you may be punished by the teacher.

2. A _____ rise in living cost[28] makes our life hard.

3. The building is a _____ 18th century church.

4. What the _____ is to temperature, the speedometer is to speed[29].

5. He has _____ evidence for his claim[30].

해답					
Practice 1	1. beat	2. contains	3. conceive	4. decorated	5. crime
Practice 2	1. elbow	2. fog	3. entrance	4. hesitated	5. furnishes
Practice 3	1. native	2. misfortune	3. match	4. loss	5. launched
Practice 4	1. privilege	2. port	3. resembles	4. roast	5. puzzle
Practice 5	1. spit	2. steep	3. typical	4. thermometer	5. substantial

27. clinical [klínikəl] *adj.* 임상(臨床)의 (a clinical thermometer : 체온계, 검온계) 28. living cost : 생활비
29. what A is to B, C is to D : A와 B와의 관계는 C와 D와의 관계와 같다   30. claim [kleim] *n.* 주장, 요구

종합 연습 문제

1 이탤릭체로 된 단어와 같은 뜻을 가진 단어를 골라 그 번호를 공란에 써넣어라.

_____ 1. to *decorate* the wall with paintings
(A) furnish　　(B) adorn　　(C) match　　(D) describe

_____ 2. a serious *offense*
(A) crime　　(B) attack　　(C) expense　　(D) misfortune

_____ 3. a *port* in the southern coast
(A) island　　(B) city　　(C) tower　　(D) harbor

_____ 4. an *outstanding* achievement
(A) unknown　　(B) impossible　(C) prominent　(D) evident

_____ 5. a *swift* glance[31]
(A) secret　　(B) wild　　(C) slight　　(D) quick

_____ 6. to *furnish* a new building
(A) decorate　　(B) equip　　(C) finish　　(D) purchase

_____ 7. to get invited to a *feast*
(A) parlor　　(B) funeral　　(C) banquet　　(D) wedding

_____ 8. a *substantial* improvement
(A) great　　(B) actual　　(C) surprising　　(D) unexpected

_____ 9. an *obvious* mistake
(A) insignificant　(B) serious　　(C) evident　　(D) real

_____ 10. a difficult *puzzle*
(A) riddle　　(B) work　　(C) language　　(D) battle

2 왼쪽에 주어진 우리말과 같은 뜻을 가진 단어를 골라 그 번호를 공란에 써넣어라.

_____ 1. 특권
(A) priest　　　　(B) character
(C) privilege　　(D) journal

_____ 2. ~을 닮다
(A) waver　　　　(B) resemble
(C) assume　　　(D) match

_____ 3. 야만인의
(A) savage　　　(B) flat
(C) native　　　(D) impossible

_____ 4. 전형적인
(A) substantial　(B) outstanding
(C) genuine　　　(D) typical

_____ 5. 지출
(A) instance　　(B) loss
(C) expense　　(D) reference

---

31. glance[glæns] ***n.*** (얼핏) 보기, 일견

Lesson 14 종합 연습 문제

3 왼쪽에 주어진 단어와 반대되는 뜻을 가진 단어를 골라 그 번호를 공란에 써넣어라.

_____ 1. noise   (A) well-being   (B) merit
                                (C) luck   (D) silence

_____ 2. gain   (A) crime   (B) loss
                                (C) virgin   (D) misfortune

_____ 3. contain   (A) divide   (B) conceive
                                (C) spit   (D) exclude

_____ 4. misfortune (A) offense   (B) feast
                                (C) luck   (D) welfare

_____ 5. exit   (A) entrance   (B) include
                                (C) encourage   (D) gain

4 괄호 속에 주어진 우리말과 같은 뜻을 가진 단어를 사용하여 문장을 완성하라.

1. It is O_____S that a blind man ought not to drive a car. (분명한)
2. The wooded R____N will be transformed into a park. (지역)
3. There is no place for S_____TS in business affairs[32]. (감상, 감정)
4. Tomorrow's weather will D_____E whether we are to go or stay. (결정하다)
5. I H_____E to ask you, but will you lend me some money? (망설이다)

5 가장 적합한 단어를 골라 빈칸을 채우라.

1. Scientists first _____ the idea of the atomic bomb in the 1930s.
    (A) contained   (B) purchased   (C) compounded   (D) conceived

2. It is the business of the police to detect[33] _____ and of the law courts to punish them.
    (A) crimes   (B) puzzles   (C) losses   (D) faults

3. The ribbon does not _____ with the hat.
    (A) resemble   (B) match   (C) appreciate   (D) allow

4. The cruel rider _____ his horse with a stick.
    (A) roasted   (B) heaped   (C) whispered   (D) beat

5. A large number of houses were burnt to _____.
    (A) victims   (B) misfortune   (C) ashes   (D) noises

---

32. business affairs : 사업상의 업무   33. detect [ditékt] *v.* 발견하다, 찾아내다

Lesson 14

6. Before we judge a person's acts, we must know all the _____.
   (A) circumstances (B) expenses (C) puzzles (D) faults

7. The king and his nobles[34] celebrated the birth of his heir[35] with a _____.
   (A) bowl (B) benefit (C) sob (D) feast

8. It is _____ to grow rice in the desert.
   (A) genuine (B) impossible (C) perilous (D) partial

9. There are many _____ in our society such as churches, schools, hospitals, and prisons.
   (A) institutions (B) foundations (C) journals (D) regions

10. He gave his friend the _____ of using his private library.
    (A) reference (B) security (C) privilege (D) expense

6 왼쪽에 주어진 단어의 적당한 파생어를 사용하여 문장을 완성하라.

1. *decorate*   The _____ of the party were bright and cheery.
2. *determine*   He has a firm _____ to do his best in the final examination.
3. *entrance*   The thief _____ through a rear window last night.
4. *expense*   The price of this radio is very _____.
5. *greedy*   His _____ for money led him to steal a painting from the museum.

Answers

1. 1. B   2. A   3. D   4. C   5. D   6. B   7. C   8. B   9. C   10. A
2. 1. C   2. B   3. A   4. D   5. C
3. 1. D   2. B   3. D   4. C   5. A
4. 1. OBVIOUS   2. REGION   3. SENTIMENTS   4. DETERMINE   5. HESITATE
5. 1. D   2. A   3. B   4. D   5. C   6. A   7. D   8. B   9. A   10. C
6. 1. decorations   2. determination   3. entered   4. expensive   5. greed

34. noble[noubl] *n.* 귀족   35. heir[ɛər] *n.* 후계자

LESSON 15

Self-test 15

적당한 단어를 골라 빈칸을 채우라.

1. Dogs _____ to be *patted*.
   (A) like   (B) hate

2. A *thirsty* person wants to have something to _____.
   (A) eat   (B) drink

3. Because of the _____ harvest of crops, there is a *scarcity* of food.
   (A) enough   (B) poor

4. He was filled with *envy* at my _____.
   (A) success   (B) failure

5. *Expedition* is a _____ made for some special purpose.
   (A) journey   (B) plan

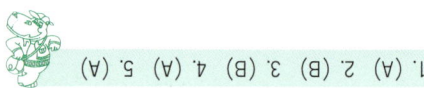
1. (A) 2. (B) 3. (B) 4. (A) 5. (A)

New Vocabulary -1

additional
[ədíʃənəl]
adj. 부가의, 추가의
v. add
n. addition
Mother needs *additional* help in the kitchen when we have guests for dinner.

aspect
[ǽspekt]
n. 국면, 양상, 정세
You must consider all *aspects* of this plan before we decide.

beard
[biərd]
n. (턱)수염
My grandfather has a long *beard* on his chin and cheeks[1].

---

1. cheek [tʃiːk] *n.* 볼, 뺨

brass
[bræs]

n. 놋쇠, 황동
He has *brass* buttons on his jackets.

carve
[kɑːrv]

v. 새기다, 조각하다
syn. inscribe
The picture was *carved* on the surface of wood.

civil
[sívil]

adj. 1. 시민의, 공민의
The judge ordered that the prisoner should lose his *civil* rights.

2. (군에 대하여) 민간의
n. civilian
The soldiers thought it would be a long time before *civil* government would be reestablished.

concern
[kənsə́ːrn]

v. 1. ~에 관계하다, ~에 관련되다
syn. affect
Don't trouble about² things that don't *concern* you.

2. 관심을 갖다, 마음을 쓰다
syn. interest
I am very much *concerned* about the future of this country.

contest
[kɔ́ntest]

n. 경쟁, 경연, 항쟁
syn. competition, struggle, conflict
The *contest* between France and England for North America ended in victory for England.

[kəntést]

v. 경쟁하다, 다투다
syn. compete
The blackbirds³ *contested* one another for nesting territory⁴.

critical
[krítikəl]

adj. 1. 비평의, 비판적인
syn. faultfinding
I don't like people who are too *critical* about everything.

2. 위기의, 위급한
His condition is reported as being very *critical*.

decrease
[dikríːs]

v. 줄다, 줄이다
ant. increase
Travel by railroad has been *decreased* because of the speed of the air travel.

---

2. trouble about ~ : ~로 고민하다   3. blackbird : (지빠귀과) 검은새   4. nesting territory : (새의) 보금자리

Practice 1

위 단어를 사용하여 아래 문장을 완성하라. 필요시 단어를 적절한 형태로 변형하라.

1. The doctor _____ himself about the health of his aged patient[5].
2. Government must protect the _____ rights of its citizens.
3. If you really understand the difficulties of the government, you wouldn't be so _____ of its policy.
4. John no longer wears a(n) _____.
5. _____ is made by mixing copper and zinc[6].

New Vocabulary -2

device
[diváis]

n. 1. 고안품, 장치
syn. design
He invented a *device* for automatically lighting a gas stove.

2. 방책, 수단
syn. method
The child's tears were a *device* to get attention.

divine
[diváin]

adj. 신(神)의, 신성의
To err[7] is human, to forgive is *divine*.

election
[ilékʃən]

n. 선거
v. elect
adj. elective
The *election* results will be broadcast tonight.

envy
[énvi]

n. 시기, 질투
adj. envious
v. envy
The boy's new bicycle was an object of *envy* to all his friends.

expedition
[ekspidíʃən]

n. 탐험(대), 원정(대)
syn. trip
A voyage of discovery or march against the enemy is an *expedition*.

---

5. aged patient : 나이든 환자   6. zinc[ziŋk] *n.* 아연, 함석   7. err[əːr] *v.* 잘못을 저지르다

feature [fíːtʃər]	*n.* 특징, 특색 syn. characteristic, quality The main *features* of Southern California are the warm climate and the beautiful scenery[8].
folly [fɔ́li]	*n.* 어리석음, 우매 syn. foolishness ant. sagacity After one year at the university he gave up[9] his studies; it was an act of the greatest *folly*.
fury [fjúəri]	*n.* 격분, 격노 syn. anger, rage *adj.* furious In his *fury* at being punished, he broke the teacher's favorite vase[10].
grief [griːf]	*n.* 슬픔, 비탄, 고뇌 syn. sorrow, suffering ant. pleasure She went nearly mad[11] with *grief* after the child died.
hide [haid]	*v.* 숨기다, 감추다 syn. conceal ant. reveal *Hide* it where no one else can find it.

Practice 2

위 단어를 사용하여 아래 문장을 완성하라. 필요시 단어를 적절한 형태로 변형하라.

1. The old man smiled sadly as he remembered the _____ of his youth.
2. He used a strange _____ to pick up the paper.
3. Some boys were full of _____ when they saw my new bicycle.
4. I _____ the broken dish behind the table yesterday.
5. His failure to live a good life was a(n) _____ to his parents.

---

8. scenery [síːnəri] *n.* 풍경, 경치   9. give up : 포기하다   10. vase [veis] *n.* 꽃병   11. go mad : 미치다

New Vocabulary -3

impression
[impréʃən]
n. 인상, 감명, 느낌
v. impress
adj. impressive
His speech made a strong *impression* on the audience.

instruct
[instrʌ́kt]
v. 가르치다, 교육하다
syn. teach
n. instruction
We have one teacher who *instructs* us in reading, English, and history.

journey
[dʒə́:rni]
n. 여행, 여정
syn. tour, excursion
Life is a long *journey* from birth to death.

lawn
[lɔ:n]
n. 잔디, 잔디밭
I spent the whole afternoon mowing[12] the *lawn* in the backyard.

lovely
[lʌ́vli]
adj. 아름다운, 귀여운
syn. beautiful, attractive
ant. ugly, unpleasant
She was wearing a very *lovely* dress at the party.

material
[mətíəriəl]
n. 재료, 원료
syn. substance
When building *materials* cost more, the price of houses increases.

mislead
[mislí:d]
v. 오해하게 하다, 잘못 인도하다
syn. misguide, misdirect
p., pp. misled
Her appearance[13] *misled* him; he thought she was young, but she wasn't.

navy
[néivi]
n. 해군, 해군력
The *navy* defends the country's shores and seas.

occasion
[əkéiʒən]
n. 때, 경우, 기회
adj. occasional
I wish to express my sorrow on this *occasion*.

---

12. mow [mou] *v.* (풀 따위를) 베다, 깎다   13. appearance [əpíərəns] *n.* 외관, 외모

overcome
[ouvərkʌ́m]

v. 이겨내다, 정복하다
syn. conquer, vanquish
In order to succeed, you must *overcome* any hardship[14].

Practice 3

위 단어를 사용하여 아래 문장을 완성하라. 필요시 단어를 적절한 형태로 변형하라.

1. Our guide[15] _____ us in the woods, and we got lost.
2. He is going to make a(n) _____ around the world.
3. Rubber is a widely used _____.
4. A birthday is not a(n) _____ for tears.
5. The child was _____ by weariness[16] and slept deeply.

New Vocabulary -4

pat
[pæt]

n. 가볍게 두드림, 애무
The child gave the dog a *pat* on the head.

v. 가볍게 두드리다, 애무하다
syn. tap
She *patted* her hair to be sure that it was neat[17].

persuade
[pəːrswéid]

v. 설득하다, 권유하여 ~하게 하다
ant. dissuade
n. persuasion
I know I should study, but he *persuaded* me to go to the movies.

portable
[pɔ́ːrtəbl]

adj. 휴대용의, 들고 다닐 수 있는
A *portable* typewriter can be easily moved from place to place.

procedure
[prəsíːdʒər]

n. 절차, 진행
The new secretary learned the *procedure* in the office.

quality
[kwɔ́ləti]

n. 질(質), 품질
ant. quantity
Quality is more important than quantity[18].

---

14. hardship[háːrdʃip] *n.* 고난, 고생   15. guide[gaid] *n.* 안내자   16. weariness[wíərinis] *n.* 피로, 권태
17. neat[niːt] *adj.* 말쑥한, 단정한   18. quantity[kwɔ́ntəti] *n.* 양(量)

register [rédʒistər]	*v.* 등록하다, 등기하다 *n.* registration You are required to *register* before the election.
resent [rizént]	*v.* 분개하다, 화내다 *n.* resentment He strongly *resents* being called a fool.
rod [rɔd]	*n.* 막대, 장대 She hung the curtains on a *rod*.
scarcity [skɛ́ərsəti]	*n.* 부족, 결핍 **syn.** lack, rarity, shortage **ant.** abundance The *scarcity* of fruit was caused by the drought[19].
series [síəri(:)z]	*n.* 연속, 일련 A *series* of rainy days spoiled their vacation.

Practice 4

위 단어를 사용하여 아래 문장을 완성하라. 필요시 단어를 적절한 형태로 변형하라.

1. He _____ the promotion[20] of his younger colleague[21] to a rank above his own.

2. It took the whole afternoon to _____ his new car.

3. She wanted to buy an orange dress, but we _____ her that the blue one was more attractive.

4. He bought a _____ television for the trip.

5. An important _____ of steel is its strength.

---

19. drought [draut] *n.* 가뭄, 한발   20. promotion [prəmóuʃən] *n.* 승급, 진급   21. colleague [kɔ́liːg] *n.* 동료

New Vocabulary -5

silly
[síli]
adj. 어리석은, 바보 같은
syn. foolish, stupid
ant. sensible, wise
It's *silly* to go out in the rain if you don't have to.

social
[sóuʃəl]
adj. 1. 사회적인, 사회의
n. society
Better housing[22] is a serious *social* problem in this country.
  2. 사교적인, 친목적인
It was a *social* meeting, and no one discussed business.

splendid
[spléndid]
adj. 화려한, 빛나는, 눈부신
syn. brilliant, magnificent
The rich man lives in a *splendid* house over there.

steer
[stiər]
n. 수송아지
syn. ox
The *steers* were fattened[23] for market.

v. 키를 잡다, 조종하다
syn. guide, navigate
We *steered* the boat toward land.

substitute
[sʌ́bstitjuːt]
v. 대체하다, 대용하다
n. substitution
We often *substitute* margarine[24] for butter.

swing
[swiŋ]
v. 흔들다, 매달리다
p., pp. swung
The big ape[25] *swung* itself from branch to branch.

thirst
[θəːrst]
n. 갈증, 목마름
adj. thirsty
The horse satisfied its *thirst* at the river.

trace
[treis]
n. 자취, 흔적, 발자국
The police were unable to find any *trace* of the thief.

---

22. housing[háuziŋ] *n.* 주택 공급, 주택   23. fatten[fǽtn] *v.* 살찌게 하다   24. margarine[mɑːrdʒərín] *n.* 인조 버터, 마가린
25. ape[eip] *n.* 원숭이

v. 밟아가다, 추적하다
syn. track
His family can *trace* its history back to the 10th century.

union
[júːnjən]

n. 연합, 결합
syn. combination
The United States of America is a federal[26] *union* of fifty-one states.

visible
[vízəbl]

adj. 보이는, 눈에 띄는
syn. perceptible
ant. hidden, invisible
The shore was barely *visible* through the fog.

whistle
[hwísl]

v. (호각, 휘파람 등을) 불다
The policeman *whistled* for the automobile to stop.

Practice 5

위 단어를 사용하여 아래 문장을 완성하라. 필요시 단어를 적절한 형태로 변형하라.

1. Sorrow had left its _____ on his face.

2. The pilot[27] _____ the ship for the harbor in the morning.

3. We _____ red balls for blue to see if the baby would notice.

4. After running 5 miles we really had a _____.

5. He was _____ his arms as he walked.

Practice 1	1. concerned	2. civil	3. critical	4. beard	5. Brass
Practice 2	1. follies	2. device	3. envy	4. hid	5. grief
Practice 3	1. misled	2. journey	3. material	4. occasion	5. overcome
Practice 4	1. resented	2. register	3. persuaded	4. portable	5. quality
Practice 5	1. traces	2. steered	3. substituted	4. thirst	5. swinging

26. federal [fédərəl] **adj.** 연방의   27. pilot [páilət] **n.** 조타수, 조종사, 키잡이

종합 연습 문제

1 네 개의 단어 중 다른 셋과 관련이 없는 것을 골라 공란에 그 번호를 써넣어라.

_____ 1. (A) overcome   (B) contest   (C) conquer   (D) vanquish
_____ 2. (A) fury   (B) anger   (C) rage   (D) folly
_____ 3. (A) loss   (B) lack   (C) rarity   (D) scarcity
_____ 4. (A) foolish   (B) stupid   (C) ugly   (D) silly
_____ 5. (A) lovely   (B) attractive   (C) divine   (D) beautiful
_____ 6. (A) procedure   (B) journey   (C) excursion   (D) travel
_____ 7. (A) mislead   (B) mistake   (C) misdirect   (D) misguide
_____ 8. (A) splendid   (B) brilliant   (C) magnificent (D) substantial
_____ 9. (A) suffering   (B) grief   (C) offense   (D) sorrow
_____ 10. (A) contest   (B) competition (C) struggle   (D) device

2 왼쪽에 주어진 우리말과 같은 뜻을 가진 단어를 골라 그 번호를 공란에 써넣어라.

_____ 1. 휴대할 수 있는   (A) portable   (B) divine
                                  (C) actual   (D) native

_____ 2. 등록하다   (A) contain   (B) furnish
                                  (C) register   (D) determine

_____ 3. 분개하다   (A) contest   (B) resent
                                  (C) steer   (D) resign

_____ 4. 턱수염   (A) fury   (B) lawn
                                  (C) series   (D) beard

_____ 5. 인상   (A) impression (B) feature
                                  (C) device   (D) quality

3 왼쪽에 주어진 단어와 반대되는 뜻을 가진 단어를 골라 그 번호를 공란에 써넣어라.

_____ 1. sensible   (A) civil   (B) wise
                                  (C) critical   (D) silly

_____ 2. abundance   (A) fury   (B) scarcity
                                  (C) quantity   (D) quality

_____ 3. grief   (A) pleasure   (B) journey
                                  (C) folly   (D) competition

_____ 4. dissuade   (A) persuade   (B) conquer
                                  (C) conceal   (D) concern

_____ 5. hidden   (A) divine   (B) visible
                                  (C) social   (D) additional

Lesson 15

종합 연습 문제

4 괄호 속에 주어진 우리말과 같은 뜻을 가진 단어를 사용하여 문장을 완성하라.

1. You have only considered one A____T of difficulty, but there are many. (양상)
2. The furniture that the store sells is known for its good Q_____Y. (품질)
3. D_____E the dose[28] of medicine when you feel better. (줄이다)
4. In our city we have an E_____N for mayor[29] every two years. (선거)
5. They lost their way in the desert[30] and died of T____T. (갈증)

5 이탤릭체로 된 단어와 같은 뜻을 가진 단어를 골라 그 번호를 공란에 써넣어라.

_____ 1. He *patted* me on the shoulder.
    (A) persuaded   (B) trimmed   (C) tapped   (D) spat

_____ 2. The early settlers[31] had many difficulties to *overcome*.
    (A) perform   (B) decrease   (C) conquer   (D) understand

_____ 3. The police *traced* the thief to his hiding place.
    (A) searched   (B) tracked   (C) vanquished   (D) located

_____ 4. They *carved* their names on the tree.
    (A) inscribed   (B) described   (C) inspired   (D) wrote

_____ 5. We *steered* the boat toward the port in the south.
    (A) hid   (B) swung   (C) spied   (D) guided

_____ 6. It is a *folly* to drink too much during the picnic.
    (A) puzzle   (B) danger   (C) foolishness   (D) feast

_____ 7. Janet is only too *critical* of Alice because she doesn't like her.
    (A) faultfinding   (B) substantial   (C) jealous   (D) negligent

_____ 8. She *hid* the toy in the drawer[32].
    (A) hit   (B) concealed   (C) disclosed   (D) put

_____ 9. Wet weather is a *feature* of life in Scotland.
    (A) characteristic   (B) quantity   (C) occasion   (D) device

_____ 10. It is no use trying[33] to argue[34] with you when you fly into a *fury* for the slightest[35].
    (A) privilege   (B) journey   (C) rage   (D) rarity

---

28. dose[dous] *n.* (약의)1회 복용량   29. mayor[méiər] *n.* 시장(市長)   30. desert[dézərt] *n.* 사막   31. settler[sétlər] *n.* 식민지, 개척자
32. drawer[drɔːr] *n.* 서랍   33. it is no use ~ing : ~해도 소용이 없다   34. argue[áːrgjuː] *v.* 논쟁하다(with)
35. the slightest : 아주 사소한 일[문제]

Lesson 15

1. 1. B 2. D 3. A 4. C 5. C 6. A 7. B 8. D 9. C 10. D

2. 1. A 2. C 3. B 4. D 5. A

3. 1. D 2. B 3. A 4. A 5. B

4. 1. ASPECT 2. QUALITY 3. DECREASE 4. ELECTION 5. THIRST

5. 1. C 2. C 3. B 4. A 5. D 6. C 7. A 8. B 9. A 10. C

LESSON 16

Self-test 16

적당한 단어를 골라 빈칸을 채우라.

1. The teacher _____ be *stern* in the discipline[1] of his pupils.
   (A) must not   (B) must

2. We visited a *gallery* of modern _____.
   (A) art   (B) cars

3. If there is a *leak* in the roof, you will have trouble in the _____ season.
   (A) rainy   (B) sunny

4. The *mayor* is the person at the head of a _____.
   (A) team   (B) town

5. He *split* the wood with _____.
   (A) fire   (B) an ax

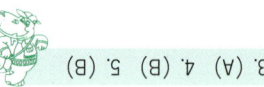
1. (B) 2. (A) 3. (A) 4. (B) 5. (B)

New Vocabulary -1

admire
[ədmáiər]
v. 찬미하다, 숭배하다, 존경하다
syn. esteem
ant. despise
n. admiration
We all *admire* a brave boy, a beautiful picture, or a fine piece of work[2].

assemble
[əsémbl]
v. 모으다, 소집하다
syn. gather
n. assembly
The students were *assembled* in the school hall.

---

1. discipline [dísəplin] *n.* 훈육, 훈련   2. a piece of work : 한 편의 작품

beast
[biːst]
n. (인간에 대한) 짐승, 금수
syn. animal
Lions, bears[3], cows and horses are *beasts*.

bravery
[bréivəri]
n. 용기, 용감성
syn. courage
ant. cowardice
A young man's *bravery* saved the child from the burning house.

castle
[kǽsl]
n. 성(城), 성곽
cf. fortress
A king once lived in the mountain *castle*.

claim
[kleim]
v. 요구하다, 청구하다
syn. demand
Every citizen may *claim* the protection[4] of the law.

conclude
[kənklúːd]
v. 결론짓다, 결론을 내리다
n. conclusion
As he didn't get[5] here at six, I *concluded* that he had been delayed[6].

contract
[kəntrǽkt]
v. 1. 계약하다, 청부 맡다
syn. bargain
Our shop *contracted* with a local clothing firm[7] for 100 coats a week.
　　2. 수축하다, 오그라들다
syn. reduce, diminish
Most metals *contract* when they cool.

crop
[krɔp]
n. 1. 농작물
Wheat, corn and cotton are three main *crops* of the United States.
　　2. 수확, 경작
The drought made the potato *crop* very small this year.

deed
[diːd]
n. 행위, 행동
syn. action, behavior
Good *deeds* should be rewarded[8] and evil *deeds* should be punished.

---

3. bear[bɛər] *n.* 곰　　4. protection[prətékʃən] *n.* 보호　　5. get (to) ~ : ~에 도착하다　　6. delay[diléi] *v.* 지연시키다, 연기시키다
7. firm[fəːrm] *n.* 회사　　8. reward[riwɔ́ːrd] *v.* 보상하다

Practice 1

위 단어를 사용하여 아래 문장을 완성하라. 필요시 단어를 적절한 형태로 변형하라.

1. The grandfather _____ all the members of his family for the annual meeting[9] last week.

2. We _____ people who succeed in spite of difficulties.

3. They _____ to pay cash[10] for the house just yesterday.

4. The injured man _____ for compensation[11] for damages at the trial[12] yesterday.

5. His _____ do not always agree with his words.

New Vocabulary -2

devote
[divóut]
v. (연구, 일, 목적 따위에) 바치다
syn. dedicate, consecrate
n. devotion
He *devoted* his efforts to the improvement of the parks in the city.

divorce
[divɔ́:rs]
v. 이혼하다, 분리하다
syn. separate
ant. marry
He has been *divorced* for a year.

n. 이혼
His wife asked him for a *divorce*.

elegant
[éligənt]
adj. 고상한, 우아한, 품위있는
syn. graceful, nice, fine
ant. vulgar
The furnishings[13] of the palace were *elegant*.

equator
[i(:)kwéitər]
n. 적도
The United States is north of the *equator*.

exist
[igzíst]
v. 존재하다, 생존하다
syn. live

---

9. annual meeting : 연례 회합   10. cash [kæʃ] n. 현금   11. compensation [kɑmpənséiʃən] n. 보상금
12. trial [traiəl] n. 재판, 공판   13. furnishings [fə́:rniʃiŋs] n. (pl.) (집, 방의) 비품, 세간 설비

	n. existence We cannot *exist* without air, food, and warmth.
federal [fédərəl]	***adj.*** 연방의, 연방 정부의 The United States has a *federal* government.
forbid [fərbíd]	***v.*** 금하다, 금지하다 **syn.** prohibit **ant.** permit, allow Smoking is *forbidden* in the bus.
gallery [gǽləri]	***n.*** 화랑, 미술관 Many pictures were hung on the walls of the *gallery*.
grind [graind]	***v.*** 갈다, 빻다, 찧다 That mill *grinds* corn into meal[14], and wheat into flour.
improve [imprú:v]	***v.*** 개선하다, 발전시키다 **syn.** develop, better ***n.*** improvement She *improved* her handwriting by constant practice.

Practice 2

위 단어를 사용하여 아래 문장을 완성하라. 필요시 단어를 적절한 형태로 변형하라.

1. The mother _____ herself to caring for[15] her sick child last week.
2. A(n) _____ is an imaginary circle around the middle of the earth at an equal distance from the North and South Poles[16].
3. What happens to the soul when it is _____ from the body?
4. In the United States foreign policy is decided by the _____ government.
5. If her father had known it, he would have _____ the marriage.

---

14. meal[mi:l] ***n.*** 가루, 굵은 가루   15. care for ~ : ~을 돌보다, 보살피다   16. the North(South) Pole : 북(남)극

New Vocabulary -3

instrument
[ínstrəmənt]
n. 도구, 기구
syn. tool
A doctor's *instruments* must be kept clean.

junior
[dʒúːnjər]
adj. 손아래의, 하급의(Jr.로도 씀)
ant. senior
This teaching course is for *junior* officers.

leak
[liːk]
n. 새는 곳, 새는 구멍
There is a *leak* in the roof.
v. 새다, 새어 나오다
The rain is *leaking* in through a crack[17] in the roof.

lower
[lóuər]
v. 내리다, 낮추다
syn. decrease, diminish
We *lower* our flag usually at six o'clock.

mayor
[méiər]
n. 시장(市長)
A *mayor* is the chief government official[18] of a city or town.

mistrust
[mistrʌ́st]
v. 불신하다, 수상히 여기다
ant. believe, trust
He keeps his money at home because he *mistrusts* banks.

neat
[niːt]
adj. 말쑥한, 단정한
The child was taught to put away her toys and clothes to keep her room *neat*.

occupy
[ɔ́kjupai]
v. 차지하다, 점령하다
n. occupation
Mr. Smith *occupies* an important position in the Ministry of Education[19].

overall
[óuvərɔːl]
adj. 전체의, 전부의
The *overall* size of the table is six feet.

patch
[pætʃ]
n. 헝겊 조각
She sewed[20] *patches* on the elbows of his jacket.

---

17. crack [kræk] *n.* (갈라진) 틈   18. official [əfíʃəl] *n.* 공무원, 관리   19. the Ministry of Education : 교육부
20. sew [sou] *v.* 꿰매다

v. 헝겊 조각을 대다
The mother *patched* the boy's trousers[21].

Practice 3

위 단어를 사용하여 아래 문장을 완성하라. 필요시 단어를 적절한 형태로 변형하라.

1. A drill[22] is one of the important _____ used by dentists[23].
2. There is a(n) _____ in the paper bag that lets sugar run out.
3. He has thousands of books, and they _____ a lot of space.
4. The _____ will lead the town meeting about taxes.
5. Her _____ handwriting[24] is easy to read.

New Vocabulary –4

phrase
[freiz]

n. 구(句), 숙어
He spoke in simple *phrases* so that the children understood him.

portion
[pɔ́:rʃən]

n. 몫, 일부
syn. share
His *portion* of the family property was the largest.

procession
[prəséʃən]

n. 행렬, 행진
syn. march
v. proceed
A funeral[25] *procession* moved along the main street.

quarrel
[kwɔ́rəl]

n. 언쟁, 말싸움, 불화
syn. argument, dispute
We have had a *quarrel* and don't speak to each other.

regret
[rigrét]

n. 유감, 섭섭함, 애석
They said goodbye with great *regret*.

v. 유감으로 여기다, 서운해 하다
I *regret* to say that I cannot help you this time.

---

21. trouser[tráuzər] *n.* (보통 *pl.*) 양복 바지   22. drill[dril] *n.* 천공기   23. dentist[déntist] *n.* 치과 의사
24. handwriting[hǽndraitiŋ] *n.* 필적, 손으로 쓴 글씨   25. funeral[fjú:nərəl] *adj.* 장례식의

reserve
[rizə́ːrv]

v. 남겨두다, 예약을 하다
n. reservation
The seats are *reserved* for old and sick people.

role
[roul]

n. 역할, 배역, 임무
syn. part
His *role* in that movie proved his acting ability[26].

scare
[skɛər]

v. 겁나게 하다, 겁주다
syn. frighten
The sudden noise *scared* her.

serious
[síəriəs]

adj. 진지한, 중대한, 심각한
syn. thoughtful
He spoke about the problem in a *serious* way.

silverware
[sílvərwɛər]

n. 은그릇, 은제품
Her *silverware* consists of knives, forks, spoons, a water pitcher[27], and candlesticks[28].

Practice 4

위 단어를 사용하여 아래 문장을 완성하라. 필요시 단어를 적절한 형태로 변형하라.

1. They were _____ at the strange sound.
2. Raising money for our club is a _____ matter.
3. The first three rows[29] of the hall are _____ for special guests.
4. The children had a _____ about the division[30] of th candy.
5. The workers marched in _____ to the minister's office.

New Vocabulary -5

sole
[soul]

adj. 유일한, 오직 하나의
syn. single, unique, only
ant. multiple
He was the *sole* heir to the fortune[31] when his rich aunt died.
n. 신바닥, 발바닥
The stone cut the *sole* of his foot.

---

26. acting ability : 연기력   27. pitcher[pítʃər] *n.* 물주전자   28. candlestick : 촛대   29. row[rou] *n.* (극장 따위의) 좌석 줄
30. division[divíʒən] *n.* 나눔, 분할   31. fortune[fɔ́ːrtʃən] *n.* 재산

split
[split]

v. 나누다, 분할하다, 쪼개다
syn. divide, crack, break
ant. unite, combine
The boys *split* the money into four shares[32].

stern
[stə:rn]

adj. 엄격한, 단호한
syn. strict, firm, severe
ant. mild, tender, lenient
He is very *stern* in his students' discipline[33].

subtract
[səbtrǽkt]

v. 빼다, 덜다, 감하다
syn. deduct
ant. add
Subtract 2 from 4, and the remainder[34] is 2.

sword
[sɔ:rd]

n. 검, 칼
Those who live by *swords* shall perish[35] by swords.

thorough
[θʌ́:rə]

adj. 철저한, 완전한
syn. complete, absolute
You must give the horse a *thorough* cleaning every day.

tradition
[trədíʃən]

n. 전통, 관례
syn. customs
It is a *tradition* that women get married in long white dress.

unite
[ju(:)náit]

v. 결합하다, 합치다, 통일하다
syn. combine, consolidate
The common interests[36] made the countries *unite*.

vision
[víʒən]

n. 1. 시력, 시각
syn. sight
The old man wears glasses because his *vision* is very poor.

2. 통찰력, 상상력
We need a man of *vision* as president.

widow
[wídou]

n. 과부
ant. widower
A *widow* is a woman whose husband had died, and who has not married again.

---

32. share[ʃɛər] *n.* 몫, 배당된 몫   33. discipline[dísəplin] *n.* 규율, 기강   34. remainder[riméindər] *n.* 나머지
35. perish[périʃ] *v.* 멸망하다, 죽다   36. common interests : 공통적인 이해 관계

Lesson 16 191

Practice 5

위 단어를 사용하여 아래 문장을 완성하라. 필요시 단어를 적절한 형태로 변형하라.

1. According to the old _____, Romulus was the founder[37] of Rome.
2. Our club was _____ by the argument[38].
3. He is a _____ scoundrel[39].
4. The pen is mightier than the _____.
5. Several firms were _____ to form one company.

해답					
Practice 1	1. assembled	2. admire	3. contracted	4. claimed	5. deeds
Practice 2	1. devoted	2. equator	3. divorced	4. federal	5. forbidden
Practice 3	1. instruments	2. leak	3. occupy	4. mayor	5. neat
Practice 4	1. scared	2. serious	3. reserved	4. quarrel	5. procession
Practice 5	1. tradition	2. split	3. thorough	4. sword	5. united

37. founder [fáundər] *n.* 창건자, 창설자   38. argument [á:rgju:mənt] *n.* 논쟁   39. scoundrel [skaundrəl] *n.* 악당, 깡패

Lesson 16

종합 연습 문제

1 이탤릭체로 된 단어와 같은 뜻을 가진 단어를 골라 그 번호를 공란에 써넣어라.

_____ 1. a *thorough* defeat
         (A) severe   (B) complete   (C) critical   (D) hidden

_____ 2. *elegant* behavior
         (A) prompt   (B) greedy   (C) typical   (D) graceful

_____ 3. to *forbid* something
         (A) order   (B) allow   (C) prohibit   (D) mistrust

_____ 4. to *devote* one's life
         (A) admire   (B) reserve   (C) bother   (D) dedicate

_____ 5. a good *deed*
         (A) contest   (B) impression (C) behavior   (D) feature

_____ 6. a medal for *bravery*
         (A) gallery   (B) quarrel   (C) courage   (D) fighting

_____ 7. a *serious* person
         (A) thoughtful (B) attactive   (C) silly   (D) thorough

_____ 8. a *stern* parent
         (A) stupid   (B) unique   (C) chilly   (D) strict

_____ 9. to *esteem* someone
         (A) envy   (B) admire   (C) permit   (D) despise

_____ 10. to *claim* something
         (A) demand   (B) assemble   (C) occupy   (D) contract

2 왼쪽에 주어진 우리말과 같은 뜻을 가진 단어를 골라 그 번호를 공란에 써넣어라.

_____ 1. 과부   (A) bachelor   (B) widow
                          (C) widower   (D) virgin

_____ 2. 전통   (A) impression   (B) procession
                          (C) expedition   (D) tradition

_____ 3. 도구   (A) instrument   (B) deed
                          (C) patch   (D) sword

_____ 4. 말쑥한   (A) neat   (B) stern
                          (C) sole   (D) obvious

_____ 5. 낮추다   (A) subtract   (B) leak
                          (C) lower   (D) fall

Lesson 16
종합 연습 문제

3. 왼쪽에 주어진 단어와 반대되는 뜻을 가진 단어를 골라 그 번호를 공란에 써넣어라.

_____ 1. vulgar   (A) ugly   (B) single
                      (C) elegant   (D) swift

_____ 2. cowardice   (A) well-being   (B) courage
                         (C) scarcity   (D) grief

_____ 3. permit   (A) discourage   (B) lower
                      (C) reserve   (D) forbid

_____ 4. combine   (A) split   (B) scare
                       (C) consolidate   (D) prohibit

_____ 5. stern   (A) abundant   (B) mild
                     (C) severe   (D) thorough

4. 괄호 속에 주어진 우리말과 같은 뜻을 가진 단어를 사용하여 문장을 완성하라.

1. I shouted suddenly to S____E her. (겁주다)

2. How do the very poor E___T on such low wage? (생존하다)

3. Practice will I_____E your handwriting. (개선하다)

4. We heard with R____T that you had failed the examination. (유감)

5. If you saw a man dressed in poor clothes, you might C_____E that he had little money.
(결론짓다)

5. 가장 적합한 단어를 골라 빈칸을 채우라.

1. A foreign firm has _____ to build a new railway across Africa.
    (A) contracted   (B) assembled   (C) subtracted   (D) occupied

2. He hits his gentle wife like a _____.
    (A) feast   (B) victim   (C) beast   (D) beard

3. _____ are better than words when people are in trouble.
    (A) Defects   (B) Visions   (C) Phrases   (D) Deeds

4. It is wrong to _____ yourself only to amusement[40].
    (A) divorce   (B) devote   (C) claim   (D) esteem

5. He did not like his daughter's boyfriend, and _____ her to meet him.
    (A) split   (B) deducted   (C) forbade   (D) mistrusted

---

40. amusement [əmjúːzmənt] ***n.*** 오락, 유흥

Lesson 16

종합 연습 문제

6. _____ is needed to try again after a defeat[41].
   (A) Quarrel   (B) Folly   (C) Bravery   (D) Gallery

7. The wheat has been _____ down to good white flour.
   (A) assembled   (B) forbidden   (C) devoted   (D) ground

8. The air conditioner soon _____ the temperature of the room.
   (A) lowered   (B) improved   (C) reserved   (D) contracted

9. They _____ some of the corn to use as seed[42].
   (A) occupied   (B) scared   (C) reserved   (D) sucked

10. She did her best to fulfil her _____ as a mother.
    (A) patience   (B) role   (C) tradition   (D) crop

6 왼쪽에 주어진 단어의 적당한 파생어를 사용하여 문장을 완성하라.

1. *procession*　After everyone was seated, the chairman _____ to announce his plans.
2. *exist*　Do you believe in the _____ of devils[43] in this world?
3. *conclude*　The astronomer's[44] _____ was that the moon was never part of the earth.
4. *reserve*　You had better make a _____ if you want to make a long trip.
5. *improve*　His schoolwork shows much _____ since last semester.

Answers

1. 1. B　2. D　3. C　4. D　5. C　6. C　7. A　8. D　9. B　10. A
2. 1. B　2. D　3. A　4. A　5. C
3. 1. C　2. B　3. D　4. A　5. B
4. 1. SCARE　2. EXIST　3. IMPROVE　4. REGRET　5. CONCLUDE
5. 1. A　2. C　3. D　4. B　5. C　6. C　7. D　8. A　9. C　10. B
6. 1. proceeded　2. existence　3. conclusion　4. reservation　5. improvement

---

41. defeat [difí:t] *n.* 패배, 실패　42. seed [si:d] *n.* 씨, 종자　43. devil [dévl] *n.* 악마, 귀신　44. astronomer [əstrɔ́nəmər] *n.* 천문학자

LESSON 17

Self-test 17

적당한 단어를 골라 빈칸을 채우라.

1. When all *assist*, the job _____ be done quickly.
   (A) can   (B) can not

2. An *insult* is an act or remark[1] which _____ another's feelings.
   (A) flatters[2]   (B) injures

3. *Clay* is used to _____ bricks, or pots.
   (A) polish   (B) make

4. Milk *spoils* quickly if it is not kept in a _____ place.
   (A) hot   (B) cold

5. Fat ladies _____ to be *lean*.
   (A) want   (B) hate

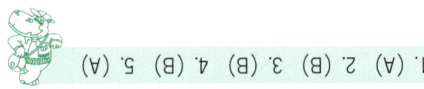
1. (A) 2. (B) 3. (B) 4. (B) 5. (A)

New Vocabulary -1

admit
[ədmít]
v. 받아들이다, 입장〔입학〕을 허가하다
n. admittance, admission
The servant opened the door and *admitted* me into the house.

assist
[əsíst]
v. 돕다, 조력하다
syn. help
She *assisted* her mother with the housework.

behave
[bihéiv]
v. 행동하다, 처신하다
n. behavior
He has *behaved* well to his wife and children as well.

---

1. remark[rimá:rk] *n.* 말, 비평   2. flatter[flǽtər] *v.* 우쭐하게 하다, 아첨하다

cattle [kǽtl]	*n.* 소, 가축 The farmer raises[3] 1,000 head[4] of *cattle* in his farm.
clay [klei]	*n.* 점토(粘土), 찰흙 *Clay* is used for making pots, dishes and bricks.
condemn [kəndém]	*v.* 비난하다, 힐난하다 syn. censure, blame All the newspapers *condemned* the general for his speech attacking a friendly nation[5].
contrary [kɔ́ntrəri]	*adj.* ~에 어긋나는, ~와 상반되는 syn. opposite If you act *contrary* to the doctor's advice, you won't get well again.
crude [kru:d]	*adj.* 1. 가공하지 않은, 자연 그대로의 syn. untreated, raw Oil and sugar are *crude* before being prepared for use. 2. 버릇없는 syn. impolite His manners were *crude* at the party.
defeat [difí:t]	*v.* 이기다, 패배시키다 syn. conquer, overcome, win We *defeated* Lincoln High School in the baseball game yesterday.
differ [dífər]	*v.* 다르다, 틀리다 syn. disagree *n.* difference The two brothers are like each other in appearance but *differ* widely in their tastes[6].

Practice *1*

위 단어를 사용하여 아래 문장을 완성하라. 필요시 단어를 적절한 형태로 변형하라.

1. The children _____ badly; their manners were bad.

2. Only 100 boys are _____ to the school every year.

3. If we had snow in summer, it would be _____ to all experience.

4. In the last class, my answer to the arithmetic[7] problem _____ from hers.

5. He _____ the enemy and was raised to the rank of general as a reward.

---

3. raise[reiz] *v.* 사육하다 4. head *n.* 마리, 수(首) 5. friendly nation : 우방국 6. taste[teist] *n.* 기호, 취미
7. arithmetic[əríθmətik] *adj.* 산술의, 셈본의

New Vocabulary -2

doll
[dɔl]
n. 인형
My granddaughter is as pretty as a little *doll*.

elementary
[eliméntəri]
adj. 초보의, 기본의
syn. introductory
ant. advanced
n. element
The *elementary* principles of mathematics are taught in the lower grades[8] at school.

equip
[ikwíp]
v. 채비를 차리다, 장비를 갖추다
syn. furnish
Is the ship fully *equipped* for its voyage[9]?

exhibit
[igzíbit]
v. 나타내 보이다, 전시하다, 진열하다
syn. show, display
ant. conceal
n. exhibition
Our men *exhibited* great bravery in the battle.

feed
[fi:d]
v. 먹이를 주다, 먹이다, 사육하다
p., pp. fed
She always *feeds* the baby with a spoon.

force
[fɔ:rs]
n. 힘, 완력
syn. strength, power
The thief took the money from the old man by *force*.

gallop
[gǽləp]
v. 질주하다, 구보하다
The wild horse *galloped* down the hill.
n. 질주, 구보
She went through[10] the work at a *gallop*[11], so it can't have been done very well.

grip
[grip]
v. 꽉 붙잡다, 단단히 쥐다
syn. seize, grab
He *gripped* the boy by the arm.

hind
[haind]
adj. 뒤쪽의, 후방의
syn. back, rear, posterior

---

8. lower grade : 저학년   9. voyage[vɔidʒ] *n.* 항해   10. go through ~ : ~을 마치다   11. at a gallop : 전속력으로

	ant. fore, front
	The *hind* wings of some insects[12] are shorter than the fore wings.
impulse [ímpʌls]	**n.** 충동, 충격
	adj. impulsive
	A sudden *impulse* of anger arose in him when he was insulted.

Practice 2

위 단어를 사용하여 아래 문장을 완성하라. 필요시 단어를 적절한 형태로 변형하라.

1. He _____ interest whenever you talk about dogs.
2. He _____ the nail[13] and pulled it out.
3. The horse rose on its _____ legs.
4. The boy found a cave and stepped in it under the _____ of curiosity.
5. The expedition[14] was fully _____ with food, tents, medical and other supplies[15].

New Vocabulary -3

insult [ínsʌlt]	**n.** 모욕, 무례
	To call a brave man a coward[16] is an *insult*.
	v. 모욕하다, 창피주다
	syn. offend
	ant. respect, honor, praise
	The man *insulted* me by calling me a liar.
jury [dʒúəri]	**n.** 배심원
	The *jury* decided the man was guilty.
lean [li:n]	**v.** 기울이다, 굽히다, 기대다
	syn. slant, slope
	He *leaned* forward to hear what she said to him.
	adj. 야윈, 마른
	syn. slender
	Do you see a *lean* lady walking across the street?

---

12. insect[ínsekt] **n.** 곤충   13. nail[neil] **n.** 못   14. expedition[ekspidíʃən] **n.** 탐험(대), 원정(대)
15. supply[səplái] **n.** (때로 *pl.*) 생활 필수품   16. coward[káuərd] **n.** 겁쟁이

loyal [lɔ́iəl]	*adj.* 충성스런, 충실한 **syn.** faithful *n.* loyalty As a *loyal* citizen, he supported his government.
meantime [míːntaim]	*n.* 동안, 중간 시간 **syn.** meanwhile Her husband left at four and returned at seven, and in the *meantime* she wrote three letters.
mixture [míkstʃər]	*n.* 혼합, 혼합물 Green is a *mixture* of yellow and blue.
needle [níːdl]	*n.* 바늘, 침(針) Mother sewed the button on my coat with *needle* and thread.
occur [əkə́ːr]	*v.* 발생하다, 일어나다 **syn.** happen *n.* occurrence The terrible car accident *occurred* last Friday.
overlook [ouvərlúk]	*v.* 내려다보다, 굽어 보다 Our garden is *overlooked* by the neighbor's window.
path [pæθ]	*n.* 길, 통로, 진로 **syn.** route The moon has a regular *path* through the sky.

Practice 3

위 단어를 사용하여 아래 문장을 완성하라. 필요시 단어를 적절한 형태로 변형하라.

1. Your refusal[17] to believe my story is a(n) _____ to me.
2. This tobacco is a(n) _____ of three different sorts.
3. It had never _____ to me to say "thanks."
4. From our house on the hillside, we can _____ the whole city.
5. Grass has grown over the _____ through the woods.

---

17. refusal[rifjúːzəl] *n.* 거절

New Vocabulary -4

physical
[fízikəl]

adj. 1. 물질적인, 물리적인
syn. material
They study the *physical* features[18] of the earth in the science class.

2. 육체적인, 신체적인
ant. spiritual, mental
The doctor's examination showed that he was in excellent *physical* condition.

positive
[pázətiv]

adj. 확실한, 명확한
syn. unquestionable
We have *positive* knowledge that the earth moves around the sum.

proclaim
[prəkléim]

v. 선언하다, 공포하다, 포고하다
syn. announce, declare
Many former colonies[19] have *proclaimed* their independence.

queer
[kwíər]

adj. 기묘한, 이상한, 별난
syn. unusual, strange
ant. ordinary, normal
There was something *queer* about the way he walked.

reign
[rein]

n. 통치, 지배
syn. rule
The queen's *reign* lasted[20] more than fifty years.

v. 통치하다, 지배하다
He *reigned* over the small country for ten years.

reside
[rizáid]

v. 1. 살다, 거주하다
syn. live
He has *resided* abroad for over ten years.

2. 존재하다, 있다
syn. exist
Her charm *resides* in her happy smile.

rooster
[rú:stər]

n. 수탉
syn. cock

---

18. feature[fí:tʃər] *n.* (*pl.*) 생김새, 모양   19. colony[káləni] *n.* 식민지   20. last[læst] *v.* 지속하다, 계속되다

	ant. hen
	A *rooster* was leading many hens.
scarf [skɑːrf]	***n.*** 목도리, 스카프 **syn.** muffler The girl wore[21] a green *scarf* over her shoulders[22].
servant [sə́ːrvənt]	***n.*** 하인, 종, 고용인 **ant.** master They have two *servants*, a cook[23] and a maid.
similarity [similéræti]	***n.*** 닮은 점, 유사성 **syn.** likeness, resemblance **ant.** difference Their differences are more noticeable than their *similarities*.

Practice 4

위 단어를 사용하여 아래 문장을 완성하라. 필요시 단어를 적절한 형태로 변형하라.

1. How much _____ is there between the two religions?

2. The ringing bells _____ the news of the birth of the prince.

3. The power to legislate _____ in the legislative[24].

4. A politician should be a _____ of the people.

5. The guard has _____ instructions not to admit anyone.

---

21. wore[wɔːr] ***v.*** wear(입다)의 과거   22. shoulder[ʃóuldər] ***n.*** 어깨   23. cook[kuk] ***n.*** 요리사   24. legislative[lédʒislətiv] ***n.*** 입법부
(*cf.* legislate : 법률을 제정하다)

New Vocabulary -5

solemn
[sɔ́ləm]
adj. 엄숙한, 진지한
syn. serious, grave
ant. playful
We watched the *solemn* ceremony in the church.

spoil
[spɔil]
v. 상하게 하다, 썩게 하다
syn. damage, ruin
She *spoiled* the meat by burning it.

stiff
[stif]
adj. 뻣뻣한, 굳은
syn. rigid
ant. flexible
Leather shoes are usually *stiff* when they are new.

subway
[sʌ́bwei]
n. 지하철, 지하도
He always goes to work by *subway*.

syllable
[síləbl]
n. 음절(音節)
There are two *syllables* in the word "button."

thread
[θred]
n. 실
Nylon thread is stronger than cotton *thread*.

trademark
[tréidmɑːrk]
n. 등록 상표
syn. label, brand
The registration[25] and protection of *trademarks* are now provided for by law.

university
[juːnivə́ːrsəti]
n. 종합 대학, 대학교
Several new *universities* have been built in the last ten years.

vocabulary
[vəkǽbjuləri]
n. 어휘, 단어
A lot of reading will increase your *vocabulary*.

wilderness
[wíldərnis]
n. 황야, 황무지
Jesus went out into the *wilderness* to think alone.

---

25. registration [redʒistréiʃən] *n.* 등록, 등기

Practice 5

위 단어를 사용하여 아래 문장을 완성하라. 필요시 단어를 적절한 형태로 변형하라.

1. She used silk _____ in sewing her dress.
2. He gave his _____ promise to defend his country.
3. A group of travellers were lost in the _____.
4. The _____ of science has grown tremendously[26] in the past 20 years.
5. A(n) _____ consists of several colleges, as of liberal arts[27], law, medicine, etc.

Practice 1	1. behaved	2. admitted	3. contrary	4. differed	5. defeated
Practice 2	1. exhibits	2. gripped	3. hind	4. impulse	5. equipped
Practice 3	1. insult	2. mixture	3. occurred	4. overlook	5. path
Practice 4	1. similarity	2. proclaimed	3. resides	4. servant	5. positive
Practice 5	1. thread	2. solemn	3. wilderness	4. vocabulary	5. university

26. tremendously [triméndəsli] *adv.* 엄청나게, 어마어마하게   27. liberal arts : 교양학과

종합 연습 문제

1 네 개의 단어 중 다른 셋과 관련이 없는 것을 골라 공란에 그 번호를 써넣어라.

_____ 1. (A) prohibit (B) declare (C) announce (D) proclaim
_____ 2. (A) likeness (B) similarity (C) resemblance (D) mixture
_____ 3. (A) hind (B) fore (C) back (D) rear
_____ 4. (A) power (B) strength (C) bravery (D) force
_____ 5. (A) admit (B) blame (C) condemn (D) censure
_____ 6. (A) queer (B) lean (C) unusual (D) strange
_____ 7. (A) grave (B) solemn (C) contrary (D) serious
_____ 8. (A) vanish (B) defeat (C) conquer (D) overcome
_____ 9. (A) untreated (B) raw (C) crude (D) stern
_____ 10. (A) exhibit (B) differ (C) display (D) show

2 왼쪽에 주어진 우리말과 같은 뜻을 가진 단어를 골라 그 번호를 공란에 써넣어라.

_____ 1. 모욕하다 (A) defeat (B) condemn (C) proclaim (D) insult

_____ 2. 종합 대학 (A) college (B) university (C) vocabulary (D) mixture

_____ 3. ~와 상반되는 (A) contrary (B) crude (C) positive (D) loyal

_____ 4. 배심원 (A) gallop (B) clay (C) jury (D) mayor

_____ 5. 내려다보다 (A) spoil (B) mistrust (C) overlook (D) regret

3 왼쪽에 주어진 단어와 반대되는 뜻을 가진 단어를 골라 그 번호를 공란에 써넣어라.

_____ 1. conceal (A) offend (B) exhibit (C) reside (D) disagree

_____ 2. difference (A) path (B) esteem (C) similarity (D) courage

_____ 3. physical (A) raw (B) stiff (C) elementary (D) mental

_____ 4. respect (A) behavior (B) insult (C) proclaim (D) differ

_____ 5. ordinary (A) queer (B) physical (C) positive (D) grave

_____ 6. servant (A) regret (B) master (C) negative (D) impulse

Lesson 17 종합 연습 문제

4 괄호 속에 주어진 우리말과 같은 뜻을 가진 단어를 사용하여 문장을 완성하라.

1. The I_____E of hunger compelled[28] the proud man to go begging for bread. (충동)
2. Cows, bulls[29], steers[30], and oxen are C____E. (가축)
3. Will you please F__D my cat for me? (먹이를 주다)
4. You must B____E well to your seniors[31]. (행동하다)
5. The N____E of compass shows we are facing north. (바늘)

5 이탤릭체로 된 단어와 같은 뜻을 가진 단어를 골라 그 번호를 공란에 써넣어라.

_____ 1. Where do you *reside* now?
    (A) reserve   (B) live   (C) reign   (D) exist

_____ 2. It had never *occurred* to me to think she was a widow.
    (A) exist   (B) behave   (C) express   (D) happen

_____ 3. He had a choice between the shorter or the better *path*.
    (A) route   (B) cock   (C) subway   (D) role

_____ 4. He wanted to be *loyal* to his firm as well as to his family.
    (A) solemn   (B) thorough   (C) faithful   (D) positive

_____ 5. The frightened boy *gripped* his mother's hand.
    (A) contracted   (B) ground   (C) spoiled   (D) seized

_____ 6. She *assisted* him in building the house.
    (A) behaved   (B) occupied   (C) forbade   (D) helped

_____ 7. What a *queer* story it is!
    (A) unusual   (B) interesting   (C) old   (D) silly

_____ 8. The heavy rain *spoiled* the crops.
    (A) subtracted   (B) ruined   (C) improved   (D) lowered

_____ 9. This paint brush is too *stiff* to use.
    (A) lean   (B) solemn   (C) rigid   (D) good

_____ 10. The child *exhibited* a bad temper[32] at an early age.
    (A) concealed   (B) showed   (C) spoiled   (D) conquered

---

28. *compel*[kəmpél] *v.* 억지로 ~시키다   29. *bull*[bul] *n.* 수소   30. *steer*[stiər] *n.* 수송아지   31. *senior*[síːnjər] *n.* 선배, 손윗사람
32. *temper*[témpər] *n.* 기질, 성미

Lesson 17 종합 연습 문제

Answers

1. 1. A 2. D 3. B 4. C 5. A 6. B 7. C 8. A 9. D 10. B

2. 1. D 2. B 3. A 4. C 5. C

3. 1. B 2. C 3. D 4. B 5. A 6. B

4. 1. IMPULSE 2. CATTLE 3. FEED 4. BEHAVE 5. NEEDLE

5. 1. B 2. D 3. A 4. C 5. D 6. D 7. A 8. B 9. C 10. B

LESSON 18

Self-test 18

적당한 단어를 골라 빈칸을 채우라.

1. Water becomes *solid* when it _____.
   (A) freezes   (B) boils

2. When a person is *exhausted*, he has _____ strength left.
   (A) much   (B) little

3. Her best *garment* is the red _____ with lace¹.
   (A) dress   (B) doll

4. It was *cruel* of him to make the donkey carry such a _____ load.
   (A) heavy   (B) light

5. This machine is _____ because of the *defects* in it.
   (A) expensive   (B) unsafe

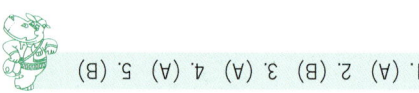

1. (A) 2. (B) 3. (A) 4. (A) 5. (B)

New Vocabulary -1

advance
[ədvǽns]

n. 1. 전진, 진출, 진행
ant. withdrawal
There were so many people that our *advance* was slow.

2. 진보, 진척, 향상
syn. progress
We had made great *advance* in airplane design.

assure
[əʃúər]

v. 보증하다, 안심시키다
syn. guarantee, convince
n. assurance
The captain *assured* the passengers² that there was no danger.

---

1. lace [leis] *n.* 레이스(각종 장식천)   2. passenger [pǽsindʒər] *n.* 승객, 여객

biology [baiɔ́lədʒi]	***n.*** 생물학 Specialists[3] in *biology* study the origin[4] and structure of plant and animal life.
brilliant [bríljənt]	***adj.*** 1. 찬란한, 빛나는 We have had a week of *brilliant* sunshine. 2. 훌륭한, 뛰어난, 혁혁한 ***n.*** brilliance Everyone likes to hear him; he is a *brilliant* speaker.
cause [kɔːz]	***n.*** 원인, 이유, 근거 **syn.** reason **ant.** consequence The flood last month was the *cause* of much damage.
colony [kɔ́ləni]	***n.*** 식민지 Canada and Australia used to be British *colonies*; now they are self-governing[5].
conduct [kɔ́ndəkt]	***n.*** 행위, 행동, 행실 **syn.** behavior The children were rewarded for good *conduct* and punished for bad conduct.
contrast [kəntrǽst]	***v.*** 대조시키다, 대비(對比)시키다 *Contrast* these foreign goods[6] with the domestic products.
cruel [krúːəl]	***adj.*** 잔인한, 무자비한 **syn.** merciless **ant.** merciful ***n.*** cruelty The *cruel* master beat his slaves mercilessly with a whip[7].
defect [difékt]	***n.*** 결점, 결함 **syn.** fault, shortcoming ***adj.*** defective The car was unsafe because of a *defect* in its construction[8].

Practice 1

위 단어를 사용하여 아래 문장을 완성하라. 필요시 단어를 적절한 형태로 변형하라.

1. The teacher _____ the hot climate of our country with the cold climate of another in the last class.

---

3. specialist[spéʃəlist] ***n.*** 전문가   4. orgin[ɔ́ridʒin] ***n.*** 기원, 발생   5. self-governing[self-gʌ́vərniŋ] ***adj.*** 자치제(自治制)의
6. foreign goods : 외국 상품   7. whip[hwip] ***n.*** 매, 채찍   8. construction[kənstrʌ́kʃən] ***n.*** 구조

2. He is much interested in plant and animal life; he will study _____ in the university.

3. A(n) _____ is a country or area under the control of a distant country and settled by people from that country.

4. We tried to _____ the nervous[9] old lady that flying in an airplane was quite safe.

5. You are old enough to know the rules of _____[10].

New Vocabulary -2

differentiate
[difərénʃieit]
v. 구별하다, 차별하다
syn. distinguish
Can you *differentiate* this kind of rose from the others?

domestic
[dəméstik]
adj. 국내의, 국산의
ant. foreign, alien
Most newspapers publish both *domestic* and foreign news.

embrace
[imbréis]
v. 포옹하다, 껴안다
syn. hug
She *embraced* the pretty baby with great affection[11].

error
[érər]
n. 잘못, 오류, 틀림
syn. mistake
adj. erroneous
I failed my test because of *errors* in spelling.

exhaust
[igzɔ́ːst]
v. 고갈시키다, (체력, 자원을) 다 소모하다
They were almost *exhausted* when they reached the top of the mountain.

festival
[féstəvəl]
n. 축제, 축전, 제전
syn. celebration
Every year the city has a summer music *festival* in August.

formation
[fɔːrméiʃən]
n. 형성, 구성
syn. structure
School life has a great influence on the *formation* of a child's character.

---

9. nervous [nə́ːrvəs] *adj.* 신경질적인, 흥분하는   10. the rules of conduct : 행동 규범   11. with great affection : 다정스럽게

garment
[gá:rmənt]

n. 의복, 옷
syn. costume
A new *garment* should be washed carefully.

groan
[groun]

v. 신음하다, 끙끙거리다
syn. moan
The wounded man lay there *groaning*, with no one to help him.

n. 신음 소리, 끙끙거리는 소리
We heard the *groans* of the man who had fallen off the cliff[12].

hire
[háiər]

v. 1. (물건을) 세내고 빌리다
He *hired* a car and a man to drive it.

2. (사람을) 고용하다
syn. employ
ant. fire
The storekeeper[13] *hired* a boy to deliver groceries[14].

Practice 2

위 단어를 사용하여 아래 문장을 완성하라. 필요시 단어를 적절한 형태로 변형하라.

1. The nation is going to have a week of _____ in honor of[15] the king's marriage.
2. The tired horse _____ under the heavy load[16].
3. The government urged the people to buy _____ goods, not foreign goods.
4. The two sisters met and _____ each other.
5. The climbing up the hill in an hour completely _____ us.

---

12. cliff [klif] *n.* 절벽, 벼랑   13. storekeeper : 상점 주인   14. grocery [gróusəri] *n.* (보통 *pl.*) 식료품
15. in honor of ~ : ~을 축하하여, ~에 경의를 표하여   16. under the heavy load : 무거운 짐에 눌려

New Vocabulary -3

incidental
[insidéntl]
adj. 부수하여 일어나는, 흔히 발생하는
n. incident
Certain discomforts[17] are *incidental* to the joys of camping out.

intelligent
[intélidʒənt]
adj. 이성적인, 지성적인
syn. clever, brilliant
ant. stupid, dull
n. intelligence
All human beings[18] are more *intelligent* than animals.

justice
[dʒʌ́stis]
n. 정의, 공정, 정당
syn. fairness, rightness
Judges should have a sense of *justice*.

leap
[li:p]
v. 뛰다, 날뛰다
syn. jump
He *leaped* with joy at a good news.

luck
[lʌk]
n. 행운, 운
adj. lucky
adv. luckily
She had the *luck* to win first prize.

measure
[méʒər]
v. 치수를 재다, 측정하다
n. measurement
The tailor *measured* me for a new suit of clothes[19].

mock
[mɔk]
v. 조롱하다, 놀리다
The naughty[20] boys *mocked* the blind beggar.

negative
[négətiv]
adj. 부정적인, 거부적인
ant. positive, affirmative
The unhappy man has a *negative* attitude toward life.

odd
[ɔd]
adj. 이상한, 괴이한, 기묘한
syn. strange, unusual
Life would be very dull without the *odd* adventures now and then[21].

---

17. discomfort[diskʌ́mfərt] *n.* 불편　　18. human being : 인간　　19. a suit of clothes : 옷 한 벌　　20. naughty[nɔ́ːti] *adj.* 장난꾸러기의, 버릇없는
21. now and then : 이따금, 때때로

owe
[ou]

v. ~에 신세지다, ~에 빚지다

He *owes* his success to good luck more than to his ability.

Practice 3

위 단어를 사용하여 아래 문장을 완성하라. 필요시 단어를 적절한 형태로 변형하라.

1. All men should be treated with _____.
2. We _____ the room and found it was 20 feet long and 15 feet wide.
3. We must know that we _____ a great deal to our parents and teachers.
4. We must take precautions[22] against dangers _____ to a soldier's life.
5. The sounds of a foreign language are always _____ to non-natives[23].

New Vocabulary -4

patience
[péiʃəns]

n. 인내, 참을성
syn. forbearance
adj. patient
It needs grant *patience* to teach little children.

physician
[fizíʃən]

n. 내과 의사
ant. surgeon
The *physician* gave his sick patient some strong medicine.

possess
[pəzés]

v. 소유하다, 가지다
syn. own
He didn't have much money, but he always *possessed* good health.

profession
[prəféʃən]

n. (전문적인) 직업
syn. occupation
adj. professional
He is preparing for the teaching *profession*.

quit
[kwit]

v. 그만두다, 끊다, 중지하다
syn. cease, stop
ant. continue
The doctor told his patient to *quit* smoking and drinking.

---

22. precaution [prikɔ́ːʃən] *n.* 예방 조치   23. non-native [nɔ́n-néitiv] *n.* 비토착민, 이국인

reject
[ridʒékt]

v. 거절하다, 거부하다, 퇴짜놓다
syn. refuse
He tried to join the army but was *rejected* because of his poor health.

resign
[rizáin]

v. 사임하다, 사직하다
ant. undertake
n. resignation
The man *resigned* from his job because of illness.

rotten
[rɔ́tn]

adj. 썩은, 부패한
ant. fresh
The apples fallen on the ground will soon become *rotten*.

scatter
[skǽtər]

v. 흩뿌리다, 분산시키다
syn. sprinkle
The farmer *scattered* seeds[24] on the field.

severe
[sivíər]

adj. 가혹한, 심한, 통렬한
syn. strict, cruel
ant. gentle
The man was given a *severe* punishment for stealing.

Practice 4

위 단어를 사용하여 아래 문장을 완성하라. 필요시 단어를 적절한 형태로 변형하라.

1. The cat watched the mouse hole[25] with great _____.

2. He was _____ from the army because of his bad eyes.

3. There is a great social difference between business and the _____.

4. He was told to _____ ashes[26] on the icy sidewalk[27].

5. She was forced to _____ her position as secretary of the club.

---

24. seed[siːd] *n.* 씨, 종자   25. mouse hole : 쥐구멍   26. ash[æʃ] *n.* (불탄 후의) 재   27. icy sidewalk : 미끄러운 보도

New Vocabulary -5

sin
[sin]

n. (종교, 도덕상의) 죄(罪), 죄악
cf. crime
Lying, stealing, dishonesty, and cruelty[28] are *sins*.

solid
[sɔ́lid]

adj. 단단한, 견고한, 고체의
syn. firm
When water freezes and becomes *solid*, we call it ice.

n. 고체
At what temperature does water become a *solid*?

spokesman
[spóuksmən]

n. 대변인, 대변자
At the meeting the *spokesman* for the government gave us the President's views[29].

still
[stil]

adj. 잠잠한, 고요한
syn. motionless, quiet
The room was *still* at the end of his speech.

suck
[sʌk]

v. 빨다, 빨아먹다
The baby *sucked* milk from its mother's breast[30].

symbolize
[símbəlaiz]

v. 상징하다, 나타내다
syn. represent
The red color *symbolizes* danger in many countries.

threat
[θret]

n. 협박, 으름장
Your *threats* will not stop me from going.

traffic
[trǽfik]

n. 통행, 교통, 교통량
The police control the *traffic* in large cities.

volcano
[vɔlkéinou]

n. 화산
A dormant *volcano*[31] may explode at any time.

wipe
[waip]

v. 닦다, 씻다
She *wiped* the dishes with paper towel.

---

28. cruelty [krúəlti] *n.* 잔학, 잔인   29. President's views : 대통령의 견해   30. breast [brest] *n.* 젖, 유방
31. dormant volcano : 휴화산(休火山)

Practice 5

위 단어를 사용하여 아래 문장을 완성하라. 필요시 단어를 적절한 형태로 변형하라.

1. The baby tried to _____ the orange juice through a straw[32].

2. That door is made of a _____ piece of wood.

3. He was the _____ for the workers in the strike against the factory owner.

4. An extinct[33] _____ has ceased to be able to explode.

5. He asked the noisy children to be _____.

Practice 1	1. contrasted	2. biology	3. colony	4. assure	5. conduct
Practice 2	1. festival	2. groaned	3. domestic	4. embraced	5. exhausted
Practice 3	1. justice	2. measured	3. owe	4. incidental	5. odd
Practice 4	1. patience	2. rejected	3. professions	4. scatter	5. resign
Practice 5	1. suck	2. solid	3. spokesman	4. volcano	5. still

32. straw [strɔː] ***n.*** 빨대, 스트로   33. extinct [ikstíŋkt] ***adj.*** 꺼진, 끊어진, 소멸된

종합 연습 문제

1 이탤릭체로 된 단어와 같은 뜻을 가진 단어를 골라 그 번호를 공란에 써넣어라.

_____ 1. to *reject* one's suggestion   (A) proclaim   (B) resign
                                                                             (C) refuse   (D) overlook

_____ 2. an old *garment*   (A) thread   (B) costume
                                                       (C) patch   (D) gallop

_____ 3. *groan* of a sick man   (A) profession   (B) regret
                                                            (C) outbreak   (D) moan

_____ 4. *merciless* punishment   (A) cruel   (B) odd
                                                         (C) crude   (D) unusual

_____ 5. *odd* behavior   (A) dangerous   (B) contrary
                                         (C) lean   (D) strange

_____ 6. my friend's *defects*   (A) errors   (B) insults
                                                     (C) shortcomings   (D) regrets

_____ 7. to lose one's *patience*   (A) justice   (B) forbearance
                                                       (C) courage   (D) strength

_____ 8. to *hire* someone   (A) reject   (B) admire
                                                 (C) employ   (D) hide

_____ 9. to *laugh* at one's behavior   (A) encourage   (B) mock
                                                             (C) mistrust   (D) assist

_____ 10. to *own* a house   (A) possess   (B) owe
                                         (C) hire   (D) equip

2 왼쪽에 주어진 우리말과 같은 뜻을 가진 단어를 골라 그 번호를 공란에 써넣어라.

_____ 1. 행위   (A) threat   (B) conduct
                     (C) cause   (D) error

_____ 2. 생물학   (A) biology   (B) colony
                       (C) surgeon   (D) vocabulary

_____ 3. 포옹하다   (A) owe   (B) possess
                         (C) assure   (D) embrace

_____ 4. 축제   (A) profession   (B) volcano
                     (C) festival   (D) gallery

_____ 5. 인내   (A) error   (B) patience
                     (C) bravery   (D) justice

Lesson 18 종합 연습 문제

3 왼쪽에 주어진 단어와 반대되는 뜻을 가진 단어를 골라 그 번호를 공란에 써넣어라.

_____ 1. merciful   (A) stiff   (B) incidental
                           (C) cruel   (D) motionless

_____ 2. foreign   (A) dangerous   (B) strange
                           (C) federal   (D) domestic

_____ 3. rotten   (A) fresh   (B) queer
                           (C) neat   (D) mild

_____ 4. hire   (A) quit   (B) fire
                           (C) scatter   (D) continue

_____ 5. withdrawal   (A) advance   (B) possess
                           (C) exhaust   (D) leap

4 괄호 속에 주어진 우리말과 같은 뜻을 가진 단어를 사용하여 문장을 완성하라.

1. I obeyed her order but only under the T____T of punishment. (협박)
2. I don't have the P_____E to hear your complaints[34] again. (참을성)
3. The J_____E of these remarks[35] was clear to everyone. (공정)
4. If you don't like your job, you may Q__T it. (그만두다)
5. There is heavy T_____C on the street during the rush hours. (교통량)

5 가장 적합한 단어를 골라 빈칸을 채우라.

1. Carelessness is often the _____ of fires.
   (A) errors   (B) cause   (C) threat   (D) consequence

2. In the elementary school there is often a prize for good _____.
   (A) conduct   (B) defect   (C) servant   (D) threat

3. He could not _____ green color from red one.
   (A) measure   (B) symbolize   (C) exhibit   (D) differentiate

4. The doctor _____ him that his child would recover from the illness.
   (A) refused   (B) assisted   (C) contrasted   (D) assured

5. _____ was with us and we won easily in the baseball game.
   (A) Defect   (B) Luck   (C) Vision   (D) Justice

6. Heat causes the _____ of the steam from water.
   (A) mixture   (B) scarcity   (C) formation   (D) profession

---

34. **complaint** [kəmpléint] ***n.*** 불평   35. **remark** [rimάːrk] ***n.*** 말, 의견

Lesson 18

종합 연습 문제

7. The thoughtless children _____ the speech of the new boy.
   (A) mocked   (B) sucked   (C) owned   (D) owed

8. A dog _____ a keen sense of smell[36].
   (A) embraces   (B) symbolizes   (C) behaves   (D) possesses

9. I _____ it to you that I am still alive.
   (A) reign   (B) hire   (C) owe   (D) own

10. A dove[37] _____ peace, whereas[38] a hawk[39] _____ war.
    (A) symbolizes   (B) contrasts   (C) assures   (D) differentiates

6 왼쪽에 주어진 단어의 적당한 파생어를 사용하여 문장을 완성하라.

1. *error*   The facts are correct, but your conclusion is _____.
2. *brilliant* The diamond glowed with a pure white _____.
3. *measure*   The _____ of individual intelligence is very difficult.
4. *incidental* The _____ has been forgotten for a long time.
5. *assure*   The plumber gave us his _____ that he would fix the pipes tomorrow.

Answers

1. 1. C   2. B   3. D   4. A   5. D   6. C   7. B   8. C   9. B   10. A
2. 1. B   2. A   3. D   4. C   5. B
3. 1. C   2. D   3. A   4. B   5. A
4. 1. THREAT   2. PATIENCE   3. JUSTICE   4. QUIT   5. TRAFFIC
5. 1. B   2. A   3. D   4. D   5. B   6. C   7. A   8. D   9. C   10. A
6. 1. erroneous   2. brilliance   3. measurement   4. incident   5. assurance

---

36. sense of smell : 후각   37. dove[dʌv] *n.* 비둘기   38. whereas[hwɛəræz] *conj.* ~에 반하여, ~하는 반면   39. hawk[hɔːk] *n.* 매

LESSON 19

Self-test 19

적당한 단어를 골라 빈칸을 채우라.

1. We _____ sugar and flour[1] at the *grocery*.
   (A) buy   (B) make

2. If someone *neglects* his duty, he gives _____ attention[2] to it.
   (A) much   (B) little

3. A *cautious* driver never drives his car too _____.
   (A) slow   (B) fast

4. Food must be _____ well to be *digested* properly[3].
   (A) chewed   (B) cooked

5. We built a new *fort* the south to _____ people.
   (A) protect   (B) carry

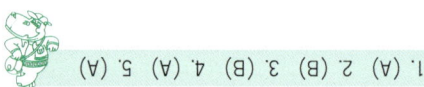

1. (A) 2. (B) 3. (B) 4. (A) 5. (A)

New Vocabulary -1

advantage　　*n.* 유리, 이익
[ədvǽntidʒ]　　syn. benefit, profit, gain
　　　　　　　　He had the *advantage* of being born into a rich family.

atmosphere　　*n.* 1. 대기(大氣), 공기
[ǽtməsfiər]　　syn. air
　　　　　　　　Most cities no longer have a clear *atmosphere*.
　　　　　　　　2. 분위기, 기분
　　　　　　　　There is an *atmosphere* of calm and peace in the country that is quite different from the *atmosphere* of a big city.

---

1. flour[flauər] *n.* 밀가루, 분말　　2. attention[əténʃən] *n.* 주의, 관심　　3. properly[prɔ́pərli] *adv.* 적당하게

broad
[brɔːd]

adj. 폭이 넓은, 광대한
syn. wide
ant. narrow
Miss Kwon, our English teacher, has *broad* experience with children.

cautious
[kɔ́ːʃəs]

adj. 주의깊은, 조심하는, 신중한
syn. careful
n. caution
A *cautious* thinker does not believe things without proof[4].

color-blind
[kʌ́lərblaind]

adj. 색맹의
A *color-blind* man can't tell red from green.

conference
[kɔ́nfərəns]

n. 회의, 회합
syn. meeting, parley
Many international *conferences* have been held at Geneva.

contribute
[kəntríbju(ː)t]

v. 1. 기여하다, 공헌하다
Honesty and hard work *contribute* to success and to happiness.

2. 기부하다, 기증하다
n. contribution
Each worker *contributed* a dollar to the Red Cross[5].

crush
[krʌʃ]

v. 눌러 부수다, 짓이기다
syn. smash, break
Wine is made by *crushing* grapes.

defend
[difénd]

v. 방어하다, 지키다
syn. guard
ant. attack
n. defense
When the dog attacked me, I *defended* myself with my stick[6].

digest
[daidʒést]

v. 소화하다
n. digestion
If you rest for half an hour after a meal, you will *digest* your food more easily.

---

4. proof[pruːf] *n.* 증거   5. the Red Cross : 적십자사   6. stick[stik] *n.* 지팡이, 막대기

Practice 1

위 단어를 사용하여 아래 문장을 완성하라. 필요시 단어를 적절한 형태로 변형하라.

1. The director of the school[7] is in _____ now; you can see him later.
2. It will be to your _____ to study Spanish before you visit Mexico.
3. Everyone was asked to _____ suggestions for the party.
4. His hat was _____ when the girl sat on it.
5. The fort cannot be _____ against an air attack.

New Vocabulary -2

dot
[dɔt]

n. 작은 점
syn. point
We watched the ship until it became a mere *dot* on the horizon.

emergency
[imə́:rdʒənsi]

n. 비상 사태, 위급한 사태
syn. crisis
I keep a box of tools and a fire extinguisher[8] in my car for use in an *emergency*.

escape
[iskéip]

v. 탈출하다, 도망하다
syn. flee
The soldier *escaped* from the enemy's prison.

executive
[igzékjutiv]

adj. 행정의, 행정상의
The *executive* branch[9] carries out the laws which have been made by the legislature[10].

fetch
[fetʃ]

v. 가져오다, 데리고 오다
Please *fetch* me the dictionary from the study room.

fort
[fɔ:rt]

n. 요새, 보루
syn. fortress
v. fortify
They decided to build a new *fort* to protect inhabitants[11] of that area.

---

7. director of the school : 학교 이사, (고등학교의) 교장   8. fire extinguisher *n.* 소화기(消火器)   9. the executive branch : 행정부
10. legislature [lédʒisleitʃər] *n.* 입법부   11. inhabitant [inhǽbitənt] *n.* 주민, 거주자

gasp
[gæsp]

n. 헐떡거림, 숨참
The fireman heard the *gasps* of a boy in the smoky room.

v. 헐떡거리다, 숨이 막히다
He *gasped* for air as he ran from the smoke-filled room.

grocery
[gróusəri]

n. 식료품점, (보통 *pl.*) 식료품
We buy our rice at the nearest *grocery*.

hollow
[hɔ́lou]

adj. 1. 속이 빈, 텅 빈
syn. empty, void, unfilled
A tube or pipe is *hollow*, and it is not heavy.

2. 움푹한, 오목한
A starving person has *hollow* eyes and cheeks.

inclination
[inklinéiʃən]

n. 경향, 성향, 성벽
syn. disposition
Most boys have a strong *inclination* for sports.

Practice 2

위 단어를 사용하여 아래 문장을 완성하라. 필요시 단어를 적절한 형태로 변형하라.

1. Please _____ me a clean handkerchief from my bedroom.

2. The President for the United States is the head of the _____ branch of the government.

3. This fire extinguisher is to be used only in a(n) _____.

4. He _____ the fire in the house by jumping out of the window when he smelled smoke.

5. The horse and rider moved further and further away until they became only a(n) _____ in the distance.

New Vocabulary -3

intend
[inténd]
v. (~할) 작정이다, (~하려고) 생각하다
syn. mean, plan, purpose
I *intended* to get up early, but forgot to set the alarm.

keen
[ki:n]
adj. 1. 날카로운, 예리한
syn. sharp, acute
ant. dull
Be careful with that knife. It's got a *keen* edge[12].

2. 신랄한, 통렬한
Like a knife, a woman's tongue is very *keen*.

leather
[léəər]
n. 가죽
His shoes are made of *leather* imported from England.

lumber
[lʌ́mbər]
n. 재목, 목재
syn. timber
They bought some *lumber* to make their fence.

mechanic
[mikǽnik]
n. 직공, 기계공, 수리공
The automobile *mechanic* repaired my car.

mode
[moud]
n. 형태, 방법, 양식
syn. method, fashion
He suddenly became wealthy, which changed his *mode* of life.

neglect
[niglékt]
v. 게을리하다, 돌보지 않다
syn. disregard, ignore
Don't *neglect* writing to your parents at least once a month.

offend
[əfénd]
v. 성나게 하다, (감정을) 상하게 하다
syn. insult
ant. appease
My friend was *offended* by the reporter's questions.

owl
[aul]
n. 올빼미
Most *owls* hunt at night and live on[13] small animals.

---

12. edge[edʒ] *n.* (칼의) 날   13. live on ~ : ~을 먹고 살다

pause
[pɔːz]

n. 중지, 멈춤
syn. stop
During the radio program there were several *pauses* for advertisements[14].

v. 중지하다, 멈추다
The dog *paused* for a moment when I called him.

Practice 3

위 단어를 사용하여 아래 문장을 완성하라. 필요시 단어를 적절한 형태로 변형하라.

1. A typewriter _____ is skilled in repairing typewriters.
2. After a(n) _____ for lunch, the man returned to work.
3. What I _____ is to finish this work before I go to bed.
4. She is wearing a(n) _____ belt.
5. Don't _____ cleaning your shoes when you go out.

New Vocabulary –4

pickpocket
[píkpɔkit]

n. 소매치기
Most *pickpockets* usually work in crowds of people.

pot
[pɔt]

n. 단지, 항아리, 독
syn. jug
Koreans usually keep soy sauce[15] in a *pot*.

profit
[prɔ́fit]

n. 수익, 이익, 이득
adj. profitable
This company makes great *profits* from manufacturing automobiles.

quiver
[kwívər]

v. 떨다, 흔들리다
syn. shake, vibrate
Her lips *quivered* like those of a child about to cry[16].

rejoice
[ridʒɔ́is]

v. 기뻐하다, 기쁘게 하다
syn. delight
They *rejoiced* when they heard she was safe.

---

14. advertisement[ədvə́ːrtismənt] *n.* 광고   15. soy sauce : 간장   16. a child about to cry : 막 울려고 하는 아이

resist
[rizíst]

v. 저항하다, 버티다
syn. oppose
ant. obey, submit
The troops[17] were no longer able to *resist* the enemy attack.

rough
[rʌf]

adj. 거칠거칠한, 울퉁불퉁한
ant. smooth
The well was made of *rough* stones.

scent
[sent]

n. 냄새, 향기
syn. odor, fragrance
The hunting dogs followed the *scent* of the fox.

v. 냄새맡다
A dog *scented* along the ground.

sew
[sou]

v. 깁다, 꿰매다, 바느질하다
The doctor *sewed* up the soldier's wound[18].

sink
[siŋk]

v. 가라앉다, 침몰하다
ant. float
The sun is *sinking* in the west.

n. 개수통
She washed the dishes in the *sink*.

Practice 4

위 단어를 사용하여 아래 문장을 완성하라. 필요시 단어를 적절한 형태로 변형하라.

1. The ship was filled with water and it _____ at last.

2. There is some water at the bottom of the _____.

3. The _____ in this business are not large.

4. The mother _____ over her son's success.

5. The _____ road made the car shake.

---

17. troop [tru:p] *n.* (보통 *pl.*) 군대   18. wound [wu:nd] *n.* 상처

New Vocabulary –5

solution
[səljúːʃən]
n. 해답, 해결
syn. answer
ant. problem
That problem was very hard; it took many hours to get its *solution*.

spot
[spɔt]
n. 1. 반점, 얼룩
syn. stain
She has a paint *spot* on her white dress.

   2. 지점, 장소
They are building their house at a beautiful *spot*.

sting
[stiŋ]
v. (벌이) 쏘다, (바늘로) 찌르다
syn. pierce, prick
Be careful or the bee will *sting* you.

n. 침(針), 바늘
A bee has its *sting* in the tail.

suffer
[sʌ́fər]
v. (고난, 고통을) 겪다, 당하다
During the war many people *suffered* from hunger.

sympathy
[símpəθi]
n. 동정, 동정심
We feel *sympathy* for a person who is ill.

thrill
[θril]
n. 전율, 오싹하는 느낌
She felt a *thrill* when she was kissed by a handsome[19] pop star.

v. 전율을 느끼다, 오싹해지다
She was *thrilled* with delight[20] when the actor winked at her.

tragic
[trǽdʒik]
adj. 비극의, 비참한
syn. disastrous, terrible
ant. comic
n. tragedy
There was a *tragic* accident on the highway yesterday.

up-to-date
[ʌ́p-tə-déit]
adj. 최신의, 최근의
syn. modern

---

19. handsome [hǽnsəm] *adj.* 잘생긴   20. delight [diláit] *n.* 기쁨, 환희

ant. out-of-date

The hotel is furnished with *up-to-date* furniture.

volume
[vɔ́lju(:)m]

n. 1. 책, 권

Our school has a library of 100,000 *volumes*.

2. 용적, 부피

The storeroom²¹ has a *volume* of 4,000 cubic feet.

wil(l)ful
[wílfəl]

adj. 1. 외고집의, 완고한

syn. stubborn

The *wilful* child would not listen to whatever you say.

2. 고의의, 계획적인

syn. intended

The police think that it was *wilful* murder.

Practice 5

위 단어를 사용하여 아래 문장을 완성하라. 필요시 단어를 적절한 형태로 변형하라.

1. We arrived at the very _____ where he was killed.

2. A bee _____ me on the neck when I was walking along the country road.

3. She was very generous²² to him, but she _____ for it when he ran away with all her money.

4. They expressed their _____ by sending flowers to her husband's funeral.

5. You can find what you want to know in the ninth _____ of the encyclopedia²³.

해답					
Practice 1	1. conference	2. advantage	3. contribute	4. crushed	5. defended
Practice 2	1. fetch	2. executive	3. emergency	4. escaped	5. dot
Practice 3	1. mechanic	2. pause	3. intend	4. leather	5. neglect
Practice 4	1. sank	2. pot	3. profits	4. rejoiced	5. rough
Practice 5	1. spot	2. stung	3. suffered	4. sympathy	5. volume

21. storeroom[stɔ́ːruːm] ***n.*** 저장실, 광   22. generous[dʒénərəs] ***adj.*** 관대한   23. encyclopedia[ensaikloupíːdjə] ***n.*** 백과 사전

Lesson 19

종합 연습 문제

1 네 개의 단어 중 다른 셋과 관련이 없는 것을 골라 공란에 그 번호를 써넣어라.

_____ 1.	(A) ignore	(B) neglect	(C) disregard	(D) suffer
_____ 2.	(A) crush	(B) spoil	(C) smash	(D) break
_____ 3.	(A) blind	(B) void	(C) hollow	(D) empty
_____ 4.	(A) sharp	(B) acute	(C) narrow	(D) keen
_____ 5.	(A) method	(B) fashion	(C) principle	(D) mode
_____ 6.	(A) fragrance	(B) odor	(C) scent	(D) atmosphere
_____ 7.	(A) mean	(B) escape	(C) intend	(D) plan
_____ 8.	(A) sting	(B) pierce	(C) resist	(D) prick
_____ 9.	(A) solution	(B) advantage	(C) gain	(D) benefit
_____ 10.	(A) quiver	(B) vibrate	(C) fetch	(D) shake

2 왼쪽에 주어진 우리말과 같은 뜻을 가진 단어를 골라 그 번호를 공란에 써넣어라.

_____ 1. 가서 가져오다	(A) crush	(B) pause
	(C) gasp	(D) fetch
_____ 2. 동정	(A) mode	(B) scent
	(C) sympathy	(D) atmosphere
_____ 3. 헐떡거리다	(A) gasp	(B) quiver
	(C) rejoice	(D) suck
_____ 4. 식료품점	(A) garment	(B) grocery
	(C) colony	(D) conference
_____ 5. 소화하다	(A) mock	(B) sew
	(C) digest	(D) suck

3 왼쪽에 주어진 단어와 반대되는 뜻을 가진 단어를 골라 그 번호를 공란에 써넣어라.

_____ 1. dull	(A) severe	(B) keen
	(C) solid	(D) careful
_____ 2. obey	(A) defend	(B) escape
	(C) rejoice	(D) resist
_____ 3. attack	(A) defend	(B) contribute
	(C) scatter	(D) suffer
_____ 4. float	(A) neglect	(B) oppose
	(C) sink	(D) leap
_____ 5. smooth	(A) stubborn	(B) rough
	(C) sharp	(D) cruel

Lesson 19 종합 연습 문제

4 괄호 속에 주어진 우리말과 같은 뜻을 가진 단어를 사용하여 문장을 완성하라.

1. I should R_____E to see you married to a good man. (기뻐하다)
2. Plenty of fresh air can C_____E to good health. (기여하다)
3. It gave her quite a T____L to shake hands with the Princess. (전율)
4. Don't N_____T to lock the door when you leave. (게을리하다)
5. I've made a mistake, though I didn't I____D to. (~하려고 생각하다)

5 이탤릭체로 된 단어와 같은 뜻을 가진 단어를 골라 그 번호를 공란에 써넣어라.

_____ 1. The duty of a soldier is to *defend* his country.
   (A) resist   (B) assure   (C) guard   (D) contribute

_____ 2. He has a red *spot* in his gown[24].
   (A) stain   (B) belt   (C) pot   (D) defect

_____ 3. You always follow your own *inclinations* instead of thinking of our feelings.
   (A) conducts (B) profits   (C) occupations (D) dispositions

_____ 4. Many teachers do not like to use *up-to-date* textbooks in their classes.
   (A) odd   (B) modern   (C) old   (D) interesting

_____ 5. We should be *cautious* in crossing a crowded street.
   (A) careful   (B) intelligent   (C) quiet   (D) weary

_____ 6. The tree fell on the roof of a car and *crushed* it.
   (A) exploded (B) smashed   (C) fetched   (D) touched

_____ 7. He *paused* for a moment, then continued speaking.
   (A) sat   (B) stood   (C) hesitated   (D) stopped

_____ 8. I *quivered* with fear at the strange sound.
   (A) shook   (B) escaped   (C) stung   (D) suffered

_____ 9. The room was filled with the *scent* of flowers.
   (A) atmosphere (B) pot   (C) feature   (D) odor

_____ 10. The senator[25] was *offended* by the reporter's silly questions.
   (A) insulted   (B) rejoiced   (C) defened   (D) rejected

---

24. gown[gaun] ***n.*** 겉옷, 가운   25. senator[sénətər] ***n.*** 상원의원

Lesson 19 종합 연습 문제

1. 1. D 2. B 3. A 4. C 5. C 6. D 7. B 8. C 9. A 10. C
2. 1. D 2. C 3. A 4. B 5. C
3. 1. B 2. D 3. A 4. C 5. B
4. 1. REJOICE 2. CONTRIBUTE 3. THRILL 4. NEGLECT 5. INTEND
5. 1. C 2. A 3. D 4. B 5. A 6. B 7. D 8. A 9. D 10. A

LESSON 20

Self-test 20

적당한 단어를 골라 빈칸을 채우라.

1. At last they *ceased* their quarrel[1]. In other words, they _____ their quarrel.
   (A) began   (B) stopped

2. A man of *dignity* has a _____ character.
   (A) noble   (B) dishonorable

3. Man has *lungs* for _____.
   (A) digestion   (B) breathing

4. This wood is too _____ to *kindle*.
   (A) wet   (B) dry

5. They *paved* the road with _____.
   (A) concrete   (B) bicycles

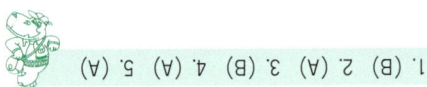

1. (B) 2. (A) 3. (B) 4. (A) 5. (A)

New Vocabulary -1

adventure
[ədvéntʃər]
n. 모험
A flight[2] in an airplane is no longer such an *adventure* as it used to be.

attach
[ətǽtʃ]
v. 붙이다, 달다
ant. detach
He *attached* a stamp on the envelope.

bitter
[bítər]
adj. 쓴, 쓰라린
ant. sweet
Good medicine tastes *bitter* to the mouth.

---

1. quarrel[kwɔ́rəl] *n.* 싸움, 말다툼   2. flight[flait] *n.* 비행

broadcast
[brɔ́ːdkæst]

v. 방송하다
p., pp. broadcast
The President's speech was *broadcast* through radio and television all over the country.

cease
[síːs]

v. 그만두다, 그치다
syn. quit, stop
ant. continue
They *ceased* their work for a few minutes to take a rest[3].

combine
[kəmbáin]

v. 1. 결합하다, 연합하다
ant. separate, split
The two countries *combined* their efforts against their enemy.
  2. 화합하다, 화합시키다
n. combination
Chemists *combine* different elements to form new compounds[4].

confess
[kənfés]

v. 자백하다, 자인하다, 실토하다
n. confession
He *confessed* that he had done wrong.

converse
[kənvɔ́ːrs]

v. 이야기를 나누다, 담화하다
syn. talk, chat
n. conversation
I'd like to *converse* with my friends about interesting subjects.

cultivate
[kʌ́ltiveit]

v. 경작하다, 갈다
The farmer *cultivated* his fields just before planting time.

delay
[diléi]

v. 늦추다, 연기하다
syn. postpone, defer
The train was *delayed* because of heavy snow.

Practice 1

위 단어를 사용하여 아래 문장을 완성하라. 필요시 단어를 적절한 형태로 변형하라.

1. The music _____ suddenly when she turned off the radio.
2. It was a(n) _____ disappointment[5] to him when he failed his examination.

---

3. take a rest : 휴식하다   4. compound [kɔ́mpaund] *n.* 합성물   5. disappointment [disəpɔ́intmənt] *n.* 실망

3. Jean _____ that she had eaten all the cakes.

4. The accident last night _____ the train for two hours.

5. After a year of studying at the university, I feel that I can _____ with anyone about anything.

New Vocabulary -2

dignity
[dígnəti]

n. 위엄, 위풍
A man's *dignity* depends not on his wealth but on what he is.

doubt
[daut]

n., v. 의심(하다)
syn. suspicion, mistrust
All his *doubt* and uncertainty[6] made him unhappy.

emotion
[imóuʃən]

n. 감정, 감격
syn. feeling
ant. reason
Love, hate, joy, and fear are *emotions*.

establish
[istǽbliʃ]

v. 설치하다, 설립하다
syn. found, institute
The university was *established* in 1850 by the government.

excuse
[ikskjúːz]

v. 용서하다
syn. pardon, forgive
Please *excuse* me for opening your letter by mistake.

fiber
[fáibər]

n. 섬유, 섬유질
Nylon is one of the most popular man-made *fibers*.

forthright
[fɔ́ːrθrait]

adj. 솔직한, 꾸밈없는
syn. candid, frank
ant. feigned
His *forthright* behavior shows that he is honest, but he seems rude[7] to some people.

gay
[gei]

adj. 즐거운, 쾌활한
syn. lively, merry

---

6. uncertainty [ʌnsə́ːrtənti] *n.* 불확실   7. rude [ruːd] *adj.* 무례한

	ant. gloomy, sad
	We were all *gay* at the thought of coming holidays.
guarantee [gǽrəntíː]	*n.* 보증, 담보
	We have a one-year *guarantee* on our new car.
	v. 보증하다, 책임지다
	syn. warrant
	The merchant *guaranteed* that the color of the material would not fade[8].
holy [hóuli]	*adj.* 신성한, 거룩한
	syn. sacred
	Jerusalem and Mecca are *holy* cities.

Practice 2

위 단어를 사용하여 아래 문장을 완성하라. 필요시 단어를 적절한 형태로 변형하라.

1. The speaker did not like the plan and made _____ objection[9] to it.

2. The young people were _____ as they prepared the hall for a dance party.

3. Don't be anxious[10]; he will come without _____.

4. I can offer my house and land as a _____.

5. The Bible and the Koran are _____ writings.

New Vocabulary -3

income [ínkəm]	*n.* (정기적) 수입, 소득
	ant. expenditure
	The government tax on *income* is called *income* tax.
interest [íntərist]	*n.* 관심, 흥미
	ant. boredom
	His two great *interests* in life are music and painting.
kindle [kíndl]	*v.* 불을 붙이다, 불붙다
	syn. ignite, inflame
	We tried to *kindle* the wood but it was wet and wouldn't *kindle* easily.

8. *fade*[feid] *v.* (색깔이) 바래다   9. *objection*[əbdʒékʃən] *n.* 반대   10. *anxious*[ǽŋkʃəs] *adj.* 걱정하는

legal
[líːgəl]

adj. 법률의, 법적인
syn. lawful
ant. illegal
Hunting is *legal* only in certain seasons.

lung
[lʌŋ]

n. 폐, 허파
That opera singer has good *lungs*.

medium
[míːdjəm]

n. 매개물, 매개체
Television can be a *medium* for giving information and opinions.

moderate
[mɔ́dərit]

adj. 적당한, 알맞은, 수수한
syn. temperate
ant. extreme, excessive
It is a large house, but the garden is of *moderate* size.

neighborhood
[néibərhud]

n. 이웃, 인근
syn. vicinity
She lives in the *neighborhood* of the mill.

odor
[óudər]

n. 냄새, 향기
syn. smell, scent
Water has neither *odor* nor color.

pace
[peis]

n. 걸음, 보폭
syn. step
The old man can walk only at a slow *pace*.

Practice 3

위 단어를 사용하여 아래 문장을 완성하라. 필요시 단어를 적절한 형태로 변형하라.

1. The whole _____ came to her birthday party.

2. The spark _____ the dry wood, so we could make fire.

3. He has a(n) _____ in collecting stamps.

4. There was a(n) _____ of roses in the air.

5. At the time of the accident, the car was running at a(n) _____ speed.

New Vocabulary -4

pave
[peiv]
v. 포장하다
n. pavement
Today most roads are *paved* with asphalt.

picturesque
[piktʃərésk]
adj. 그림 같은, 그림처럼 아름다운
There was a *picturesque* old mill at the foot of the mountain.

pour
[pɔːr]
v. 붓다, 내쏟다
She *poured* milk from the bottle into the glasses.

progress
[próugrəs]
n. 진보, 향상
syn. development, growth, advance
He is showing rapid[11] *progress* in his studies.

v. 진보하다, 진전하다
His work is *progressing* smoothly as we expected.

quote
[kwout]
v. 인용하다, 따다 쓰다
syn. cite
The judge *quoted* various cases[12] in support of his opinion.

relate
[riléit]
v. 1. 이야기하다, 말하다
syn. tell
We listened as he *related* his adventures.

2. 관련시키다, 관계시키다
syn. connect
n. relation
It is difficult to *relate* these results to her mistake.

resolve
[rizɔ́lv]
v. 결심하다, 결의하다
syn. decide, determine
He *resolved* to do better work in the future.

royal
[rɔ́iəl]
adj. 왕의, 왕다운
The nobleman is a man of the *royal* family.

scheme
[skiːm]
n. 안(案), 설계, 계획
syn. plan, plot

---

11. rapid[rǽpid] *adj.* 빠른   12. case[keis] *n.* 판례

Their *scheme* of building the road has failed.

v. 입안(立案)하다, 계획하다
They *schemed* for the overthrow[13] of the government.

situate
[sítʃueit]

v. 위치시키다, 위치를 정하다
syn. place, locate
n. situation
The city is *situated* by the river.

Practice 4

위 단어를 사용하여 아래 문장을 완성하라. 필요시 단어를 적절한 형태로 변형하라.

1. The building of the new school _____ quickly during the last summer.
2. The discovery of electricity[14] _____ the way for many inventions.
3. Many people _____ to quit smoking and never do.
4. He tried to _____ from the Bible to support his beliefs.
5. The firehouse[15] is so _____ that the fireman can easily reach all parts of the town.

New Vocabulary -5

somewhat
[sʌ́mhwət]

adv. 다소, 어느 정도
syn. slightly
I was *somewhat* surprised to hear the bad news.

spray
[sprei]

v. 물안개를 뿜다, 물보라를 날리다
Jane was *spraying* green paint on the wall.

stir
[stəːr]

v. 휘젓다, 동요시키다
ant. calm, pacify
She *stirred* her coffee with a teaspoon.

suitable
[súːtəbl]

adj. 적합한, 어울리는
syn. proper
The park is a *suitable* place for a picnic.

---

13. overthrow [ouvərθróu] *n.* 전복, 타도   14. electricity [ilektrísəti] *n.* 전기   15. firehouse [fáiərhaus] *n.* 소방서

tale
[teil]

n. 이야기, 설화
syn. story
Father likes to tell us *tales* of his boyhood.

throat
[θrout]

n. 목구멍, 인후
The murderer cut the old man's *throat*.

tramp
[træmp]

v. 1. 터벅터벅 걷다, 뚜벅뚜벅 걷다
syn. stride
The soldiers *tramped* along the street.

   2. 짓밟다
Someone *tramped* on my toes on the crowded bus.

urge
[əːrdʒ]

v. 몰아내다, 강요하다, 다그치다
syn. force
Hunger *urged* him to steal a piece of bread.

vow
[vau]

n. 맹세, 서약
syn. promise, oath
All the men made a *vow* of loyalty to their leader.

v. 맹세하다, 서약하다
They *vowed* vengeance[16] against the oppressor[17].

witch
[witʃ]

n. 마녀, 여자 마법사
It was thought that *witches* generally used their power to do evil.

Practice 5

위 단어를 사용하여 아래 문장을 완성하라. 필요시 단어를 적절한 형태로 변형하라.

1. Choose the most _____ word for the blank of the sentence.

2. We have arrived _____ late, I'm afraid.

3. He was _____ by the doctor to rest more.

4. On returning from the war, he told us _____ of fear and sadness.

5. She felt so homesick[18] that she _____ never to leave home again when she was back home.

---

16. vengence [véndʒəns] *n.* 복수   17. oppressor [əprésər] *n.* 박해자   18. homesick [hóumsik] *adj.* 고향을 그리워하는, 향수병의

Practice 1	1. ceased	2. bitter	3. confessed	4. delayed	5. converse
Practice 2	1. forthright	2. gay	3. doubt	4. guarantee	5. holy
Practice 3	1. neighborhood	2. kindled	3. interest	4. odor	5. moderate
Practice 4	1. progressed	2. paved	3. resolve	4. quote	5. situated
Practice 5	1. suitable	2. somewhat	3. urged	4. tales	5. vowed

Lesson 20

1 이탤릭체로 된 단어와 같은 뜻을 가진 단어를 골라 그 번호를 공란에 써넣어라.

_____ 1. to *cite* the Bible   (A) read   (B) attack
                                                  (C) cover   (D) quote

_____ 2. an unpleasant *odor*   (A) procedure   (B) emotion
                                                  (C) smell   (D) stain

_____ 3. a *vow* of loyalty   (A) oath   (B) plan
                                                  (C) break   (D) doubt

_____ 4. to *cease* doing something   (A) begin   (B) quit
                                                  (C) start   (D) delay

_____ 5. to *converse* with someone   (A) fight   (B) talk
                                                  (C) contract   (D) rejoice

_____ 6. to *establish* a school   (A) found   (B) mistrust
                                                  (C) destroy   (D) guarantee

_____ 7. to *delay* something   (A) defend   (B) decide
                                                  (C) claim   (D) postpone

_____ 8. *forthright* behavior   (A) stubborn   (B) cruel
                                                  (C) candid   (D) merry

_____ 9. a *holy* cup   (A) strange   (B) sacred
                                                  (C) hollow   (D) solid

_____ 10. in the *neighborhood*   (A) place   (B) medium
                                                  (C) wood   (D) vicinity

2 왼쪽에 주어진 우리말과 같은 뜻을 가진 단어를 골라 그 번호를 공란에 써넣어라.

_____ 1. 고백하다   (A) confess   (B) converse
                                (C) relate   (D) forgive

_____ 2. 법률의   (A) royal   (B) executive
                                (C) legal   (D) incidental

_____ 3. 감정   (A) sorrow   (B) anger
                                (C) odor   (D) emotion

_____ 4. 결심하다   (A) quote   (B) resolve
                                (C) defer   (D) resist

_____ 5. 즐거운   (A) gay   (B) dull
                                (C) gloomy   (D) acute

Lesson 20 종합 연습 문제

3 왼쪽에 주어진 단어와 반대되는 뜻을 가진 단어를 골라 그 번호를 공란에 써넣어라.

_____ 1. continue (A) combine (B) pour
　　　　　　　　　　　　(C) cease　　(D) contribute

_____ 2. boredom   (A) reason　 (B) interest
　　　　　　　　　　　　(C) progress (D) dignity

_____ 3. moderate (A) hollow　 (B) legal
　　　　　　　　　　　　(C) cautious (D) excessive

_____ 4. attach   (A) detach　 (B) confess
　　　　　　　　　　　　(C) urge　　 (D) resolve

_____ 5. gloomy   (A) extreme (B) gay
　　　　　　　　　　　　(C) keen　　 (D) forthright

4 괄호 속에 주어진 우리말과 같은 뜻을 가진 단어를 사용하여 문장을 완성하라.

1. A person's yearly I____E is all the money that he gets in a year. (수입)
2. He has a S____E for extracting[19] gold from sea water. (계획)
3. Will you P__R me out a cup of tea, please? (붓다)
4. The newspaper is an advertising M____M. (매개체)
5. I have no I_____T in politics. (관심)

5 가장 적합한 단어를 골라 빈칸을 채우라.

1. The thief _____ to the police that he had stolen the money.
　　(A) offended　(B) ceased　(C) confessed　(D) contributed

2. I have no _____ that you will pass the examination.
　　(A) fiber　　(B) doubt　　(C) mode　　(D) sympathy

3. The trip to Alaska was quite a(n) _____ for her.
　　(A) spot　　(B) mode　　(C) adventure　(D) medium

4. A deaf and blind man shows _____ by facial[20] expressions and gestures.
　　(A) adventure　(B) grocery　(C) profession　(D) emotions

5. Soldiers usually have to bear[21] _____ hardship during the war.
　　(A) queer　(B) royal　(C) gay　(D) bitter

6. We will _____ the party for a week and hold it next Saturday.
　　(A) advance　(B) differ　(C) delay　(D) forgive

---

19. extract[ikstrǽkt] *v.* 추출하다, 짜내다　　20. facial[féiʃəl] *adj.* 얼굴의　　21. bear[bɛər] *v.* 참다

7. This clock is _____ for one year.
   (A) urged   (B) situated   (C) determined   (D) guaranteed

8. Prices in this hotel are _____, not high at all.
   (A) moderate   (B) broad   (C) excessive   (D) bitter

9. There is some beautiful scenery in our _____.
   (A) atmosphere   (B) neighborhood   (C) fashion   (D) scheme

10. He _____ this sentence from a speech by the President.
    (A) invented   (B) attached   (C) quoted   (D) symbolized

6 왼쪽에 주어진 단어의 적당한 파생어를 사용하여 문장을 완성하라.

1. *combine*   The _____ of yellow and blue forms green.
2. *situate*   The store is in an ideal _____ to draw tourists.
3. *confess*   The thief's _____ of guilt closed the case.
4. *relate*   There is no _____ between the nations.
5. *converse*   He had a long telephone _____.

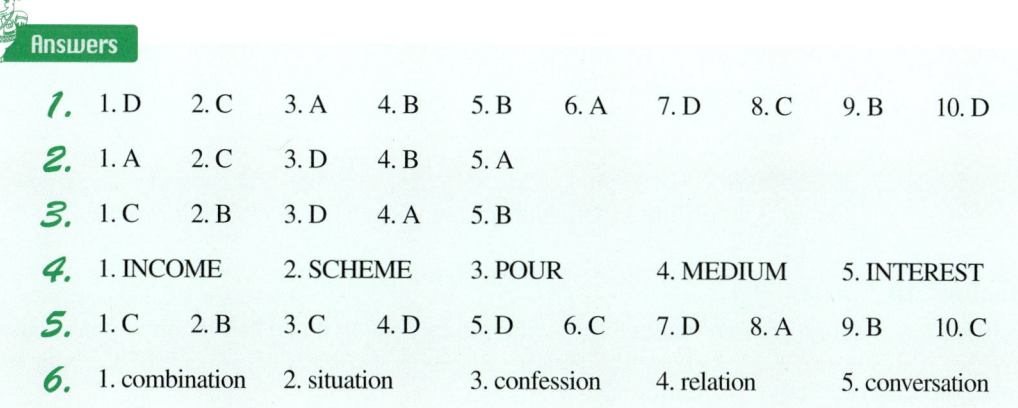

Answers

1. 1. D   2. C   3. A   4. B   5. B   6. A   7. D   8. C   9. B   10. D
2. 1. A   2. C   3. D   4. B   5. A
3. 1. C   2. B   3. D   4. A   5. B
4. 1. INCOME   2. SCHEME   3. POUR   4. MEDIUM   5. INTEREST
5. 1. C   2. B   3. C   4. D   5. D   6. C   7. D   8. A   9. B   10. C
6. 1. combination   2. situation   3. confession   4. relation   5. conversation

Lesson 20   243

LESSON 21

Self-test 21

적당한 단어를 골라 빈칸을 채우라.

1. We could see the *dim* outline of buildings _____.
   (A) in the dark   (B) in the bright daylight

2. The *kite* has _____ to maintain¹ its balance.
   (A) two legs   (B) a tail

3. A _____ man doesn't have much *leisure*.
   (A) free   (B) busy

4. A *blacksmith* makes and repairs things made of _____.
   (A) iron   (B) wood

5. The ice on the road *melted* in the _____.
   (A) cold   (B) sunshine

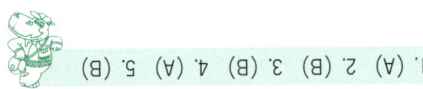
1. (A) 2. (B) 3. (B) 4. (A) 5. (B)

New Vocabulary -1

advertise
[ǽdvərtaiz]
v. 광고하다, 선전하다
syn. publicize
They *advertised* in the newspaper that they had a used car² for sale.

attack
[ətǽk]
v. 공격하다, 습격하다
syn. assault
ant. defend
On the 25th of June, 1950, North Korea began to *attack* South Korea.

blacksmith
[blǽksmiθ]
n. 대장장이
A *blacksmith* makes things with iron by heating it and hammering it into shape.

1. maintain[meintéin] *v.* 유지하다   2. used car : 중고차

brook
[bruk]

n. 시내, 개울
syn. stream, creek
A *brook* is a natural waterway[3] smaller than a river.

ceiling
[síːliŋ]

n. 천장
Lying on the sofa, he could see the *ceiling* of the room.

comfort
[kʌ́mfərt]

v. 위로하다, 위안하다
ant. grieve
I tried to *comfort* Jean after her mother's death.

confine
[kənfáin]

v. 1. 제한하다, 국한하다
syn. limit, restrict
Please *confine* your remark[4] to the subject we are talking about.

2. 가둬넣다, 감금하다
syn. imprison, restrain
John was *confined* to bed for a week with his cold.

convert
[kənvə́ːrt]

v. 바꾸다, 전환하다
syn. change
Give me time and I'll *convert* her to our political party.

cunning
[kʌ́niŋ]

adj. 교활한, 간교한, 교묘한
syn. sly, clever
He is as *cunning* as a fox.

delegate
[déligit]

n. 대표자
syn. representative
Our club sent two *delegates* to attend the meeting.

Practice *1*

위 단어를 사용하여 아래 문장을 완성하라. 필요시 단어를 적절한 형태로 변형하라.

1. Because of heavy rain he was _____ to his room all day.
2. We should _____ those who are in sorrow.
3. _____ can mend[5] tools and horseshoes.
4. When people lose something valuable, they usually _____ it in the newspaper.
5. John was _____ to Buddhism[6] by a Chinese priest.

---

3. waterway[wɔ́ːtərwei] *n.* 수로(水路)   4. remark[rimáːrk] *n.* 말, 의견   5. mend[mend] *v.* 수선하다, 수리하다
6. Buddhism[búdizəm] *n.* 불교

New Vocabulary -2

dim
[dim]
adj. 어둠침침한, 어둑한
syn. dark
ant. bright
The light is too *dim* for me to see.

drag
[dræg]
v. 끌다, 끌어당기다
syn. haul, pull
ant. push
The horse was *dragging* a heavy load[7].

emperor
[émpərər]
n. 황제, 제왕
ant. empress
Napoleon was the *Emperor* of France.

estate
[istéit]
n. 땅, 토지, 재산
syn. property
The rich man left a great *estate* when he died.

exclaim
[ikskléim]
v. 외치다, 부르짖다
syn. shout, yell
"It's eight o'clock." His mother *exclaimed* how late it was.

fierce
[fiərs]
adj. 사나운, 맹렬한
syn. violent
ant. gentle
He bought a *fierce* dog to guard[8] his house.

fortunate
[fɔ́:rtʃənit]
adj. 운이 좋은, 행운의, 다행한
syn. lucky
ant. miserable
n. fortune
You are *fortunate* in having such a fine family.

gaze
[geiz]
v. 응시하다, 바라보다
syn. stare
For hours[9] she sat *gazing* at the stars.

---

7. load [loud] *n.* 짐   8. guard [gɑ:rd] *v.* 지키다, 경계하다   9. for hours : 몇 시간 동안

habit	***n.*** 버릇, 습성, 습관
[hǽbit]	**syn.** practice, custom
	Some people say that smoking is a bad *habit*.

hop	***v.*** 깡충 뛰다, 훌쩍 뛰다
[hɔp]	He had hurt his foot and had to *hop* along.

Practice 2

위 단어를 사용하여 아래 문장을 완성하라. 필요시 단어를 적절한 형태로 변형하라.

1. Are you in the _____ of going to bed early and rising early?
2. The child had _____ at the stranger for a few minutes before answering his questions.
3. You are _____ to have such rich parents.
4. He has a beautiful _____ 40 miles from Seoul with a country house and a swimming pool[10] on it.
5. He was _____ out of his hiding place.

New Vocabulary -3

independence	***n.*** 독립, 자주
[indipéndəns]	**syn.** freedom
	adj. independent
	Korea gained[11] *independence* from Japan in 1945.

international	***adj.*** 국제적인, 국제간의
[intərnǽʃənəl]	**ant.** domestic, national
	A treaty[12] is an *international* agreement.

kite	***n.*** 연
[kait]	A *kite* was flying in the air at the end of a long string.

leisure	***n.*** 여가, 한가한 시간
[léʒər]	She spends at least half part of her *leisure* in reading.

machinery	***n.*** 기계류, 기계 장치
[məʃíːnəri]	The factory has much new *machinery*.

---

10. swimming pool : 수영장   11. gain [gein] ***v.*** 얻다, 획득하다   12. treaty [tríːti] ***n.*** 조약

melt
[melt]

v. 녹다, 녹이다
syn. dissolve
ant. freeze
The ice will *melt* when the sun shines on it.

modest
[mɔ́dist]

adj. 겸손한, 겸허한
syn. humble
ant. arrogant
The hero was very *modest* about his great deeds[13].

nervous
[nə́ːrvəs]

adj. 신경 과민의, 신경질적인, 신경의
n. nerve
A person who has been overworking is likely to become *nervous*.

offer
[ɔ́fər]

v. 제공하다, 제안하다
syn. propose, tender
He *offered* a few ideas to improve[14] the plan.

pack
[pæk]

v. 꾸리다, 싸다
She *packed* a suitcase for the trip.

n. 짐, 꾸러미, 보따리
syn. package, parcel, packet, bundle
The camper had cooking equipment in his *pack*.

Practice 3

위 단어를 사용하여 아래 문장을 완성하라. 필요시 단어를 적절한 형태로 변형하라.

1. Six nations have signed a(n) _____ trade agreement.

2. When you begin to earn[15] money, you can live a life of _____.

3. I like a(n) _____ girl, who is neither shy[16] nor loud.

4. She is so _____ that she jumps at the slightest[17] noise.

5. He _____ twenty dollars for a new stove, but the seller refused to see it at that price.

---

13. deed[diːd] *n.* 행위, 업적   14. improve[imprúːv] *v.* 개선하다, 향상시키다   15. earn[əːrn] *v.* 벌다, 얻다
16. shy[ʃai] *adj.* 수줍어하는   17. slight[slait] *adj.* 사소한

New Vocabulary –4

paw
[pɔː]
n. (개, 고양이의) 발
The dog lifted his two front *paws* before his master.

pigeon
[pídʒin]
n. 비둘기
syn. dove
Pigeons are often trained to carry messages.

poverty
[pávərti]
n. 가난, 빈곤
ant. wealth
adj. poor
His ragged[18] clothes and broken furniture indicated his *poverty*.

project
[prɔ́dʒekt]
n. 계획, 기획
syn. plan, scheme
A *project* to build a new church was discussed at the meeting.

reduce
[ridjúːs]
v. 줄이다, 낮추다
syn. decrease, lessen
ant. enlarge, increase
She is now 150 pounds; she has to *reduce* her weight.

reply
[riplái]
v. 응답하다, 대답하다
syn. answer, respond
She *replied* to my letter right away.

n. 응답, 대답
He made no *reply* to my question.

rifle
[ráifl]
n. 소총
syn. musket
A *rifle* is usually fired from the shoulder.

salary
[sǽləri]
n. 봉급, 급료
syn. wage
His *salary* will be increased next year.

section
[sékʃən]
n. 구분, 구획
syn. division
Mother cut the pie into eight *sections*.

---

18. ragged[rǽgid] *adj.* 누덕누덕한, 해진

	v. 구분하다, 세분하다
	syn. divide, classify
	The teacher *sectioned* the history class by ability ratings[19].
shoot	*v.* 쏘다, 사격하다
[ʃuːt]	**syn.** fire
	He *shot* at a bird, but missed it.

Practice 4

위 단어를 사용하여 아래 문장을 완성하라. 필요시 단어를 적절한 형태로 변형하라.

1. I asked him where to go, but he didn't _____.

2. Don't drive so fast; _____ speed, please.

3. The _____ of his family made it impossible for him to go to school.

4. Soldiers are equipped with the _____ and trained to use them.

5. I _____ an arrow at the spot on the wall, but the arrow didn't even reach the wall.

New Vocabulary -5

slope	*n.* 경사, 비탈
[sloup]	**syn.** slant, incline
	We climbed the steep[20] *slope* of the hill.
	v. 경사지다, 비탈지다
	The railroad *slopes* up slightly[21] at this point.
spider	*n.* 거미
[spáidər]	A *spider* is a small animal with eight legs.
starve	*v.* 굶주리다, 굶다
[staːrv]	*n.* starvation
	They got lost in the desert and *starved* to death.
structure	*n.* 1. 구조, 조직
[strʌ́ktʃər]	The *structure* of English is quite different from that of Korean.

19. rating [réitiŋ] *n.* 등급, 급수   20. steep [stiːp] *adj.* 가파른   21. slightly [sláitli] *adv.* 약간

2. 건물, 구조물
syn. building
The city hall[22] is a large stone *structure*.

swallow
[swɔ́lou]

v. 삼키다, 들이키다
syn. gulp, engulf
We *swallowed* all our food and drink.

n. 제비
In the early evening, the air was filled with graceful *swallows*.

tender
[téndər]

adj. 부드러운, 연한
syn. soft
ant. tough
Cook the meat a long time so that it's really *tender*.

v. 내놓다, 제출하다
syn. offer, propose
He *tendered* us money as payment for the book he had lost.

trust
[trʌst]

n. 신임, 신용
syn. confidence, reliance
A child put *trust* in his parents.

v. 신임하다, 신용하다
syn. rely (on), depend (on)
You shouldn't *trust* him; he is dishonest[23].

vest
[vest]

n. 조끼
syn. waistcoat
He likes to wear a *vest* under his jacket.

weed
[wi:d]

n. 잡초
Many *weeds* are growing among the flowers.

v. 잡초를 뽑다
He spent the whole afternoon *weeding* in the garden.

yield
[ji:ld]

v. 1. 산출하다, 생산하다
syn. produce
This land *yields* good crops.

---

22. city hall : 시청   23. dishonest[disɔ́nist] *adj.* 부정직한

2. 굴복하다
syn. submit
The enemy finally *yielded* to our soldiers.

Practice 5

위 단어를 사용하여 아래 문장을 완성하라. 필요시 단어를 적절한 형태로 변형하라.

1. The man said he would _____ rather than beg for food[24].
2. Most _____ make webs to catch insects[25] for food.
3. The _____ of that roof is very steep.
4. Yesterday he _____ his resignation[26] to the Prime Minister[27].
5. He is not the sort of man to be _____.

Practice 1	1. confined	2. comfort	3. Blacksmiths	4. advertise	5. converted
Practice 2	1. habit	2. gazed	3. fortunate	4. estate	5. dragged
Practice 3	1. international	2. independence	3. modest	4. nervous	5. offered
Practice 4	1. reply	2. reduce	3. poverty	4. rifles	5. shot
Practice 5	1. starve	2. spiders	3. slope	4. tendered	5. trusted

24. beg for food : 음식을 구걸하다   25. insect [insekt] ***n.*** 곤충   26. resignation [rezignéiʃən] ***n.*** 사표, 사직
27. Prime Minister : 국무총리

종합 연습 문제

1 네 개의 단어 중 다른 셋과 관련이 없는 것을 골라 공란에 그 번호를 써넣어라.

_____	1.	(A) parcel	(B) pack	(C) part	(D) packet
_____	2.	(A) progress	(B) scheme	(C) plan	(D) project
_____	3.	(A) cunning	(B) tender	(C) clever	(D) sly
_____	4.	(A) drag	(B) haul	(C) pull	(D) delay
_____	5.	(A) brook	(B) broom	(C) stream	(D) creek
_____	6.	(A) respond	(B) reply	(C) relate	(D) answer
_____	7.	(A) vow	(B) confidence	(C) trust	(D) reliance
_____	8.	(A) practice	(B) custom	(C) habit	(D) comfort
_____	9.	(A) reduce	(B) yield	(C) lessen	(D) decrease
_____	10.	(A) exclaim	(B) yell	(C) proclaim	(D) shout

2 왼쪽에 주어진 우리말과 같은 뜻을 가진 단어를 골라 그 번호를 공란에 써넣어라.

_____ 1. 신경 과민의 (A) tragic (B) violent (C) nervous (D) cautious

_____ 2. 여가 (A) patience (B) lack (C) independence (D) leisure

_____ 3. 굶다 (A) escape (B) starve (C) sting (D) quiver

_____ 4. 광고하다 (A) advertise (B) broadcast (C) contract (D) purchase

_____ 5. 빈곤 (A) doubt (B) servant (C) poverty (D) cowardice

3 왼쪽에 주어진 단어와 반대되는 뜻을 가진 단어를 골라 그 번호를 공란에 써넣어라.

_____ 1. arrogant (A) smooth (B) modest (C) soft (D) dull

_____ 2. grieve (A) sorrow (B) gloomy (C) comfort (D) lucky

_____ 3. push (A) delay (B) drag (C) seize (D) pour

_____ 4. increase (A) reduce (B) melt (C) dissolve (D) enlarge

_____ 5. miserable (A) tender (B) modest (C) fortunate (D) clever

Lesson 21 종합 연습 문제

4 괄호 속에 주어진 우리말과 같은 뜻을 가진 단어를 사용하여 문장을 완성하라.

1. I asked him, but he made no R___Y. (응답)
2. Don't S_____W the hot coffee; your throat may burn. (삼키다)
3. Tiberius was the E_____R of Rome during the life of Jesus Christ. (황제)
4. He went hunting with a R___E in his hand. (소총)
5. The children chose one D_____E to buy the flowers. (대표자)

5 이탤릭체로 된 단어와 같은 뜻을 가진 단어를 골라 그 번호를 공란에 써넣어라.

_____ 1. This factory *yields* cars of good quality.
　　　　　　(A) sells　　(B) buys　　(C) produces　　(D) offers

_____ 2. He has just bought an *estate* in the country.
　　　　　　(A) pasture　(B) property　(C) house　　(D) castle

_____ 3. We *gazed* at the man, wondering who he was.
　　　　　　(A) conceived (B) conversed　(C) mocked　(D) stared

_____ 4. The general[28] decided to *attack* the enemy's positions.
　　　　　　(A) offend　(B) oppose　(C) guard　　(D) assault

_____ 5. A man was killed by a *fierce* wolf[29].
　　　　　　(A) violent　(B) bitter　(C) stubborn　(D) nervous

_____ 6. The rough material hurt the child's *tender* skin.
　　　　　　(A) gay　　(B) beautiful　(C) soft　　(D) tough

_____ 7. The snow soon *melted* away when the warm weather came.
　　　　　　(A) resolved　(B) dissolved　(C) destroyed　(D) reduced

_____ 8. Coal can be *converted* to gas by burning.
　　　　　　(A) reduced　(B) yielded　(C) changed　(D) separated

_____ 9. The young actress is very *modest* about her success.
　　　　　　(A) humble　(B) proud　(C) merry　　(D) serious

_____ 10. A team of four horses *dragged* the big log[30] out of the forest.
　　　　　　(A) fetched　(B) pulled　(C) pushed　(D) carried

---

28. general[dʒénərəl] *n.* 장군, 장성　　29. wolf[wulf] *n.* 이리, 늑대　　30. log[lɔg] *n.* 통나무

Answers

1. 1. C 2. A 3. B 4. D 5. B 6. C 7. A 8. D 9. B 10. C
2. 1. C 2. D 3. B 4. A 5. C
3. 1. B 2. C 3. B 4. A 5. C
4. 1. REPLY 2. SWALLOW 3. EMPEROR 4. RIFLE 5. DELEGATE
5. 1. C 2. B 3. D 4. D 5. A 6. C 7. B 8. C 9. A 10. B

LESSON 22

Self-test 22

적당한 단어를 골라 빈칸을 채우라.

1. *Delicate* machines should be handled¹ with great _____.
   (A) force (B) care

2. The farmers *drained* the swamp² to get more _____ for crops.
   (A) land (B) water

3. With *brooms* we _____ our rooms.
   (A) clean (B) decorate

4. _____ voices *hailed* us as we entered the hall.
   (A) Angry (B) Cheerful

5. The *foul* air in this room should be _____.
   (A) changed (B) cooled down

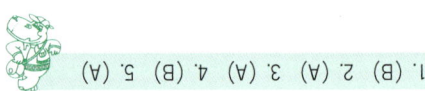
1. (B) 2. (A) 3. (A) 4. (B) 5. (A)

New Vocabulary -1

affair | *n.* 1. 일, 업무, 용무
[əfέər] | syn. business, job
| When he asked me how much money I earned, I told him to mind³ his own *affairs*.
| 2. 사건
| syn. event, happening
| The meeting was a noisy *affair*.

attempt | *v.* 시도하다, 꾀하다
[ətémpt] | syn. try
| I *attempted* to speak but was told to be quiet.

---

1. handle[hǽndl] *v.* 다루다 2. swamp[swɔmp] *n.* 늪, 늪지 3. mind[maind] *v.* 주의하다, 돌보다

blade
[bleid]

n. (칼의) 날, (풀의) 잎

A razor[4] should have a very sharp *blade*.

broom
[bru:m]

n. 비, 빗자루

We swept the broken glass into a pile[5] with a *broom*.

cell
[sel]

n. 1. 작은 방

Bees store[6] honey in the *cells* of a honeycomb[7].

2. 세포

All animals and plants are made of *cells*.

command
[kəmǽnd]

v. 명령하다, 지휘하다

syn. order

ant. obey

The officer *commanded* his men[8] to fire at the enemy.

confirm
[kənfə́:rm]

v. 확실히 하다, 확증하다

syn. approve

n. confirmation

The rummor that there was flooding[9] was *confirmed* by a news broadcast.

convince
[kənvins]

v. 확신시키다, 납득시키다

syn. persuade, assure

We *convinced* Anne to go by train rather than by plane.

cure
[kjuər]

v. 치료하다, 고치다

syn. remedy, heal

This medicine should *cure* you of your cold.

n. 치료, 치유, 완쾌

He has tried all sorts of *cures* but he is still ill.

delicate
[délikit]

adj. 섬세한, 정교한

syn. dainty, fine

ant. crude, coarse

A pianist or a violinist must have a *delicate* sense of touch.

---

4. razor[réizər] *n.* 면도칼   5. pile[pail] *n.* 더미   6. store[stɔːr] *v.* 저장하다   7. honeycomb[hʌ́nikoum] *n.* 벌집
8. man : 병사, 부하   9. flood[flʌd] *v.* 범람하다

Practice 1

위 단어를 사용하여 아래 문장을 완성하라. 필요시 단어를 적절한 형태로 변형하라.

1. Scientists sometimes need very _____ instruments.
2. Rest in bed will often _____ a cold.
3. The mistakes you made _____ me you had not studied your lesson.
4. He sent the written request[10] to _____ his telephone order.
5. The captain[11] of a ship _____ all the officers and men.

New Vocabulary -2

dip
[dip]
v. 담그다, 적시다
syn. immerse, plunge
She *dipped* her hand into the pool to see how cold the water was.

drain
[drein]
v. 배수하다, 물을 빼다
ant. irrigate
You should dig trenches[12] to *drain* away the water.

emphasis
[émfəsis]
n. 강조, 중점
syn. stress
v. emphasize
Some schools put much *emphasis* on studies that prepare their students for college.

estimate
[éstimeit]
v. 평가하다, 어림잡다
syn. evaluate
The gardener[13] *estimated* that it would take four hours to weed[14] the garden.

figure
[fígjər]
n. 모습, 모양, 형체
syn. appearance
I saw a *figure* approaching in the darkness.

foul
[faul]
adj. 불결한, 더러운, 탁한
syn. dirty, unclean
We opened the windows to let out the *foul* air.

---

10. request[rikwést] *n.* 요청   11. captain[kǽptin] *n.* 선장, 육군 대위   12. trench[trentʃ] *n.* 도랑   13. gardener[gáːrdnər] *n.* 정원사
14. weed[wiːd] *v.* 잡초를 제거하다

gem [dʒem]	*n.* 보석 syn. jewel Diamonds and rubies are well-known *gems*.	
hail [heil]	*v.* 환호하다, 환호하여 맞이하다 syn. cheer, greet The crowd *hailed* the new boxing champion.	
horizon [həráizn]	*n.* 수평선, 지평선 We saw a small ship on the *horizon*.	
indicate [índikeit]	*v.* 가리키다, 지시하다 syn. designate, show The arrow on the sign *indicates* the way to go.	

Practice 2

위 단어를 사용하여 아래 문장을 완성하라. 필요시 단어를 적절한 형태로 변형하라.

1. A writer sometimes underlines important words for _____.
2. He _____ his spoon into the soup and began breakfast.
3. The wall was covered with _____ of birds and flowers.
4. The air in this room is _____; open the window!
5. The crown of the queen sparkled[15] with _____.

New Vocabulary –3

interrupt [intərʌ́pt]	*v.* 방해하다, 저지하다 syn. intervene Don't *interrupt* me when I am busy.
kneel [niːl]	*v.* 무릎을 꿇다 *p., pp.* knelt She *knelt* down to pull weeds from the flower bed[16].
lessen [lésn]	*v.* 적어지다, 낮아지다 syn. diminish ant. increase The child's fever[17] *lessened* during the night.

---

15. sparkle [spɑːrkl] *v.* 반짝반짝 빛나다   16. flower bed : 화단   17. fever [fíːvər] *n.* 열(熱)

magic
[mǽdʒik]

n. 마법, 마술, 요술
syn. witchcraft
In fairy tales[18] witches[19] often use *magic* to change persons into animals or birds.

mend
[mend]

v. 고치다, 수선하다
syn. repair, fix
My brother *mended* the broken doll for me.

moist
[mɔist]

adj. 습기가 있는, 축축한
syn. damp, wet
ant. dry
v. moisten
The thick steam in the room had made the walls *moist*.

nest
[nest]

n. (새의) 둥우리, 보금자리
Most birds lay their eggs in their *nests*.

official
[əfíʃəl]

n. 공무원, 관리
The President is the most powerful government *official*.

adj. 공무상의, 공식적인
The letter should be written in an *official* style.

package
[pǽkidʒ]

n. 꾸러미, 소포
syn. parcel
He carried a large *package* of books under his arm.

payroll
[péiroul]

n. 급료, 지불, 명부
Don't do the work until he puts you on the *payroll*.

Practice 3

위 단어를 사용하여 아래 문장을 완성하라. 필요시 단어를 적절한 형태로 변형하라.

1. He made a trip to Seoul on _____ business.
2. The birds build their _____ with twigs[20] and leaves.
3. Her eyes got _____ when she heard the bad news.
4. I don't want to be _____ in my business.
5. I _____ down and gave God thanks for my recovery[21] from sickness.

---

18. fairy tale : 요정(妖精) 이야기   19. witch [witʃ] *n.* 마녀   20. twig [twig] *n.* 작은 가지   21. recovery [rikʌ́vəri] *n.* 회복

New Vocabulary -4

pile
[pail]

n. 더미, 쌓아 올린 것
syn. stack
The room was full of *piles* of old books.

v. 쌓이다, 쌓아 올리다
syn. heap
The snow *piled* so high in front of the door that we couldn't go out.

practical
[prǽktikəl]

adj. 실제적인, 실용적인
ant. theoretical
His plan was interesting but not *practical*.

prompt
[prɔmpt]

adj. 신속한, 기민한, 지체없는
syn. immediate, swift
His *prompt* action prevented serious trouble.

refer
[rifə́ːr]

v. 참조하다, 문의하다
If you don't know what this means, *refer* to the dictionary.

represent
[reprizént]

v. 나타내다, 표현하다
syn. symbolize, stand for
On the map, blue *represents* water and brown represents land.

righteous
[raitʃəs]

adj. 정의의, 정당한
syn. just
ant. wrong
He is a *righteous* man; he always behaves[22] justly.

sandwich
[sǽndwitʃ]

n. 샌드위치
He ate *sandwiches* for lunch.

v. 끼워넣다, 사이에 끼우다
Their house was *sandwiched* between two tall buildings.

secure
[sikjúər]

adj. 안전한, 확실한, 안심되는
syn. safe
n. security
He has a *secure* position as a university lecturer[23].

---

22. behave[bihéiv] *v.* 행동하다   23. lecturer[lékt∫ərər] *n.* 강사

***v.* 1.** 안전하게 하다, 지키다

syn. protect

We must *secure* ourselves against the dangers of the coming storm.

2. 확보하다, 획득하다

syn. get, obtain

He's lucky to have *secured* himself such a good job.

shortage
[ʃɔ́ːrtidʒ]

n. 부족, 결핍

syn. lack

ant. surplus

The rice crop will be poor because of the *shortage* of rain.

smart
[smaːrt]

adj. 재치있는, 영리한

syn. clever

Both of his children are very *smart*.

Practice 4

위 단어를 사용하여 아래 문장을 완성하라. 필요시 단어를 적절한 형태로 변형하라.

1. You'd better _____ to the dictionary for the meaning of the word.

2. The red lines on the map _____ railways.

3. The fort was _____ against any surprise attack[24].

4. I expect your _____ answer to my question.

5. There is a _____ of grain[25] because of poor crops.

New Vocabulary -5

spill
[spil]

v. 엎지르다, 흘리다

The child *spilled* the milk on the floor.

statesman
[stéitsmən]

n. 정치가

syn. politician

Winston Churchill was a famous English *statesman*.

---

24. surprise attack : 기습 공격   25. grain [grein] ***n.*** 곡물, 곡물류

struggle
[strʌ́gl]

v. 애쓰다, 고투하다, 몸부림치다
syn. labor, strive, toil
The widow[26] *struggled* to send her six children to college.

sway
[swei]

v. 흔들리다, 흔들다
syn. swing, wave
The branches of the trees were *swaying* in the wind.

n. 동요, 진동
The *sway* of the pail[27] caused some milk to spill out.

term
[tə:*r*m]

n. 1. 기일, 기간
syn. duration
The President is elected for a five-year *term*.

2. 학기
syn. semester
Are there any examinations at the end of this *term*?

3. (*pl.*) 말, 용어
syn. word, vocabulary
The author uses many technical *terms* in this book.

4. (*pl.*) 조건
syn. conditions
The *terms* of the contract are unfair.

toil
[toil]

v. 고되게 일하다, 애써 나아가다
syn. labor, effort, struggle
They *toiled* with their hands for a living.

n. 1. 노고, 고생
He succeeded after years of *toil*.

2. (*pl.*) (짐승 잡는) 그물, 올가미
syn. snare
A lion was caught in the *toils*.

tune
[tju:n]

n. 곡조, 가락
syn. melody
There are *tunes* that are easy to remember.

v. 조율하다, 조정하다
A man is *tuning* the piano.

---

26. widow [wídou] *n.* 과부   27. pail [peil] *n.* 양동이, 통

vice
[vais]

n. 악, 악덕
syn. evil
ant. virtue
He loves drinking beer; it is one of his *vices*.

weep
[wi:p]

v. 눈물을 흘리다, 울다
syn. cry
He lost control of his feelings and began to *weep*.

zone
[zoun]

n. 지대, 지역
syn. area
The demilitarized *zone*[28] divides the Korean Peninsula[29].

Practice 5

위 단어를 사용하여 아래 문장을 완성하라. 필요시 단어를 적절한 형태로 변형하라.

1. Who has _____ the ink on my notebook?

2. We honored[30] him as our leading _____.

3. She _____ to get on the bus during the rush hours[31].

4. In spite of the police, there is usually a certain amount of _____ in all big cities.

5. Do you know the _____ of this song?

해답					
Practice 1	1. delicate	2. cure	3. convinced	4. confirm	5. commands
Practice 2	1. emphasis	2. dipped	3. figures	4. foul	5. gems
Practice 3	1. official	2. nests	3. moist	4. interrupted	5. knelt
Practice 4	1. refer	2. represent	3. secure	4. prompt	5. shortage
Practice 5	1. spilled	2. statesman	3. struggled	4. vice	5. tune

28. demilitarized zone : 비무장지대   29. peninsula[pininsjulər] *n.* 반도   30. honor[ɔ́nər] *v.* 존경하다
31. rush hour : (혼잡한) 출퇴근 시간

종합 연습 문제

1 이탤릭체로 된 단어와 같은 뜻을 가진 단어를 골라 그 번호를 공란에 써넣어라.

_____ 1. a famous *statesman*   (A) lawyer   (B) soldier
                                                                                       (C) businessman (D) politician

_____ 2. a *smart* boy   (A) dirty   (B) swift
                                                                (C) clever   (D) small

_____ 3. a *secure* position   (A) safe   (B) good
                                                                        (C) modest   (D) bad

_____ 4. a *righteous* man   (A) practical   (B) just
                                                                       (C) clever   (D) fierce

_____ 5. to put *stress* on something   (A) spot   (B) emphasis
                                                                                         (C) emotion   (D) trust

_____ 6. to *cure* illness   (A) vanish   (B) repair
                                                                (C) heal   (D) diminish

_____ 7. to *stand for* something   (A) hail   (B) refer
                                                                      (C) confirm   (D) represent

_____ 8. a safety *zone*   (A) area   (B) rule
                                                                  (C) vest   (D) device

_____ 9. to *repair* something   (A) reduce   (B) mend
                                                                    (C) respond   (D) refer

_____ 10. to *convince* someone   (A) interrupt   (B) approve
                                                                          (C) convert   (D) assure

2 왼쪽에 주어진 우리말과 같은 뜻을 가진 단어를 골라 그 번호를 공란에 써넣어라.

_____ 1. 축축한   (A) modest   (B) moist
                                                  (C) moderate   (D) dim

_____ 2. 신속한   (A) prompt   (B) magic
                                                (C) fierce   (D) smart

_____ 3. 공무원   (A) senator   (B) mayor
                                                (C) instructor   (D) official

_____ 4. 시도하다   (A) refer   (B) toil
                                                (C) attempt   (D) pile

_____ 5. 보석   (A) gold   (B) gem
                                                (C) silver   (D) cell

Lesson 22 종합 연습 문제

3 왼쪽에 주어진 단어와 반대되는 뜻을 가진 단어를 골라 그 번호를 공란에 써넣어라.

_____ 1. virtue   (A) spider   (B) lack
                             (C) leisure   (D) vice

_____ 2. crude   (A) weak   (B) delicate
                             (C) safe   (D) moist

_____ 3. foul   (A) dirty   (B) clean
                             (C) dry   (D) damp

_____ 4. obey   (A) reduce   (B) interrupt
                             (C) command   (D) yield

_____ 5. surplus   (A) shortage   (B) leisure
                             (C) evil   (D) wage

4 괄호 속에 주어진 우리말과 같은 뜻을 가진 단어를 사용하여 문장을 완성하라.

1. My high school puts great E_____S on studies that are practical in our daily life. (강조)

2. Please C_____M your telephone message. (확인하다)

3. It is not polite to I_____T when someone is talking. (방해하다)

4. The poor beggar had to S_____E for a living. (고투하다)

5. It took many hours to C_____E John of his wife's guilt[32]. (확신시키다)

5 가장 적합한 단어를 골라 빈칸을 채우라.

1. She _____ for joy when she won the award.
   (A) piled   (B) struggled   (C) confessed   (D) wept

2. Leave me alone! Mind your own _____.
   (A) affairs   (B) defects   (C) dignity   (D) virtue

3. A colonel[33] is an officer who _____ a regiment[34].
   (A) confines (B) assaults   (C) commands   (D) obeys

4. He had the _____ of his skate sharpened.
   (A) slopes   (B) backs   (C) tunes   (D) blades

5. The prisoners[35] _____ to escape but failed.
   (A) swayed   (B) attempted   (C) exclaimed   (D) intervened

6. Parents try to _____ their children of bad habits.
   (A) cure   (B) dissolve   (C) drain   (D) yield

---

32. guilt[gilt] *n.* 범죄, 죄   33. colonel[kə́ːrnəl] *n.* 육군 대령   34. regiment[rédʒimənt] *n.* 연대   35. prisoner[príznər] *n.* 죄수

Lesson 22

종합 연습 문제

7. He has _____ himself that his method is the best.
   (A) convinced   (B) restrained   (C) indicated   (D) represented

8. We _____ that it would take three months to finish the work.
   (A) attempted   (B) estimated   (C) converted   (D) interrupted

9. The _____ machine can record even very slight changes.
   (A) dull   (B) fierce   (C) foul   (D) delicate

10. She went into the church and _____ down to pray.
    (A) melt   (B) piled   (C) knelt   (D) spilt

Answers

1. 1. D 2. C 3. A 4. B 5. B 6. C 7. D 8. A 9. B 10. D

2. 1. B 2. A 3. D 4. C 5. B

3. 1. D 2. B 3. B 4. C 5. A

4. 1. EMPHASIS 2. CONFIRM 3. INTERRUPT 4. STRUGGLE 5. CONVINCE

5. 1. D 2. A 3. C 4. D 5. B 6. A 7. A 8. B 9. D 10. C

LESSON 23

Self-test 23

적당한 단어를 골라 빈칸을 채우라.

1. Most flowers would *perish* when _____ comes.
   (A) winter   (B) summer

2. *Experts* knows a lot about _____ things.
   (A) special   (B) general

3. They look so _____ each other that we thought they were *twins*.
   (A) alike   (B) unlike

4. I was most *grateful* to John for his _____.
   (A) kindness   (B) cruelty

5. Most _____ turn *purple* when they ripen[1].
   (A) apples   (B) grapes

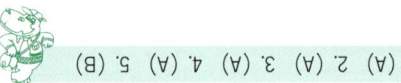
1. (A) 2. (A) 3. (A) 4. (A) 5. (B)

New Vocabulary -1

acid
[ǽsid]
n. 산(酸)
Some *acids* burn holes in cloth and wood.

approach
[əpróutʃ]
v. ~에 가까이 가다, ~에 접근하다
syn. near
As we *approached* the man, we saw that he was blind[2].

battle
[bǽtl]
n. 전투, 싸움
syn. combat
It is interesting to watch a *battle* between two lions.

1. ripen[raipn] *v.* 익다   2. blind[blaind] *adj.* 눈이 먼

bough
[bau]

n. 큰 가지
syn. branch
The *bough* bent under the weight of the snow.

capable
[kéipəbl]

adj. 유능한, 능력있는
syn. proficient, competent, able
n. capability
Mr. Smith is a man *capable* of doing anything.

choke
[tʃouk]

v. 질식시키다, 숨막히게 하다
syn. suffocate
The smoke from the burning building almost *choked* the firemen[3].

comrade
[kɔ́mrid]

n. 동무, 전우
syn. companion, fellow
The two boys were close *comrades* and did everything together.

consult
[kənsʌ́lt]

v. 상의하다, 상담하다
syn. confer
Have you *consulted* your doctor about your illness?

credit
[krédit]

n. 신용(信用)
syn. trust, confidence
If you pay your bills[4] on time, your *credit* will be good.

declare
[diklɛ́ər]

v. 선언하다, 포고하다
syn. announce
When will the results of the election be *declared*?

Practice 1

위 단어를 사용하여 아래 문장을 완성하라. 필요시 단어를 적절한 형태로 변형하라.

1. The rabbits[5] hid under a pile of _____ cut from the tree.

2. As winter _____, the weather grew colder.

3. Some airplanes are _____ of flying 1,000 miles an hour.

4. You'd better _____ a dictionary for the meaning of a new word.

5. Fighting had been going on for a year but war had not yet been _____.

---

3. fireman[fáiərmən] *n.* 소방수   4. bill[bil] *n.* 계산서   5. rabbit[rǽbit] *n.* 토끼

New Vocabulary -2

destroy
[distrɔ́i]

v. 파괴하다, 못쓰게 하다
syn. demolish
ant. construct, establish
n. destruction
Careless children *destroy* all their toys.

disturb
[distə́:rb]

v. 소란하게 하다, 방해하다
syn. bother
n. disturbance
She opened the door quietly so as not to *disturb* the sleeping child.

effective
[iféktiv]

adj. 효력있는, 유효한, 효과적인
ant. ineffective
His efforts to improve[6] the school have been very *effective*.

entire
[intáiər]

adj. 전체의, 전부의
syn. whole, total, complete
The *entire* people in the country were surprised at the news that the earthquake[7] was coming.

expert
[ékspə:rt]

n. 전문가, 숙련자
ant. beginner, learner
She is an *expert* in teaching small children.

favor
[féivər]

n. 호의, 친절, 은혜
syn. kindness
adj. favorable
A mother shouldn't show too much *favor* to one of her children.

flutter
[flʌ́tər]

v. 퍼덕거리다, 펄럭이다
syn. flap
The wings of the bird still *fluttered* after it had been shot down.

fur
[fə:r]

n. 모피, 털
The *fur* coat will keep you warm during the winter.

---

6. improve[imprú:v] *v.* 개선하다, 향상하다   7. earthquake[ə́:rθkweik] *n.* 지진

grateful
[gréitfəl]

adj. 감사하는, 고마워하는
syn. thankful
I am *grateful* to the friends who have helped me.

hell
[hel]

n. 지옥
ant. heaven
Wicked[8] persons are said to be punished in the *hell* after death.

Practice 2

위 단어를 사용하여 아래 문장을 완성하라. 필요시 단어를 적절한 형태로 변형하라.

1. He did all he could do to win[9] her _____.
2. The new system of taxation[10] will be _____ from next May.
3. Our hope of a picnic was completely _____ by the heavy rain.
4. She was wearing a very expensive _____ coat.
5. The curtains were _____ in the breeze[11].

New Vocabulary -3

immense
[iméns]

adj. 광대한, 막대한
syn. huge, vast
ant. tiny
An ocean[12] is an *immense* body of water.

instant
[ínstənt]

adj. 즉각의, 즉시의
syn. immediate
adv. instantly
The medicine gave *instant* relief[13] from pain.

join
[dʒɔin]

v. 접합하다, 연결하다
syn. combine, connect, unite
ant. disconnect, separate
Those two towns are *joined* by a railway.

---

8. wicked[wíkid] *adj.* 사악한   9. win : 얻다   10. taxation[tekséiʃən] *n.* 과세   11. breeze[briːz] *n.* 산들바람, 미풍
12. ocean[óuʃən] *n.* 대양   13. relief[rilíːf] *n.* (고통의) 제거

lash
[læʃ]

n. 채찍질, 태형(笞刑)
The prisoner received ten *lashes*.

v. 채찍으로 치다
syn. whip
He *lashed* the horse until it ran.

lodge
[lɔdʒ]

v. 묵다, 숙박하다
syn. reside, dwell
We *lodged* in a hotel on our trip.

mast
[mæst]

n. 돛대
The ship has four *masts* for its sails.

mirror
[mírər]

n. 거울
A woman usually carries a small *mirror* in her bag.

nail
[neil]

n. 1. 손톱, 발톱
Many women have long *fingernails* for beauty.

2. 못, 징
He hammered[14] some *nails* into the piece of hard wood.

observe
[əbzə́:rv]

v. 1. 관찰하다, 관측하다
syn. notice, watch
n. observation
Did you *observe* anything strange in that boy's behavior?

2. 지키다, 준수하다
syn. keep, follow
n. observance
A careful driver *observes* the traffic rules[15].

outlook
[áutluk]

n. 조망, 경치
syn. scene
From my study window I have a pleasant *outlook* over mountains and valleys.

Practice 3

위 단어를 사용하여 아래 문장을 완성하라. 필요시 단어를 적절한 형태로 변형하라.

1. Please _____ the rule about not walking on the grass.

---

14. hammer[hǽmər] *v.* 망치로 치다   15. traffic rule : 교통 법규

2. The driver saw in his driving _____ that a police car was following him.

3. One of the sailors[16] climbed up the _____ to see what was on the horizon.

4. The shipwrecked[17] sailors were _____ in the hotel.

5. The horse didn't run very fast, so he _____ it over the back with his whip.

New Vocabulary -4

passage
[pǽsidʒ]

n. 1. 통과, 통행
The old bridge is not strong enough to allow the *passage* of heavy trucks.

2. 통로, 길
syn. path, route
The *passage* between the two houses was blocked[18].

perish
[périʃ]

v. 멸망하다, 죽다
syn. die
ant. persist
Hundreds of people *perished* in the earthquake.

politician
[pɔlitíʃən]

n. 정치가, 정객
syn. statesman
Politicians are very busy when the election time comes.

primary
[práiməri]

adj. 으뜸가는, 제일의
syn. principal, chief, prime
His *primary* reason for studying was to get a better job.

purple
[pə́ːrpl]

n. 자주빛, 진홍색
The artist likes to use *purple* in his paintings.

reflect
[riflékt]

v. 1. 반사하다, 반영하다
The sunlight was *reflected* from the water.

2. 숙고하다, 깊이 생각하다
syn. meditate, ponder, think
n. reflection
Take enough time to *reflect* before doing important things.

---

16. sailor [séilər] *n.* 선원   17. shipwrecked [ʃíprekt] *adj.* 난파당한   18. block [blɔk] *v.* 차단하다

require
[rikwáiər]

v. 필요로 하다, ~할 필요가 있다
syn. need, demand
n. requirement
Every foreign[19] student is *required* to take an English examination.

risk
[risk]

n. 위험, 모험
syn. danger, peril
ant. safety
There are always some *risks* in every adventure.

sauce
[sɔːs]

n. 소스, 양념
The vegetables[20] were eaten with a cheese *sauce*.

seek
[siːk]

v. 추구하다, 탐구하다
syn. search, look for
He is going to Canada to *seek* his fortune[21].

Practice 4

위 단어를 사용하여 아래 문장을 완성하라. 필요시 단어를 적절한 형태로 변형하라.

1. The police opened a _____ through the crowd for the President.
2. The _____ cause of Tom's failure is his laziness[22].
3. After _____ for a time, he decided not to go.
4. All passengers[23] are _____ to show their tickets.
5. Fishermen face a lot of _____ in their daily lives.

---

19. foreign [fɔ́ːrin] *adj.* 외국의   20. vegetable [védʒitəbl] *n.* 야채   21. fortune [fɔ́ːrtʃən] *n.* 부(富)   22. laziness [léizinis] *n.* 나태
23. passenger [pǽsindʒər] *n.* 여객, 승객

New Vocabulary -5

shriek
[ʃriːk]

n. 비명
syn. scream
A *shriek* of pain came from the wounded[24] man.

v. 비명을 지르다
The girls were all *shrieking* with laughter.

snatch
[snætʃ]

v. 잡아채다, 갑자기 빼앗다
syn. seize, grasp, grab
The thief *snatched* her handbag and ran away.

n. 잡아챔, 강탈
He made a *snatch* at the rope but missed.

spine
[spain]

n. 척추, 등뼈
syn. backbone
His *spine* was broken in the accident.

stem
[stem]

n. (초목의) 줄기, 대
The *stem* of a tree supports its branches or leaves.

stumble
[stʌmbl]

v. 발이 걸리다, 걸려 넘어지다
He *stumbled* over a stone on the rough path.

sweep
[swíːp]

v. 쓸다, 청소하다
syn. clean
While her mother was cooking, Mary *swept* the floor.

territory
[téritəri]

n. 영토, 영역
syn. land, region
Some people like to travel through unknown *territory*.

torture
[tɔ́ːrtʃər]

v. 고문하다, 괴롭히다
syn. torment
Most of the civilized[25] nations do not *torture* prisoners.

n. 고문
The sight of his sick brother was an unbearable[26] *torture* to him.

---

24. wounded[wúːndid] *adj.* 부상당한 25. civilized[sívilaizd] *adj.* 문명화한, 개화된 26. unbearable[ʌnbέərəbl] *adj.* 참기 어려운, 견딜 수 없는

twin
[twin]

n. 쌍둥이, 한 쌍
I can't tell[27] one *twin* from the other; they look just alike.

vine
[vain]

n. 덩굴, 포도나무
syn. grapevine
Melons and pumpkins[28] grow on *vines*.

whip
[hwip]

v. 채찍질하다, 매질하다
syn. beat, lash
The boy was *whipped* for telling a lie.

n. 채찍, 매질
It is cruel to use a *whip* to punish a little child.

Practice 5

위 단어를 사용하여 아래 문장을 완성하라. 필요시 단어를 적절한 형태로 변형하라.

1. He was _____ by his father for bad manners.

2. Much _____ in the northern part of Africa is desert.

3. Many bridges were _____ away by the floods.

4. If you are not careful, you'll _____ over that box.

5. The boy was _____ from his home by two armed men[29].

해답					
Practice 1	1. boughs	2. approached	3. capable	4. consult	5. declared
Practice 2	1. favor	2. effective	3. destroyed	4. fur	5. fluttering
Practice 3	1. observe	2. mirror	3. mast	4. lodged	5. lashed
Practice 4	1. passage	2. primary	3. reflecting	4. required	5. risks
Practice 5	1. whipped	2. territory	3. swept	4. stumble	5. snatched

27. tell A from B : A와 B를 분간하다   28. pumpkin[pʌ́mpkin] *n.* 호박   29. armed man : 무장한 남자〔병사〕

Lesson 23 종합 연습문제

1 네 개의 단어 중 다른 셋과 관련이 없는 것을 골라 공란에 그 번호를 써넣어라.

_____	1.	(A) lodge	(B) dwell	(C) reside	(D) exist
_____	2.	(A) route	(B) zone	(C) path	(D) passage
_____	3.	(A) primary	(B) principal	(C) practical	(D) chief
_____	4.	(A) seek	(B) require	(C) need	(D) demand
_____	5.	(A) seize	(B) snatch	(C) grasp	(D) confirm
_____	6.	(A) fellow	(B) comrade	(C) delegate	(D) companion
_____	7.	(A) capable	(B) prompt	(C) proficient	(D) competent
_____	8.	(A) terror	(B) danger	(C) risk	(D) peril
_____	9.	(A) unite	(B) combine	(C) join	(D) command
_____	10.	(A) whole	(B) complete	(C) vast	(D) entire

2 왼쪽에 주어진 우리말과 같은 뜻을 가진 단어를 골라 그 번호를 공란에 써넣어라.

_____ 1. 전문가 (A) expert (B) comrade (C) companion (D) statesman

_____ 2. 영토 (A) estate (B) property (C) horizon (D) territory

_____ 3. 쓸다 (A) seek (B) sweep (C) sway (D) lash

_____ 4. 호의, 친절 (A) emotion (B) trust (C) favor (D) comrade

_____ 5. 효과적인 (A) candid (B) effective (C) practical (D) clever

3 왼쪽에 주어진 단어와 반대되는 뜻을 가진 단어를 골라 그 번호를 공란에 써넣어라.

_____ 1. hell (A) shortage (B) horizon (C) virtue (D) heaven

_____ 2. construct (A) bother (B) destroy (C) acquire (D) establish

_____ 3. peril (A) safety (B) favor (C) comfort (D) grief

_____ 4. perish (A) dwell (B) stumble (C) repair (D) persist

_____ 5. tiny (A) entire (B) primary (C) immense (D) effective

Lesson 23 종합 연습 문제

4 괄호 속에 주어진 우리말과 같은 뜻을 가진 단어를 사용하여 문장을 완성하라.

1. We must try to O_____E any kind of regulations. (준수하다)
2. If you drive carefully, there is no R__K accident. (위험)
3. Mirrors R_____T our faces. (반사하다)
4. You'd better C_____T a doctor when you are sick. (~을 찾아보라)
5. I felt I_____T relief from pain after taking a dose[30] of medicine. (즉각적인)

5 이탤릭체로 된 단어와 같은 뜻을 가진 단어를 골라 그 번호를 공란에 써넣어라.

_____ 1. The building was completely *destroyed* in the fire.
   (A) defended   (B) reflected   (C) choked   (D) demolished

_____ 2. Do you give *credit* to his account[31] of what happened?
   (A) confidence   (B) favor   (C) emphasis   (D) interest

_____ 3. The bird *fluttered* its wings in the cage.
   (A) snatched   (B) flapped   (C) lashed   (D) reflected

_____ 4. He *choked* when a piece of meat stuck[32] in his throat.
   (A) struggled   (B) cried   (C) stumbled   (D) suffocated

_____ 5. Do not *disturb* the baby; he is asleep.
   (A) bother   (B) whip   (C) approach   (D) insult

_____ 6. He *declared* himself a member of their party.
   (A) indicated   (B) announced   (C) consulted   (D) convinced

_____ 7. The boys *shrieked* when they saw the terrible accident.
   (A) hailed   (B) disturbed   (C) approached   (D) screamed

_____ 8. The police *tortured* the man to make him confess the crime.
   (A) lashed   (B) required   (C) tormented   (D) whipped

_____ 9. We saw the *immense* statue[33] of the hero, thirty times life size.
   (A) entire   (B) huge   (C) divine   (D) magnificent

_____ 10. I feel *grateful* for your help.
   (A) competent   (B) nervous   (C) proud   (D) thankful

---

30. dose[dous] ***n.*** (약의) 1회 복용량   31. account[əkaunt] ***n.*** 설명, 이야기   32. stuck[stʌk] ***v.*** stick (들러붙다)의 과거형
33. statue[stǽtjuː] ***n.*** 상, 조상(彫像)

Lesson 23

6 왼쪽에 주어진 단어의 적당한 파생어를 사용하여 문장을 완성하라.

1. *require*   Experience in a related field is a _____ for this job.
2. *reflect*   He gave much _____ to the problem but still had no answer.
3. *observe*   This telescope[34] is used for the _____ of distant stars.
4. *disturb*   You can work in here without any _____.
5. *destroy*   The fire caused the _____ of two buildings.

Answers

1. 1. D   2. B   3. C   4. A   5. D   6. C   7. B   8. A   9. D   10. C
2. 1. A   2. D   3. B   4. C   5. B
3. 1. D   2. B   3. A   4. D   5. C
4. 1. OBSERVE   2. RISK   3. REFLECT   4. CONSULT   5. INSTANT
5. 1. D   2. A   3. B   4. D   5. A   6. B   7. D   8. C   9. B   10. D
6. 1. requirement   2. reflection   3. observation   4. disturbance   5. destruction

34. telescope[téliskoup] *n.* 망원경

LESSON 24

Self-test 24

적당한 단어를 골라 빈칸을 채우라.

1. He *declined* my offer[1] to have lunch together, so I _____ have lunch with him.
   (A) may   (B) may not

2. An *efficient* worker _____ time and money in doing his job.
   (A) saves   (B) wastes

3. A *stupid* person behaves _____.
   (A) bravely   (B) foolishly

4. The room is like a *furnace*; it is terribly _____.
   (A) hot   (B) cold

5. _____ houses are more *permanent* than _____ houses.
   (A) Wooden, brick   (B) Brick, wooden

1. (B) 2. (A) 3. (B) 4. (A) 5. (B)

New Vocabulary -1

acquire
[əkwáiər]
v. 획득하다, 손에 넣다
syn. gain, attain, obtain
n. acquisition
He *acquired* the money for his trip by working at night.

apron
[éiprən]
n. 앞치마, 행주 치마
Wear an *apron* over the front part of your clothes to keep them clean while cooking.

bead
[bi:d]
n. 구슬, 염주알
She was wearing a string[2] of green *beads* around her neck.

---

1. offer[ɔ́fər] *n.* 제의   2. string[striŋ] *n.* 실, 끈

boundary
[báundəri]

n. 경계, 경계선
cf. border
The new *boundaries* were fixed after the war.

career
[kəríər]

n. 경력, 이력, 생애
syn. occupation, vocation
We can learn much by reading about the *careers* of great men[3].

chop
[tʃɔp]

v. 팍팍 찍다, 잘게 패다
syn. cut
He was *chopping* wood into small, short pieces for burning.

conceal
[kənsíːl]

v. 숨기다, 감추다
syn. hide
n. concealment
He *concealed* himself behind a large tree.

contact
[kɔ́ntækt]

n. 접촉, 맞닿음
syn. touch
If you bring fire into *contact* with gunpowder[4], there will be an explosion[5].

creep
[kriːp]

v. 기다, 포복하다
p., pp. crept
We *crept* through the bushes[6] towards the enemy.

decline
[dikláin]

v. 거절하다, 사절하다
syn. refuse, reject
ant. accept, consent
I said I would give him ten dollars for the horse, but he *declined* my offer.

Practice 1

위 단어를 사용하여 아래 문장을 완성하라. 필요시 단어를 적절한 형태로 변형하라.

1. He tried to _____ the fact that he broke the window glass.
2. Churchill's _____ proves that he was a great man.
3. To bring fire into _____ with gasoline may cause an explosion.
4. The cat _____ quietly nearer to the bird, but the bird flew away.
5. I am sorry to _____ your invitation to dinner because I have to study for the examination.

---

3. great man : 위인   4. gunpowder [gʌ́npaudər] *n.* 화약   5. explosion [iksplóuʒən] *n.* 폭발   6. bush [buʃ] *n.* 관목, 덤불

New Vocabulary -2

detail
[díːteil]
n. 세부, 세목
syn. particular
Everything in her story is correct to the smallest *detail*.

ditch
[ditʃ]
n. 도랑, 개천, 수로
A *ditch* is a long, narrow place dug in the earth to carry off water.

efficient
[ifíʃənt]
adj. 능률적인, 효율적인
syn. competent
n. efficiency
Our *efficient* new machines are cheaper than old ones.

entitle
[intáitl]
v. (~)의 칭호를 붙이다
syn. denominate, name, designate
The author *entitled* his book "Treasure Island"[7].

experiment
[ikspérimənt]
n. 실험, 시험
Scientists test out theories[8] by *experiments*.

favorite
[féivərit]
adj. 매우 좋아하는, 가장 좋아하는
What is your *favorite* flower?

n. 마음에 드는 것[사람]
Among those records, Beethoven's Fifth Symphony is one of my *favorites*.

foam
[foum]
n. 거품, 포말
The breaking waves[9] make *foam* near the coast.

furnace
[fɚːrnis]
n. 화로, 용광로
An oil *furnace* heats our school buildings in winter.

grave
[greiv]
n. 무덤, 묘, 산소
syn. tomb
We visited her *grave* and put flowers on it.

herd
[həːrd]
n. (짐승의) 떼, 무리
We saw a big *herd* of cattle on the farm.

---

7. Treasure Island : 보물섬   8. theory [θíːəri] *n.* 이론   9. breaking wave : 부딪쳐 부서지는 파도

Practice 2

위 단어를 사용하여 아래 문장을 완성하라. 필요시 단어를 적절한 형태로 변형하라.

1. We found a(n) _____ of elephants[10] running together.

2. We buried[11] the dead cat in a little _____ dug in the backyard.

3. Some people learn by _____ and others by experience.

4. A(n) _____ worker deserves[12] good pay.

5. _____ are usually used to irrigate[13] fields and carry off water.

New Vocabulary -3

import
[impɔ́ːrt]

v. 수입하다
ant. export
The United States *imports* coffee from Brazil.

n. 수입
Last year we reduced[14] the amount of *import* and expanded that of export.

instinct
[ínstiŋkt]

n. 본능, 천성
He has an *instinct* for always doing and saying the right thing.

joint
[dʒɔint]

n. 집합점, 매듭
v. join
The *joints* of the chair were very loose.

latter
[lǽtər]

adj. 후반의, 후자의
ant. former
Of these two men, the former is dead, but the *latter* is still alive.

lonesome
[lóunsəm]

adj. 외로운, 쓸쓸한
The old woman was *lonesome* without children.

masterpiece
[mǽstərpiːs]

n. 걸작, 명작
All of his paintings were considered as *masterpieces*.

---

10. elephant [élifənt] *n.* 코끼리   11. bury [béri] *v.* 파묻다, 매장하다   12. deserve [dizɔ́ːrv] *v.* ~을 받을 가치가 있다
13. irrigate [írigeit] *v.* (토지에) 물을 끌어 넣다, 관개하다   14. reduce [ridjúːs] *v.* 줄이다

miserable
[mízərəbl]

adj. 불쌍한, 비참한
syn. pitiable, wretched
ant. happy
n. misery
The child is hungry, tired, and homeless; he is a *miserable* child.

naked
[néikid]

adj. 벌거벗은, 나체의
syn. unclothed, bare, nude
Some *naked* boys were swimming in the river.

obtain
[əbtéin]

v. 얻다, 손에 넣다, 획득하다
syn. acquire, get
ant. lose
It is necessary to *obtain* a permit[15] to hunt or fish in this State.

output
[áutput]

n. 생산고, 생산품, 출력
ant. input
What is the daily *output* of automobiles of this factory?

Practice 3

위 단어를 사용하여 아래 문장을 완성하라. 필요시 단어를 적절한 형태로 변형하라.

1. _____ during the last five years were greater than exports.

2. He fell and put his knee out of _____.

3. Most animals have a(n) _____ to protect their young[16].

4. The _____ sailor was all alone in a strange town across the sea from his home.

5. Cold weather caused the leaves to fall and left the trees _____.

---

15. permit[pə́ː*r*mit] *n.* 허가증, 면허장   16. young[jʌŋ] *n.* (동물의) 새끼

New Vocabulary –4

passionate
[pǽʃənit]
adj. 열렬한, 열정적인
n. passion
They soon fell in *passionate* love with[17] each other.

permanent
[pə́ːrmənənt]
adj. 영구적인, 영속하는
syn. enduring, perpetual
ant. temporary
After doing temporary[18] jobs for a month, he got a *permanent* position as a clerk[19] in a store.

populous
[pápjuləs]
adj. 인구가 조밀한, 인구 밀도가 높은
n. population
Korea is one of the *populous* countries.

principle
[prínsəpl]
n. 원리, 원칙
The students are studying the *principles* of democracy[20].

pursue
[pərsúː]
v. 추적하다, 추구하다
syn. chase, seek
ant. flee
n. pursuit
The police are now *pursuing* the escaped prisoner.

reform
[rifɔ́ːrm]
v. 개혁하다, 개선하다
syn. improve
n. reformation
The new President promised to *reform* the government.

rescue
[réskjuː]
v. 구출하다, 구원하다
syn. save
The passengers were *rescued* from the sinking[21] ship.

rival
[ráivəl]
n. 경쟁자, 호적수
The two boys were *rivals* for the first prize.

---

17. fall in love with ~ : ~와 사랑에 빠지다   18. temporary [témpərəri] *adj.* 일시적인, 잠시의   19. clerk [kləːrk] *n.* 점원, 사무원
20. democracy [dimákrəsi] *n.* 민주주의   21. sinking [síŋkiŋ] *adj.* 가라앉는

saucy
[sɔ́:si]

adj. 1. 건방진, 불손한
ant. polite
The girl was *saucy* to her mother.

2. 멋있는, 산뜻한
The girl was wearing a *saucy* new hat.

seize
[síːz]

v. 1. 붙잡다, 잡다
syn. hold, grab
Mother *seized* the child by the arm.

2. 빼앗다, 압수하다
syn. confiscate
The weapons[22] hidden in the house were *seized* by the police.

Practice 4

위 단어를 사용하여 아래 문장을 완성하라. 필요시 단어를 적절한 형태로 변형하라.

1. Brick walls are more _____ than wooden fences.
2. A _____ country has many people per square mile[23].
3. The flow of water in a river is explained by the _____ of gravity[24].
4. We should try to _____ criminals[25] rather than punish them.
5. The fireman tried to _____ the child from the burning house.

New Vocabulary -5

shut
[ʃʌt]

v. 닫다, 닫히다
syn. close
ant. open
Shut the gate so that the dog can't get out.

soak
[souk]

v. 1. 적시다, 담그다
syn. wet
She *soaked* the clothes before washing them.

2. 빨아들이다
syn. absorb
Use this cloth to *soak* up the spilled milk.

---

22. weapon[wépən] *n.* 무기, 병기   23. per square mile : 1평방 마일 당   24. gravity[grǽvəti] *n.* 중력, 무게
25. criminal[krímənəl] *n.* 범죄자, 범인

spirit
[spírit]

n. 정신, 영혼
syn. soul
ant. body, flesh
Though he is dead, he is with us in *spirit*.

stepmother
[stépmʌðər]

n. 계모
cf. stepfather, stepson, stepbrother
Mary didn't get along with[26] her *stepmother*.

stupid
[stjú:pid]

adj. 어리석은, 바보 같은
syn. foolish, silly
ant. bright
It was *stupid* of you to run away from the accident.

swell
[swel]

v. 부풀다, 불어나다
syn. expand
Wood often *swells* when it is wet.

theme
[θi:m]

n. 주제, 논지
syn. topic, subject
The *theme* of his talk was the need of education.

tough
[tʌf]

n. 강인한, 질긴, 끈기 있는
syn. strong
Only *tough* breeds[27] of sheep can live in the mountains.

twist
[twist]

v. 꼬다, 뒤틀다
She *twisted* her hair round her fingers to make it curl[28].

violence
[váiələns]

n. 폭력, 완력
adj. violent
The policeman had to use *violence* to arrest the murderer[29].

whirl
[hwə:rl]

n. 소용돌이, 빙빙 돌기
The dancer suddenly made a *whirl*.

v. 빙빙 돌다
The leaves *whirled* in the wind.

---

26. get along with ~ : ~와 잘 지내다   27. breed[bri:d] ***n.*** (동식물의) 품종   28. curl[kə:rl] ***v.*** (머리털이) 곱슬곱슬해지다
29. murderer[mə́:rdərər] ***n.*** 살인자

Practice 5

위 단어를 사용하여 아래 문장을 완성하라. 필요시 단어를 적절한 형태로 변형하라.

1. He _____ his eyes and tried to sleep.
2. The _____ is willing[30] but the flesh is weak.
3. John's real mother died last year, and now he lives with his _____.
4. Her ankle[31] _____ up after she fell down.
5. Patriotism[32] was his _____ when he spoke at our school.

Practice 1	1. conceal	2. career	3. contact	4. crept	5. decline
Practice 2	1. herd	2. grave	3. experiment	4. efficient	5. Ditches
Practice 3	1. Imports	2. joint	3. instinct	4. lonesome	5. naked
Practice 4	1. permanent	2. populous	3. principle	4. reform	5. rescue
Practice 5	1. shut	2. spirit	3. stepmother	4. swelled	5. theme

30. will [wil] *v.* 의지를 발동하다   31. ankle [ǽŋkl] *n.* 발목   32. patriotism [péitriətizəm] *n.* 애국심

종합 연습 문제

1 네 개의 단어 중 다른 셋과 관련이 없는 것을 골라 공란에 그 번호를 써넣어라.

```
_____  1.   (A) enduring     (B) permanent    (C) instant      (D) perpetual
_____  2.   (A) chase        (B) pursue       (C) seek         (D) seize
_____  3.   (A) acquire      (B) obtain       (C) save         (D) gain
_____  4.   (A) theory       (B) theme        (C) topic        (D) subject
_____  5.   (A) silly        (B) efficient    (C) stupid       (D) foolish
_____  6.   (A) unclothed    (B) passionate   (C) bare         (D) naked
_____  7.   (A) scheme       (B) vocation     (C) career       (D) occupation
_____  8.   (A) entitle      (B) name         (C) designate    (D) reside
_____  9.   (A) miserable    (B) populous     (C) wretched     (D) pitiable
_____ 10.   (A) resolve      (B) decline      (C) reject       (D) refuse
```

2 왼쪽에 주어진 우리말과 같은 뜻을 가진 단어를 골라 그 번호를 공란에 써넣어라.

```
_____ 1. 능률적인      (A) magic         (B) efficient
                            (C) clever        (D) instant

_____ 2. 실험          (A) instrument    (B) expedition
                            (C) project       (D) experiment

_____ 3. 걸작, 명작    (A) expert        (B) master
                            (C) masterpiece   (D) feast

_____ 4. 원리          (A) principle     (B) principal
                            (C) subject       (D) theme

_____ 5. 본능          (A) emphasis      (B) instinct
                            (C) emotion       (D) passion
```

3 왼쪽에 주어진 단어와 반대되는 뜻을 가진 단어를 골라 그 번호를 공란에 써넣어라.

```
_____ 1. latter        (A) former        (B) better
                            (C) lower         (D) slower

_____ 2. temporary     (A) lonesome      (B) cold
                            (C) immediate     (D) permanent

_____ 3. reveal        (A) disclose      (B) conceal
                            (C) obtain        (D) improve

_____ 4. flesh         (A) rotten        (B) bone
                            (C) soul          (D) stupid

_____ 5. lose          (A) obtain        (B) perish
                            (C) tight         (D) unite
```

Lesson 24 종합 연습 문제

4 괄호 속에 주어진 우리말과 같은 뜻을 가진 단어를 사용하여 문장을 완성하라.

1. The stream forms a B_____Y between your land and mine. (경계선)
2. Who is your F_____E Korean folk singer? (가장 좋아하는)
3. Have you been in C_____T with your sister recently? (접촉)
4. The fathers of our country were P_____E believers in freedom. (열렬한)
5. I have to D_____E your invitation because my mother expects me at home. (거절하다)

5 가장 적합한 단어를 골라 빈칸을 채우라

1. The poet has _____ fame all his life, but has never experienced it.
   (A) concealed   (B) declined   (C) acquired   (D) pursued

2. He _____ my hand and said how glad he was to see me.
   (A) seized   (B) twisted   (C) pursued   (D) required

3. The boy's eyes were _____ with tears.
   (A) choked   (B) drained   (C) swollen   (D) swept

4. He _____ a good knowledge of English by studying hard.
   (A) disturbed   (B) acquired   (C) revealed   (D) demanded

5. He _____ the block of wood in two with a single blow[33].
   (A) twisted   (B) snatched   (C) chopped   (D) crept

6. It is interesting to read the _____ of great men.
   (A) beads   (B) boundaries   (C) purples   (D) careers

7. What is your _____ food?
   (A) passionate   (B) favorite   (C) populous   (D) effective

8. The burglar[34] _____ into the house and up the stairs.
   (A) rescued   (B) whirled   (C) crept   (D) declined

9. Birds do not learn to build their nests but build them by _____.
   (A) instinct   (B) passion   (C) principle   (D) theory

10. They started their holiday on a _____ day; it was cold and the rain never stopped.
    (A) stupid   (B) saucy   (C) willful   (D) miserable

---

33. with a single blow : 단 일격에   34. burglar [bə́ːrɡlər] **n.** 밤도둑, 강도

1. 1. C 2. D 3. C 4. A 5. B 6. B 7. A 8. D 9. B 10. A

2. 1. B 2. D 3. C 4. A 5. B

3. 1. A 2. D 3. B 4. C 5. A

4. 1. BOUNDARY 2. FAVORITE 3. CONTACT 4. PASSIONATE 5. DECLINE

5. 1. D 2. A 3. C 4. B 5. C 6. D 7. B 8. C 9. A 10. D

찾아보기

A

abroad 8
absolute 18
academic 30
accentuate 42
accept 54
accidental 66
accompany 78
accomplish 90
accord 102
account 114
accustom 125
ache 137
achieve 149
acid 268
acquire 280
actual 161
additional 172
admire 184
admit 196
advance 208
advantage 220
adventure 232
advertise 244
affair 256
affect 8
agency 18
ahead 30
aim 42
alarm 54
ambition 66
amuse 78
anchor 90
angle 114
ankle 125
apparent 137
appreciate 149
approach 268

apron 280
ash 161
aspect 172
assemble 184
assist 196
assure 208
atmosphere 220
attach 232
attack 244
attempt 256
attend 8
attitude 18
attraction 30
audience 42
author 54
authority 66
avoid 79
awaken 90
award 102
aware 114

B

bachelor 125
barn 137
basis 150
battle 268
bead 280
beard 172
beast 185
beat 161
behave 196
biology 209
bitter 232
blacksmith 244
blade 257
blame 9
blank 19
blaze 31
bless 43
blind 55

blossom 67
blush 91
boast 102
bold 115
bomb 79
border 126
bore 138
bother 150
bough 269
boundary 281
bowl 162
brass 173
bravery 185
brilliant 209
broad 221
broadcast 233
brook 245
broom 257
bubble 9
bulk 19
bundle 43
burden 55
bureau 67
burial 79
bush 91
butcher 102

C

cabin 115
calm 126
canal 138
candle 150
capable 269
career 281
carpenter 162
carve 173
castle 185
cattle 197
cause 209
cautious 221

cease 233	confirm 257	**D**
ceiling 245	conflict 9	
cell 257	confuse 19	damp 31
cemetery 9	congress 31	darken 43
ceremony 19	connect 43	dash 55
challenge 31	conquer 55	dawn 67
characteristic 43	conscience 67	deafen 79
charitable 55	consent 79	debate 91
charm 67	consequence 91	debt 103
chase 79	consist 103	decay 115
cheat 91	consolation 115	decent 126
cheek 103	consolidate 126	decisive 138
cheer 115	constant 138	deck 150
chew 126	constitute 150	declare 269
chilly 138	consult 269	decline 281
choice 150	contact 281	decorate 162
choke 269	contain 162	decrease 173
chop 281	contest 173	deed 185
circumstance 162	contract 185	defeat 197
civil 173	contrary 197	defect 209
claim 185	contrast 209	defend 221
clay 197	contribute 221	delay 233
colony 209	converse 233	delegate 245
color-blind 221	convert 245	delicate 257
combine 233	convince 257	delicious 10
comfort 245	cooperate 9	delight 20
command 257	copper 19	demand 31
commendation 9	correction 31	deny 44
commerce 19	correspond 43	deposit 56
commit 31	costume 55	depress 68
communicate 43	cottage 67	derive 80
companion 55	counterpart 79	descend 92
comparison 67	courage 91	describe 103
compel 79	crack 103	deserve 116
compete 91	crash 115	despair 127
competent 103	crawl 126	desperate 139
complain 115	create 138	despise 150
complex 126	credit 269	destroy 270
compose 138	creep 281	detail 282
compound 150	crime 162	determine 163
comrade 269	critical 173	device 174
conceal 281	crop 185	devote 186
conceive 162	crude 197	differ 197
concern 173	cruel 209	differentiate 210
conclude 185	crush 221	digest 221
condemn 197	cultivate 233	dignity 234
conduct 209	cunning 245	dim 246
conference 221	cure 257	dip 258
confess 233	curious 9	direct 10
confine 245	curse 19	

disappear	20
disappoint	32
discharge	44
disclose	56
discourage	68
display	80
dispose	92
dispute	104
distinction	116
distress	127
distribute	151
district	139
disturb	270
ditch	282
divide	163
divine	174
divorce	186
doll	198
domestic	210
dot	222
doubt	234
drag	246
drain	258
draw	10
drift	20
drown	32
dull	44
dumb	56
dusk	68
dust	80

E

earnest	92
ease	104
echo	116
edge	127
edible	139
educate	151
effective	270
efficient	282
elbow	163
election	174
elegant	186
elementary	198
embrace	210
emergency	222
emotion	234
emperor	246

emphasis	258
empire	10
employ	20
encourage	32
endeavor	44
endure	56
energetic	80
enforce	92
engage	104
enormous	116
enterprise	127
entertain	139
enthusiastic	151
entire	270
entitle	282
entrance	163
envy	174
equator	186
equip	198
error	210
escape	222
establish	234
estate	246
estimate	258
event	10
evidence	20
evident	32
excellence	44
exception	56
exchange	68
excuse	234
exclaim	246
executive	222
exhaust	210
exhibit	198
exist	186
expedition	174
expense	163
experiment	282
expert	270
explode	151
explore	139
export	127
expose	116
express	104
extend	92
extent	80
extraordinary	68
extreme	56

F

fable	32
faculty	20
fade	45
failure	10
faint	69
fairy	80
faithful	93
fancy	104
farewell	116
fasten	127
fate	139
fault	151
favor	270
favorite	282
feast	163
feature	174
federal	187
feed	198
festival	210
fetch	222
fiber	234
fierce	246
figure	258
file	10
financial	20
firm	32
fist	45
flame	57
flash	69
flatter	80
flavor	93
flee	104
fleet	116
flesh	127
float	139
flood	151
flutter	270
foam	282
fog	163
folly	175
forbid	187
force	198
formation	210
fort	222
forthright	234
fortunate	246
foul	258

frank.................................10
freight...............................20
frequent............................33
frighten.............................45
frost..................................69
frown................................81
frustrate............................93
fulfill................................104
function...........................117
fund.................................128
fundamental...................140
funeral............................152
fur....................................270
furnace...........................282
furnish.............................163
fury..................................175

G

gallery.............................187
gallop..............................198
garment..........................211
gasp................................223
gay..................................234
gaze................................246
gem.................................259
generate...........................11
generous..........................21
genius..............................33
ghost................................45
glance..............................57
gleam...............................69
glimpse.............................81
glorious............................93
grace..............................105
gradual...........................117
graduate.........................128
grand..............................140
grant...............................152
grateful...........................271
grave..............................282
greedy............................164
grief................................175
grind...............................187
grip..................................198
groan..............................211
grocery...........................223
guarantee.......................235

H

habit................................247
hail..................................259
halt....................................11
handy..............................21
harbor..............................33
hardship..........................45
hardware.........................57
harness............................69
harvest.............................81
haste................................93
haunt..............................105
hay..................................117
heal.................................128
healthy............................140
heap................................152
hell..................................271
herd................................282
hesitate..........................164
hide.................................175
hind.................................198
hire..................................211
hollow.............................223
holy.................................235
hop..................................247
horizon............................259
horn..................................11
horrible.............................21
howl..................................33
huge.................................46
humble.............................57
hymn................................70

I

identify.............................94
ignorant..........................117
illustrate..........................128
imagine...........................140
immediate......................152
immense.........................271
import.............................283
impossible......................164
impression......................176
improve..........................187
impulse...........................199
incidental........................212

inclination.......................223
income............................235
independence................247
indicate...........................259
individual..........................11
industrious.......................21
infamous..........................34
inferior..............................46
influence..........................58
inform...............................70
inhabit..............................81
injure................................94
innocent.........................105
inquire............................117
insist...............................128
inspire.............................140
instance.........................152
instant............................271
instinct............................283
institution........................164
instruct...........................176
instrument......................188
insult...............................199
intelligent.......................212
intend.............................224
interest...........................235
international...................247
interrupt.........................259
interval.............................11
intimate............................21
introduce.........................34
invent...............................46
investigate.......................58
invite................................70
involve.............................81
irregular...........................94
issue...............................105
item................................118

J

jar...................................128
jealous...........................140
jewel..............................152
join.................................271
joint................................283
journal............................164
journey...........................176
junior..............................188

INDEX 295

jury..199
justice..212

K

keen..224
kindle..235
kite..247
kneel...259
knot...11
knowledge......................................22

L

labor..34
lack..58
ladder...70
lamb..82
lame..94
landlord..105
landscape.....................................118
lane..128
lantern..141
lap...152
lash...272
latter..283
launch...165
lawn..176
leak...188
lean...199
leap...212
leather..224
legal..236
leisure...247
lessen..259
liberal..12
liberty...22
lid..34
lighten..46
lightning..58
limb..70
liquid...82
liquor...94
literature.....................................106
liver..118
loan..129
local..141
locate...153

lodge..272
lonesome....................................283
loss..165
lovely..176
lower..188
loyal..200
luck...212
lumber...224
lung..236

M

machinery....................................247
magic...260
magnificent.................................12
majesty..22
majority...34
male...46
mammal......................................58
manage..70
manly..94
manufacture.............................106
manuscript................................118
maple..129
marble..141
marvel...153
mast..272
masterpiece..............................283
match..165
material......................................176
mayor..188
meantime...................................200
measure.....................................212
mechanic...................................224
medium......................................236
melt..248
mend...260
mental...12
mention..22
mercy..34
merit..46
method...70
mighty...82
mild..94
military..106
millionaire..................................118
mingle...129
minor...141
minute...153

mirror..272
miserable...................................284
misfortune..................................165
mislead.......................................176
mistrust.......................................188
mixture..200
mock..212
mode...224
moderate...................................236
modest.......................................248
moist...260
momentary..................................12
monument...................................22
moral..34
mortal..46
motion..58
motive..70
mount..82
mourn..94
multiply......................................106
murder.......................................118
muscle.......................................129
mutual..141
mysterious................................153

N

nail..272
naked...284
native...165
navy..176
neat..188
needle..200
negative....................................212
neglect......................................224
neighborhood..........................236
nervous.....................................248
nest..260
neutral...12
nickname....................................22
nod...34
normal...58
nostril..70
notify...82
notion..94
numerous.................................106

O

obey 118
object 129
objective 141
oblige 153
observe 272
obtain 284
obvious 165
occasion 176
occupy 188
occur 200
odd 212
odor 236
offend 224
offer 248
official 260
omit 12
onion 22
operate 34
opportunity 46
oppose 58
oral 71
orbit 82
order 95
ordinary 106
organization 118
origin 129
ornament 141
outbreak 153
outlook 272
output 284
outstanding 165
overall 188
overcome 177
overlook 200
owe 213
owl 224

P

pace 236
pack 248
package 260
painful 35
palace 47
palm 59
pang 71
paradise 82
paragraph 95
pardon 106
parliament 119
parlor 130
partial 142
participate 153
passage 273
passionate 285
pasture 166
pat 177
patch 188
path 200
patience 213
pause 225
pave 237
paw 249
payroll 260
peacock 13
peak 23
pearl 35
peasant 47
peck 59
peculiar 71
peer 82
penalty 95
peninsula 106
pepper 119
perceive 130
perform 142
perilous 154
perish 273
permanent 285
personality 166
persuade 177
phrase 189
physical 201
physician 213
pickpocket 225
picturesque 237
pigeon 249
pile 261
pioneer 13
pit 23
pitch 35
pity 47
planet 59
plate 71
pledge 83
pluck 95
plunge 107
poetry 119
poisonous 130
polish 142
polite 154
politician 273
populous 285
port 166
portable 177
portion 189
positive 201
possess 213
pot 225
pour 237
poverty 249
practical 261
pray 13
preach 23
precious 35
preface 47
preparation 59
preserve 71
pressure 83
pretend 95
prevent 107
preview 119
previous 130
priceless 142
priest 154
primary 273
principle 285
privilege 166
procedure 177
procession 189
proclaim 201
profession 213
profit 225
progress 237
project 249
prompt 261
pronounce 13
proof 23
property 35
proportion 47
proposal 59
prospect 71
prosper 83
protect 95
protest 107
provide 119

province 130
publish 142
purchase 154
purple 273
pursue 285
puzzle 166

Q

quality 177
quarrel 189
queer 201
quit 213
quiver 225
quote 237

R

race 13
rag 23
rage 36
range 47
rapid 59
rare 72
raw 83
realize 96
rear 107
reckless 119
recognize 142
recommend 130
reduce 249
refer 261
reference 154
reflect 273
reform 285
region 166
register 178
regret 189
reign 201
reject 214
rejoice 225
relate 237
relative 13
release 23
relieve 36
religious 47
remarkable 59

remedy 72
remind 83
remove 96
rent 107
repair 119
repeat 142
replace 130
reply 249
represent 261
request 154
require 274
rescue 285
resemble 166
resent 178
reserve 190
reside 201
resign 214
resist 226
resolve 237
resort 13
responsibility 23
restless 36
resume 48
retain 60
retire 72
retreat 83
reveal 96
revenge 107
reward 143
ridiculous 130
rifle 249
righteous 261
ripe 154
risk 274
rival 285
roast 166
rod 178
role 190
rooster 201
rotten 214
rough 226
royal 237
rub 13
rude 23
rug 36
ruin 48
rust 60

S

sacred 84
sacrifice 96
saddle 108
saint 119
sake 143
salary 249
sandwich 261
satisfy 154
sauce 274
saucy 286
savage 166
scarcity 178
scare 190
scarf 202
scatter 214
scent 226
scheme 237
scorn 23
scout 36
scrape 48
scratch 60
scream 72
screen 84
screw 96
seal 108
search 119
secret 143
section 249
secure 261
security 155
seek 274
seize 286
sentiment 166
series 178
serious 190
servant 202
severe 214
sew 226
shadow 14
shallow 24
shame 36
sharp 48
shave 60
shed 72
shelf 84
shell 97

shelter 108	sphere 131	structure 250
sheriff 119	spider 250	struggle 263
shield 143	spill 262	stuff 156
shift 130	spin 155	stumble 275
shoot 250	spine 275	stupid 287
shortage 262	spirit 287	substantial 167
shortcoming 155	spit 167	substitute 179
shriek 275	splendid 179	subtract 191
shut 286	split 191	subway 203
silence 167	spoil 203	suck 215
silly 179	spokesman 215	suffer 227
silverware 190	spot 227	suitable 238
similarity 202	spray 238	suitcase 14
sin 215	spread 14	sum 24
sink 226	sprinkle 24	summon 37
situate 238	spy 37	superintendent 49
situation 14	square 49	supreme 61
sketch 37	squirrel 61	surface 73
skill 48	staff 73	surgeon 85
slant 60	stability 85	surrender 97
slavery 73	stain 97	surround 109
sleeve 84	stake 109	survey 120
slender 97	stalk 120	suspect 144
slice 108	stare 144	suspicion 131
slight 143	startle 131	swallow 251
slip 131	starve 250	sway 263
slope 250	statesman 262	sweat 156
smart 262	steady 155	sweep 275
smash 155	steep 167	swell 287
snatch 275	steer 179	swift 167
soak 286	stem 275	swing 179
sob 167	stepmother 287	sword 191
social 179	stern 191	syllable 203
sole 190	stiff 203	symbolize 215
solemn 203	still 215	sympathy 227
solid 215	sting 227	
solution 227	stir 238	
somewhat 238	stomach 14	# T
sore 14	stoop 24	
soul 24	storage 37	tale 239
sound 37	stout 49	talent 14
sour 49	strain 61	talkative 25
sow 61	straw 73	tame 37
spacious 73	strawberry 85	tangle 49
spare 85	stream 97	tap 61
sparkle 97	stretch 109	task 85
spear 109	strict 120	tasty 97
specialist 120	string 144	tavern 109
spell 144	stroke 131	temper 120

temperature 144
temple 131
tender 251
term 263
terrible 156
territory 275
theme 287
thermometer 168
thirst 179
thread 203
thorough 191
threat 215
thrill 227
throat 239
throne 15
throughout 25
thrust 37
thumb 49
thunder 61
tick 73
tide 85
tight 97
timber 109
tin 120
tissue 144
toad 132
toil 263
torch 156
torture 275
tough 287
tower 168
trace 179
trademark 203
tradition 191
traffic 215
tragic 227
tramp 239
transfer 15
transport 25
trap 37
treaty 49
tremble 61
tremendous 73
trial 85
tribe 97
trick 109
trim 121

troop 144
troublesome 132
trust 251
tune 263
turtle 156
twin 276
twist 287
typical 168

U

union 180
unite 191
university 203
up-to-date 227
urge 239
usage 15
utter 25

V

vaccinate 38
vanish 49
vapor 61
variety 73
vast 85
vein 110
venture 121
verse 144
vessel 132
vest 251
vice 264
victim 156
vine 276
violence 287
virgin 168
visible 180
vision 191
vocabulary 203
volcano 215
volume 228
vow 239
vowel 15
voyage 25

W

wage 38
warfare 49
warrior 61
waterfall 73
waterproof 86
weaken 110
wealthy 121
weapon 98
weary 145
web 132
weed 251
weep 264
welfare 156
whip 276
whirl 287
whisper 168
whistle 180
widow 191
wilderness 203
willful 228
wipe 215
witch 239
withdraw 15
wither 25
witness 38
witty 50
woe 61
worm 73
worsen 86
wreck 98
wring 110
wrist 120

Y

yell 132
yield 251

Z

zone 264